Norton
MOTOR CYCLES
FROM 1950 TO 1986

Norton
MOTOR CYCLES
FROM 1950 TO 1986

Steve Wilson

PSL

Patrick Stephens Limited

This book substantially comprises material first
published in 1986 in
BRITISH MOTOR CYCLES SINCE 1950
Volume 3 – Greeves, Hesketh, Indian, James,
Norman and Norton roadsters of 250cc and over

British Library:
A catalogue record for this book is available from
the British Library

ISBN 1 85260 573 1

Library of Congress catalog card no. 96 78554

Patrick Stephens Limited is an imprint of Haynes
Publishing, Sparkford, Nr Yeovil, Somerset,
BA22 7JJ

Typeset and printed in Great Britain by
J. H. Haynes & Co. Ltd, Sparkford

Contents

Acknowledgements

Grateful thanks to Bert Hopwood for 'The Norton', and above all to John Hudson, who burned the midnight oil on this 'Norton' as he did so often on the metal ones – well above and beyond what others would consider the call of duty. To Graham Sanderson of the late lamented *Motor Cycle Weekly* for kind permission for the use of photos; and now thanks to *Classic Bike* magazine and *The Classic Motor Cycle* magazine for kind permission for the use of photos which are currently copyright of EMAP National Publications Ltd. Also thanks to Cyril Ayton of *Motor Cycle Sport* for photos, as well as others too numerous to mention. Once again to the model of typists for typists everywhere, Sandra den Hertog. And as before, to all the scribes, smudgers and illustrators of the golden years, without whose long work this pint-size distillation would never have been possible. Good roads to you all.

Introduction

In a sense this is the saddest introduction to these new editions which I shall have to write. Just over ten years ago when the work contained in this book first appeared as part of *British Motor Cycles since 1950* Vol 3, Norton were poised to go into production for the first time in ten years, with a civilian model of their rotary-engined twin.

Since then the dream has come and gone. It encompassed some rideable machines and some heroic shoe-string racing victories, culminating in the 1992 TT win. But I'm not too sorry that book production constraints mean I have not been required to bring the story up to date.

Less than a thousand machines were actually completed over the eight years from 1987 to 1994, before the entire enterprise foundered in a complicated welter of confused and disputed ownership which would be laughable if it did not involve the probable finish of Norton production forever. Company in-fighting, wasted potential and financial skullduggery — not much of an end to the story of integrity and sound engineering begun by 'Pa' Norton.

There is a good case to be made, however, that Norton never really recovered from the move from its traditional home at Bracebridge Street, Birmingham, to the parent AMC factory at Plumstead, South-East London; and certainly not from its subsequent takeover by Dennis Poore in 1966 when AMC went under, and Poore created Norton-Villiers. I am happy with the broad outlines of the story as recounted in the Norton history section of the book, but subsequent journalistic work for *Classic Bike Guide* magazine (CBG), has given me the opportunity to hear some further details of the Norton-Villiers saga, as well as some reasons for the actions and attitudes of those involved.

Tony Denniss, for instance, an ex-Plumstead man actively involved in the genesis of the Commando and subsequently much else, was able to pinpoint for me one factor in the company's internal rivalry between the old Villiers works in Wolverhampton, where from mid-1969 Commando engines were built, and Plumstead plus later Andover, where Commandos were assembled. Why the ill-feeling, which continued after Plumstead Norton people had transferred up to Wolverhampton, and which frequently led to important improvements to the motorcycles being blocked? 'Villiers and AMC didn't get on very well', Tony explained. 'It went back to the days of the trouble over the two-strokes.'

This referred to the way in which AMC had attempted to undercut the ubiquitous Villiers two-stroke engines which they had up till then, like many other manufacturers, used in their James and Francis-Barnett lightweights. But from 1956, after a dispute with Villiers, they had initiated their own, Piatti-designed two-stroke series. These were neither reliable nor successful — and in the end Plumstead even had to get Villiers at Marston Road to assemble the engines for them. 'When Wolverhampton later took over the Commando', Tony went on, 'some of their people, particularly production people, wanted to get their own back.' And he was able to give specific instances of how this affected the Commando's quality and fortunes.

The design of the Commando's alloy primary chaincase, after a careful look at that of the Royal Enfield range, was one which was simply fixed with a single central bolt, rather than a mass of screws around its periphery. This chaincase was only sealed around its edge with a sealing band, and inevitably prototype examples at Plumstead were found to bow if the central bolt was overtightened, and to then leak oil. 'So', said Tony, 'we arranged that the back end of the chaincase was cast at the foundry so that it tapered out and was shallower at each end. This was carried out by Lavenders, who did a lot of casting work for AMC, and it worked. Until engine

Nearly the last of the 'real' Norton singles, 500cc ES2 from 1959, with classic Wideline Featherbed frame.

production was transferred to Wolverhampton, who didn't bother with this, so the case leaked.'

A fundamental difference of attitude underlay the problem. 'Both sides were proud of their production methods', Tony went on. AMC's had been a quality product, with an active competition element to keep things up to the mark. 'When we wanted more power from the Combat engine, I knew from work with Wally Wyatt at Plumstead that this would require the RHP barrel-roller main bearings, to cope with flexing cranks. But Villiers were very mass-production orientated, and said that the bearings were unnecessary — they could always blame Bernard Hooper' (the Commando's principal designer) 'when things went wrong . . .' As they did with the Combat so spectacularly in 1972.

The move of actual Commando assembly to Andover in late '69 had not exactly helped matters, as NV's ace salesman Mike Jackson now admits. Production soon reached around 150 machines a week, but 'I cannot say I was over-impressed', Jackson recalled in notes for the Norton Owners' Club calendar, 'with some of the folk they had hired, on the management side . . . In charge at Andover was Philip Sellars, who had made a success of running a "widget" factory for Dennis Poore at Camberley, Surrey. He was a career MD with no great love or sympathy for the product. He had gathered about him at Andover a number of "experts", all drawn from the widget factory, who were incapable of making the Commando as good as they said it was in the sales brochures.'

There were flaws not only at the top. Not many of the workforce from Plumstead had made the move to Hampshire, and as Tony Denniss

confirmed, 'they used "green" labour at Andover and could never get the place to assemble Commandos quite right — more than once, gangs from Wolverhampton had to be sent down'. The problems discouraged Poore, but 'it was also political; Villiers was declining, people there wanted to keep the Commando and in the end they won'. Before long, Commando production moved up to Wolverhampton.

This, however, was not the end of the problems, far from it. In this book, for instance, I mention the fact that some later Commando frames were sourced from Italy rather than at Reynolds Tubes, and that these caused some problems. The truth in detail was even more surprising. Alan Sargent, after a spell at BSA/Triumph, became Poore's Chief Development Engineer in mid-1972, at Wolverhampton. 'What a place!' he laughed ruefully, recalling the antiquated 17½ acre works, yet with some affection. 'Not much of the site was being used by then, and even the bit we were using was pretty derelict, mucky and dirty . . .'

On the new frames, he soon noticed considerable variations in the handling of individual Commandos, and set out to find why. By then around half the frames were being sourced from Italy; they were distinguishable by a mark on the front petrol tank mounting, and according to Alan, road testers 'with any sense got themselves a non-Italian one'. There was a frame acceptance gauge in the Inspection department, and those from Reynolds usually fitted correctly. But after several Italian-framed machines had proved difficult to steer straight, Alan investigated and found out why.

It emerged that the acceptance gauge

Coil ignition and Reynolds-built Featherbed frame. But testing this beautiful original 1959 ES2 single taught the author about the comparative harshness of its engine.

consisted of a blunt lump dubbed 'the donkey's dick', which was supposed to fit loosely through the steering head when the frame was aligned in blocks at each side of the mounting points. But if the 'dick' didn't fit an Italian frame, the Inspector was in the habit of *hammering it in* until it did. In addition, said Alan, 'half the time the tubes on the Italian jobs were not even to the right gauge'. So why use the Italian frames at all? Tony Denniss supplied the insider's answer. 'They were 60% of the price of the British-built ones. And Reynolds themselves, like all British manufacturers at that time, were going through a difficult period, so there was also the possibility of their ceasing to make frames for us.'

Beneath this however, Alan Sargent knew, lay a deeper malaise at Wolverhampton. 'There seemed to be an inner wheel there which let non-conforming components through.' The reason? So as not to upset Chairman Poore, and keep

production, which was by then mostly for export, going strong. Poore badly needed this to justify his motorcycle venture to his parent Board at Manganeze Bronze Holdings, at a time of declining NV profitability; and then to expedite the stroke he put together to extricate himself from that situation, the takeover of BSA/Triumph.

Denniss, Jackson and Sargent all had a high opinion of the late Mr Poore personally, but Tony Denniss did note the Chairman's habit of secretively running projects in parallel within the Group, something which angered Alan Sargent after he had worked on a rubber-mounted B50 project, when he then found Doug Hele had been tasked by Poore to produce an alternative version at the same time, without Alan's knowledge. As Denniss said, 'at NVT we would discuss things, agree on something — and then each go away and do our own thing. This was Mr Poore's

SON OF A BITCH.

REAR SUSPENSION
Race-developed rear shock absorber with pre-load, compression and rebound adjustment.

FRONT SUSPENSION
State of the art technology by White Power as used in the racing machine. Upside-down front fork assembly with compression and rebound damping adjustment.

FRONT BRAKES
320 mm floating double discs for maximum pad-to-disc contact. Brembo 4-pot opposed piston calipers.

REAR BRAKE
230 mm fixed disc. Brembo 2-pot opposed piston caliper.

FRAME
Hand-crafted twin-spar construction, beam frame in aluminium alloy. High lateral rigidity, developed and proven under race conditions.

POWER UNIT
New 588 ccm liquid-cooled rotary engine with hydraulically operated clutch. High power-to-weight ratio with few moving parts. 5-speed constant-mesh gearbox. Maintenance-free electronic ignition.

WHEELS & TYRES
17" 3-spoke cast aluminium alloy wheels shod by race-bred ultra-low profile radial tyres.

THE NORTON F1
RACE BRED THROUGH AND THROUGH

Publicity expletive for 1990 F1 rotary race replica could well be applied to the company's subsequent performance . . .

method, which did fragment our thoughts and our way forward'.

Under the circumstances, perhaps the Shenstone rotary follies were a logical progression from all this — and the Commando was a better bike to ride than it had any right to be! I don't have a Norton in my stable right now; I got rid of my much-loved 750 Commando after eight years, just as this book was first published, and then some years later tried a Mk III 850. But soon a con rod with 80,000 miles on it decided to let go at 95 mph in the fast lane of the M25 during the rush hour, which brought that one to an end, though the trusty Commando stayed upright and got me, dead-engine and with the flywheel exposed, to the central reservation.

But I still like the big bendies, as well as nearly every other Norton I've been privileged to try.

That road-test experience has caused me to modify a few of the judgements about specifics on the bikes treated in the book. I could have mentioned, for instance, that the absence of an engine-shaft shock absorber on the ES2/Model 50 singles makes them rather harsher engines than their BSA equivalents. Also a couple of tests on Wideline Featherbed-frame bikes has convinced me that, for a six footer at least, they are definitely a more comfortable ride than their Slimline successors. But warts, omissions and all, I do hope this book continues to be of some use to Norton riders everywhere.

Wantage
Oxfordshire
September 1996

How to use this book

The book is arranged in the following way:
1 A brief history of the marque.
2 More detailed consideration of the major categories within the factory's road-going output during the period (ie, usually broken down into single and twin cylinder machines, but with separate sections for unusual and exceptional designs like the International).
3 These are followed by a table of *production dates*. Here, though production generally shifted during August and a new machine would usually be on display in November at the annual show of say, 1950, I have followed the makers' intentions and referred to it as the 1951 model or model for 1951. Next come some necessarily brief *technical specifications* for each range of machines.
4 These are followed by a detailed *year-by-year survey* of each range, noting developments and modifications. (Like the book, these are 'British', since with the information available it has not been possible to include export specifications.) This should help with the identification of particular models, but it should be noted that sometimes there were changes made either gradually or mid-year.
5 A final section with details of the marque's *engine and frame numbers* (where available), and *colour schemes*.

The following further points should be borne in mind. The *production dates* quoted are in general

those for availability in the UK rather than for export. *Weights:* all weights quoted in the technical specifications are the weight dry (unless otherwise stated). They have usually derived from *Motor Cycling* magazine's 'Buyer's Guide' section, and occasionally inaccuracies have come to light, either from a failure to update or from optimism by the factory which supplied the figures. *Speeds:* top and cruising speeds for most models are to be found in the text, not the specifications, and are approximate figures. This is because not all machines were road-tested, and not all those tested underwent timed runs at MIRA. Also the author feels that top speeds on road test machines were not always representative, since they could feature non-standard high-performance parts fitted by the factories. *MPG:* petrol consumption figures are also approximate, being subject to the variables of state of tune, prevailing conditions and the hand at the throttle.

Owners' Clubs: For up-to-date information on Owners' Clubs, telephone the BMF (British Motorcyclists Federation) in London on 0181-942-7914.

Please also note that in the interests of space-saving, the following abbreviations have been used for periodicals throughout the text:
MCS — Motor Cycle Sport; MCN — Motor Cycle News; MCW — Motor Cycle Weekly; and *MCM — Motor Cycle Mechanics.*

Left: *Five styles of cafe racer customizing for Norton Commandos in 1971.*

Norton

Norton Motors Ltd, Bracebridge Street, Birmingham 6

Probably the noblest name in the whole range of British marques, Norton epitomized all that was best in our manufacturers' tradition — racing success, technical ingenuity, and in our period a series of roadsters, pre-eminently twins, which were fast, strong, tractable, and above all set standards of handling and roadholding by which all others were judged. Even the name's swansong to 1985, the Commando, while more controversial, is still arguably the ultimate British parallel twin. Known since 1908 as 'The Unapproachable Norton', the machines bearing the curly 'N' earned a place in history that made this proud assertion truly so.

The distinctive Norton character was well established — massiveness (as far back as 1913 their TT machines weighed in at 265 lb against the 200-odd lb of the Triumph), extreme ruggedness and an aura of unmistakeable masculinity —

'Nortons always were sexy', Barry Sheene was to say, and showbiz connections, with Norton enthusiasts including George Formby and Sir Ralph Richardson, tended to confirm this. Against the lightness and delicacy of a Scott, a Triumph, a cammy Velo, the Bracebridge Street singles in particular presented an uncompromising brute power — tall-engined, heavy, requiring a strong kick to start, and with a barking exhaust note 'like a distant Bofors gun', as Titch Allen recalled.

The ruggedness was not confined to the image; when the firm's founder James Landsdowne 'Pa' Norton had claimed that 'the Big 4 pulls a sidecar like a locomotive', he knew whereof he spoke. In 1921, at the age of 52, for three solid months he had toured extensively in South Africa, mostly in mud and dust. During the whole time his outfit had needed none of the spares which he had carried. The legend was to live on into the 1950s with John Masterman's 1928 Model 19 'Old Faithful' which in four decades covered over three

Below left *The roots in racing. The 1920 TT and Norman Brown (Norton) negotiates Ballaugh Bridge.*

Right *An early WD 16H—equipped for overseas duty with massive air-cleaner and upswept pipe.*

quarters of a million miles on three continents, all on the original big end and without being cleaned!

In 1950 Norton racing successes at a world level were about to take a last quantum leap forward again due to the Featherbed frame. The devotees of the traditional roadster singles, with their customary massive ruggedness suited for sidecar and solo work alike, were keeping demand for these 'Edwardian motor cycles' ticking over gently. More significantly, the range had recently been revitalized with the arrival of the Bert Hopwood-designed 500 cc Dominator 7 Twin, one of the sweetest twin-cylinder motors on the market. The Norton name at its Bracebridge Street, Aston, home appeared undimmed. Or was it?

Bracebridge Street itself was a large part of the problem. In 1916 Norton Motors had moved from their tiny Bradford Street workshops into premises on Philips Street, backing on to the Aston Brook Street works of their fellow company, toolmakers R. T. Shelley with whom they had been associated since 1913. Later Bracebridge Street was added as the third parallel road, and that's the way things stayed for the next 47 years. Premises that were stretched producing 4,500 machines a year in 1923, now during the boom following the Second World War were sometimes turning out double that number. The result was the paradox that Norton were world leaders who operated out of a slum.

Worse than the rabbit warren of Small Heath, worse than the 'vertical assembly-line' of AMC's Plumstead where finished bikes ended up on the fourth floor, Bracebridge Street was feelingly described by Bert Hopwood as 'a slummy shambles'. As late as 1960 new road-tester John Gill arrived at the alleyway entrance, glassed over like a conservatory, with the walls painted green and what appeared to be a black carpet on the floor. He soon discovered this to be concrete, with a thick covering of oil and dirt. Hopwood had to design the Dominator engine sitting back-to-back with colleague Jack Moore in 'an eight-foot square office' which he observed drily was 'reasonably quiet, and did not let in too much rain'.

Water also abounded, liberally dosed with oil, whenever the antiquated dynamometer for the production Manx and International machines was employed; it spewed the mixture copiously out into Aston Brook Street, so that when it was in use a labourer had to sweep away the flood in the street, to forestall complaints from pedestrians and Police. The building also housed more than men and machines. John Gill describes the then head tester, a man whom he says rode infrequently, who once interrupted his kitting-up

process prior to one of his rare runs to suddenly caper around the shop. The explanation came when eventually he wrenched off his skid-lid to reveal a scratched bald pate. This had been caused by a mouse which had been nesting in his helmet!

These incidents make amusing anecdotes in retrospect, but as anyone who has worked in an unhealthy, noisy and ill-lit environment for more than a few days can tell you, it's actually no joke; and certainly not the sanitary environment which precision engineering and assembly demands. There was of course another side to it all. As Norton man John Hudson recalls of the mid-50s, 'when Ivor Smith was testing one of Joe Craig's late 350s and it was buzzing at 8,000 plus we loved to hear it, it was music to our ears. Our toilets weren't posh but they were adequate and were certainly not smothered with rude graffiti. The important thing was that we worked as a team and if extra work involving overtime was needed, there was never any shortage of volunteers. . . the experience (at the experimental shop) was most rewarding and I consider myself privileged to have worked in there.' Yet there were civilized offices in the building, and a modern leak-free dynamometer (and even a spare). But these, together with what in Hopwood's estimation amounted to 90 per cent of the engineering effort, were reserved for 'The Wizard of Waft'—Joe Craig and the racing side, an operation so exclusive that if managing director

Gilbert Smith knocked on Craig's door and received no instructions to enter, he would go away again.

Craig had been with the company since 1925. He was rightly held in awe for the way in which, apart from wartime interludes at BSA and AMC, he had squeezed extra horsepower every year from the basic 1930 Arthur Carroll-designed ohc single cylinder racing engines. A dour, taciturn Ulsterman, normally as unapproachable as Nortons themselves, Craig had presided in the '30s when Nortons unquestionably dominated the TT and the international GP scene, and at times held more world speed records than any other manufacturer. By the '50s he was just about reaching the limit, at around 52 bhp, with variations of the Carroll engine, and he knew it.

After the handling of the McCandless brothers' Featherbed frame and the riding wizardry of Geoff Duke won a brief and glorious reprieve, Craig negotiated to buy rights on a transverse four-cylinder machine from French independent designer Henri Nougier (which the parent company wouldn't authorize) and was experimenting with a transverse four of his own. He enlisted the help of the design team responsible for the original BRM racing car engine. By autumn 1953, a single cylinder of 125 cc had been bench tested, representing one quarter of a dohc liquid-cooled 500. By 1954 Craig had also nearly completed work on a flat 'F' type engine—a horizontally-inclined single with a unit

Far left *Though up to 1,000 WD Nortons a week were produced at one time—here trick photography has been employed to discourage the enemy.*

Left *'Nortons are sexy' I—Ava Gardner goes side-saddle on a model 18 500 single while filming 'Bhowani Junction'.*

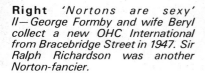

Right *'Nortons are sexy' II—George Formby and wife Beryl collect a new OHC International from Bracebridge Street in 1947. Sir Ralph Richardson was another Norton-fancier.*

gearbox—in response to the threat from the very similar machines of Moto Guzzi. This followed the abortive attempt to gain another edge for the Norton singles from the handling and low frontal area of the FIM-banned 'kneeler' frame. At that point the works racing effort ceased abruptly and in 1955 Craig left the company.

Up to that time Craig's efforts had undeniably consumed a disproportionate amount of the company's time, resources and money. Why did Craig persevere? Once a distinguished competitor and TT rider himself, his concentrated dedication was never in question. But Bert Hopwood supplies a revealing new angle on the man's motives, previously available to insiders only. In *Whatever Happened to the British Motorcycle Industry?* he states that Craig's contract, since the days when he had been racing manager, linked his wage scale to his competition successes. This was understandable while Craig was racing director, but when in 1946 he was appointed Norton's director of engineering, the contract should have been changed.

It may have made sense of the racing effort to Craig, but as Hopwood says, 'the managing director did not realize, until it was too late, that it was commercial suicide to have racing as a first priority'. In the factory itself the involvement at all levels was there—Geoff Duke recalls that when he came to them in 1950 'the enthusiasm of the workforce at Bracebridge Street had to be seen to be believed'. But the Nortons that were

manufactured to sell were almost entirely different from the works racers. They might have been tinged with the glamour of track successes and 'Built in the Light of Racing Experience', but the facilities available for their building now suffered in very real ways from absence of the money that had gone into the racing effort.

There was no metallurgist at the works; and the Dominator engine had to be sand-cast, since there were no facilities (or money) for die-casting. There was practically no design department. When the McCandless brothers came up with the all-welded Featherbed frame, they had to bring their jigs to the factory from Northern Ireland and manufacture the first batch themselves, as the Norton facilities were geared only to the older method of construction, with tubes hearth-brazed into cast lugs. The results were heavy and the process slow; the 'garden gate' plunger frame of the period was obsolete requiring as it did no less than 96 time-consuming machinery operations per frame. World War 2 experience of welding tubular assemblies, had paved the way for volume production of all-welded frames like the Featherbed. For this reason Featherbed frames were always manufactured at tubing specialists Reynolds, under the direction of experts Bill Barnett and (later) Ken Sprayson.

Furthermore, until as late as 1955, cylinder heads for the twins were iron rather than alloy, the reason being the most significant Bracebridge Street deficiency of all—there was no money. Of

A 1937 start at the German circuit where Scots Norton rider Jimmy Guthrie suffered his fatal crash.

a slightly later period, Hopwood was to recall that 'money was so short we used to stand on the front steps looking for the postman to arrive with orders'. This was combined with the absence of a modern production line; right until the end in 1963, there was simply an assembly track with machines pushed along on a trolley, twelve to fifteen at a time. Together, all these factors limited output to a maximum of around thirty a day, representing no more than 9,000 to 10,000 in a good year; one eighth of BSA's output, and not sufficient to generate the profit necessary for retooling and expansion. Hopwood cites 7 per cent profit before tax, with sister company R. T. Shelley generating the majority even of that.

The result was to be the takeover of Norton Motors by the South London-based Associated Motor Cycles organization early in 1953. In the early '50s AMC, which by then incorporated James and Francis-Barnett as well as AJS and Matchless, achieved annual profits of around half a million pounds. This would easily allow the absorption of Norton and R. T. Shelley, which it is said they acquired for rather less than £1 million. As we shall see, the takeover led directly to a further decline, steady but not uninterrupted, until the parent company foundered in 1966. Then the Norton name was to experience another troubled decade of production under the ownership of

Dennis Poore's Norton Villiers (later NVT).

The situation in 1950 which led to all this was the result of trying to live on history.

By 1950, with the exception of the Dominator, the roadster range was as old-fashioned as it looked. The singles were undeniably heavy, and they clattered, vibrated, leaked oil and were slow. A partial exception in terms of speed were the ohc 'International' models, but the other factors applied, and BSA's Gold Stars were soon to displace them as the acme of road-going racing singles. Even the over-the-counter Manx racers were down on power. Journalist Vic Willoughby in his book *Exotic Motorcycles* states bluntly that for 1953 the production 350, still with its long-stroke motor in contrast with that year's works model (he rode both) 'would hardly dislodge skin from a rice pudding'. This was the price of living on history.

It is true there were some benefits still from the racing, among them a not inconsiderable income from sponsors; the hardcore loyalty to the name among the big-single brigade and the workforce's enthusiasm.

The sport's governing body, the FIM, in their wisdom had banned supercharging when World War 2 ended. This was bad for AJS, who were left with an unblown and unreliable version of their 'Porcupine' twin, but good for Norton whose

Right *Maestro. Geoff Duke in action on a Featherbed racer, Scarborough 1958.*

Below right *Little acorns. The 1950 show and schoolboys try Geoff Duke's winning garden gate racer for size.*

steady pegging away at the single racers led to gradual power increases for the 500s, from an initial 29 bhp at 5,500 rpm, to 34-35 bhp at 5,750 rpm for the dohc engines just pre-war, and 44-45 bhp for the short-stroke motors after it. The rise in rpm is relevant, as Vic Willoughby points out in his definitive book *The Racing Motorcycle*. For higher bore/stroke ratios, in conjunction with the careful matching of cam forms to valve-spring characteristics, was one of two ways in which the single could work to remain competitive against the inherently superior output of an equivalent capacity multi. The other way was increasing brake mean effective pressure, the effectiveness of each individual engine cycle. This was done by endless methodical attention to downdraught angles, port shapes, valve sizes and included angles, inlet and exhaust resonances, plus squish forms and surface/volume ratios in the combustion chamber.

These were the areas that Norton race chief Joe Craig exploited, being suited for development rather than design by both his history (he lacked formal engineering training) and his temperament (he disliked change, made no secret of his aversion to a redesign, and would just not allow the demonstrable theoretical superiority of four-valve heads, multis, and the shape of the future, two-strokes). It took time for the competition's theoretical advantages to become actual, and in the meantime Craig had, in the words of Edgar Franks, 'a sound basic design, thoroughly developed over the years, embodying the highest possible grade of materials and workmanship'. Craig hung on to this, as Titch Allen writes, 'to the exclusion of consideration for any other person' or for Norton's or the sponsors' resources. 'He spared neither the firm's expense nor the feelings of loyal workers nor of his riders'—he was, as Vic Willoughby wrote, 'widely suspected [of being] more concerned for his bikes than his riders.' All this paid off on the tracks, where if the works machinery was not accessible to the public, some of the virtues that prevailed were—patient experiment, meticulous preparation, and then all-out riding, with handling and tactics contributing as much as sheer output. The secretive, inscrutable Craig kept tight control of the works team tactics; as Freddie Frith said, 'Joe arranged the bicycles to suit his plan of who should win. . . On the start line Joe would say who was to win,' at least until the mid-thirties when the BMW/Gilera threat became serious.

But aside from establishing a tradition of British pride and skill on the track that was to linger for many years, there was another way that Craig's obsession paid. Despite his secretiveness at the time, there remained the fruits of his continuous experimentation, as well as of those whom he enrolled to assist him. These included not only factory personnel but outside talent like Leo Kozmicki (until his departure for Vanwall in the mid '50s) Francis Beart, the McCandless brothers and tuner Harry Weslake, who helped in the '40s on airflow studies, valve port design and investigation into turbulence. All fell out with Craig to a greater or lesser degree, and their contracts specifically forbade them to take credit for their share in the Norton success story, which was always associated with Craig alone.

In this way there built up what in modern terms would be called a data bank, and it was further increased at the end of the '50s, after Joe had departed and the works team had been disbanded, with the hundred or so Manx engines built each year as production racers under the leadership of Bert Hopwood and his partner Doug Hele. These men, in contrast to Craig, took pains to link this specialist activity with production engineering as much as possible. This experience guided them with later designs, and as Hopwood was to write, 'we were able, at last, to understand a great deal more about the ideal bores and strokes for various cylinder capacities, and also the most desirable connecting rod and crank ratios to satisfy certain parameters. . . we were also able, once and for all, to arrive at some basic formula which transformed the handling characteristics of the single track vehicle, and which were later to be

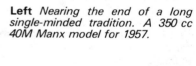

Left *Nearing the end of a long single-minded tradition. A 350 cc 40M Manx model for 1957.*

Above right *Another kind of winner—the excellent 500T trials for 1949; like the Featherbed frame, a fruit of the McCandless brothers' genius.*

used in endowing certain British machines with a standard of road-holding and stability which was the envy of motor cycle manufacturers throughout the world.' Since Hopwood and then Hele moved to Meriden in the early 1960s, some of the machines in question almost certainly bore the badges of Norton's great rival, Triumph! It was the indirect route, but roadsters did eventually benefit from the process that Craig had initiated, and once more Norton was a benefactor to the industry as a whole.

Norton racing supremacy set the tone and the attitude for much of the industry. A hangover from the glory days of the 1930s combined with little real technical innovation and forward thinking to lead to a scene where both key manufacturing personnel, as well as many dealers, were often ex-competition men, and the emphasis was not on service and the 'horses for courses' of commuting and touring, but on hot sportsters. Mechanical soundness and simplicity, quietness and styling, were looked upon as the province of foreigners and sissies. Could you really blame the rude boys of the '50s and early '60s, the rockers? Their café racers were just an

expression of this prevailing ethos in the industry, a search for performance at all costs, including comfort and reliability. It created a scene with plenty of flavour, but overall certainly did sales, and probably motor cycling as a whole, little good.

For the racing singles there were two further avenues both of which would be explored by Moto-Guzzi's Guilio Carcano; namely lightening, and streamlining. For Norton these were to be less Craig's province than, in the latter instance, the McCandless brothers with the sensational 'Kneeler' or Silver Fish 350 prototype of 1953 with its ultra-low frontal area plus streamlining front and rear, somewhat capriciously excluded by the authorities from the TT, but ridden by Ray Amm to take a string of world records. But as Rex McCandless asserted recently in *Classic Bike*, 'because the kneeler was not Craig's idea, he was always against it.' A sometime associate of the McCandless outfit (Rex's brother Cromie rode for him), ace tuner Francis Beart also understood the advantages of lightness very well, to the extent of marketing a list of light alloy goodies for Norton's racers, keyed to Norton's spares list. At the 1951 TT this brought down the wrath of Norton MD Gilbert Smith—until Beart pointed out to him that examples of these products of his had featured on works Nortons for the last couple of years, and that he had Craig's official order for them to prove it!

So the company had reached a crossroads in early 1953 when they were taken over by AMC. Bert Hopwood had designed the Dominator and left early in 1949. The association with the McCandless brothers had born its fruit in the form of the Featherbed frame and also the successful and well-loved 500T and 350T trials singles; but the works trials team, which had included Jeff Smith, was disbanded after 1952, surely not by coincidence in the year of the takeover by AMC with their own competitive works team. One resounding bonus from this tail-end involvement with trials had been the recruitment to the squad by Gilbert Smith in 1948 of the young Lancashire rider Geoff Duke, who from 1949 went on to distinguish himself in another sphere, and with other skilled works riders like Artie Bell and Ray Amm, held on to Norton's GP supremacy until 1953. Then Duke, too, went, in this case to Gilera and the Italians, a move that signalled the end of the long Norton domination. The McCandless brothers too turned to other fields after 1953.

Their brainchild and Duke's tool, the Featherbed frame, was not exploited commercially, since Craig was still in residence. Ex-Norton racer Ken Kavanagh confirmed

1951, and Norton lead with the model 7 Dominator—but also remember the TT.

recently that Norton had an ES2 500 cc motor in a Featherbed frame in 1951, but as Rex McCandless claimed, there was resistance to using his design among Norton management and design staff, with the excuse given that the frame might not be strong enough for sidecar work. This fear was subsequently proved to be unfounded, as Eric Oliver demonstrated in the 1958 sidecar TT. So the singles failed to acquire it until as late as 1959 (the Featherbed Dominator went into production in 1953). Excellent as it was, up till then the twins' presence alone had not been enough to put the company on a sound financial footing. Production was low, never more than 180 a week, and there was virtually no commercial outlet in the lucrative market of the United States. There, according to Hopwood, Hap Jones took only a token four or five machines a year, a pitiful failure to exploit both the 1949 devaluation of the pound against the dollar, and the triumph of tuner Francis Beart and the works riders at Daytona from 1949 to 1951 with much resultant publicity in America. For these successes, which were honoured by a Savoy luncheon and brought congratulations from the Duke of Edinburgh, in another demonstration of the company's parsimony, Beart was paid (grudgingly) £20 a week plus expenses.

After the AMC takeover C. A. Vandervell, chairman since 1913 and famous as the originator of CAV battery and lighting sets, stood down (and died in 1955). His son left to form the Vanwall

bearing concern; Craig's departure has already been discussed, and Gilbert Smith (a protegé of Pa Norton himself since 1916) only stayed on as MD because his contract had not expired. That Smith stayed under protest is clear from Hopwood's comment that the MD 'was opposed to AMC policy (if one could call it that) . . . [and] never disguised what appeared to be total dislike and opposition to all connections with Associated Motor Cycles.' He had some grounds; Donald Heather of AMC was not an inspiring leader, and the merger had meant the instant elbow for several Norton projects. These included not just Craig's racing projects but also a 250 cc high-cam ohv single, which according to Bob Collier, a long-time Norton road-tester and experimental engineer, was a sweet, fast, good-handling piece of work from Jack Moore, then Norton's chief designer. There had also been for 1953 a 500 cc side-valve twin cylinder motor intended for military use, the first to feature alternator electrics. Housed in the frame of the 16H single, it proved a pleasant and flexible machine; but in this case it was the Army's possession of £45,000-worth of the Triumph TRW spares which gave it the thumbs down.

Smith soldiered on until 1957. He was in his early sixties, and as Hopwood points out, not only loved everything about the company—he had once said 'the name Norton means more to me than the name Smith'—but also 'had much to offer, with his vast experience, and his entree to the trade as a whole.' But when his service agreement ran out, Woolwich decided not to offer a renewal. When Hopwood went in to bat for him he was asked 'which side are you working for?' Smith died shortly after leaving the company at the age of 62, and Hopwood was not alone in believing that 'the sadness associated with this enforced relinquishment of all his lifelong interests in this famous old firm, shortened his life by many years.' Craig, too, had died (in a car accident) a year after leaving.

But this was far from the end of the Norton story; there were still good men at work there, though their priorities were to be different from those of the previous generation. Foremost was Hopwood himself. In 1949 as chief designer he was dismissed (though on the point of resigning) after Craig's domination of the firm's engineering facilities and delaying tactics on the release of the Dominator had 'worn him down'. While he had succeeded in persuading Smith to recruit more technical personnel, too much time had gone on things such as winning the 'silly fight' over the construction of a new two-storey drawing office and development shop. Obstructed by management, architects and builders from getting the natural light he felt such a place required, Hopwood had had to redesign the building himself! He left to go to BSA but after some brilliant work there he resigned due both to company politics—Triumph's Edward Turner, both his collaborator and antagonist of old, was achieving ascendancy in the group—and probably because, as he once told BSA's Bert Perrigo, 'people who move seem to do better for themselves.'

In 1955 Hopwood was hired as a director of both Norton Motors and R. T. Shelley, 'with full executive control of the works including production, engineering and product design', rather than design engineering as such. He walked into a nest of problems, foremost among them being the dominance of AMC and the 'great jealousy at Woolwich of any Norton successes.' There was also industrial action, a damaging strike, which began the day he arrived, over the dismissal of 26 redundant workers; this was to drag on for six months. Gilbert Smith handled the dispute, from which Hopwood says he learned valuable lessons on industrial relations, not the least being that 'the official trade union attitude was to fight for any cause, whether worthy or not.' That does seem to have been the case in this dispute, since all the redundant men had found jobs in their own trade at comparable wages. Later, Hopwood was to make a point of a weekly walk through the works, and by personal contact achieved a strike-free three years when he became managing director. 'Hopwood would have a technical discussion and call everyone in,'

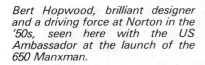

Bert Hopwood, brilliant designer and a driving force at Norton in the '50s, seen here with the US Ambassador at the launch of the 650 Manxman.

recalled John Hudson, a twenty-year Norton man. 'He'd listen to the office boy or a junior tester if they had an opinion to express.' In Hopwood's own words, 'a unique team spirit' was forged, and the shop stewards even presented him with a tankard when he left.

The strike was the first of many obstacles to be overcome, and Hopwood acknowledges in particular the vital role of the company secretary, Alec Skinner, who had been newly promoted to the board. Skinner's updated weekly financial statements, simple and easy to understand, made financial control possible in circumstances that were often difficult, as the economic climate was then worsening. Gilbert Smith, too, though initially suspicious, became Hopwood's ally until his dismissal in 1957. Then in 1958, after an interim period during which AMC sales director Jock West had turned down the job, Hopwood took over as Norton's MD.

Smith's tendency had been 'to go it alone almost as a dictator', and there had been 'no regular management meetings' — those that there

were taking the form of 'a series of statements from the MD on generally trivial matters'. This had enforced the company's disposition to simply struggle from crisis to crisis, with little or no forward product plan. Hopwood set about correcting this as best he could, aided by some men of outstanding ability. Doug Hele had arrived from Douglas, and was promoted by Hopwood to chief engineer. John Hudson had come as a tester in the 'holy of holies' experimental department in 1955, and became an unusually gifted technical writer, one-man Norton service department and trouble-shooter, both before and after the move to Plumstead. His extraordinary efforts on behalf of owners often single-handedly upheld the Norton reputation, and he is now, rightly, the president of the NOC. Bill Pitcher, Hopwood's design engineer on the original Dominator, continued to assist with its development as the clamour for bigger and bigger twins began to sweep the market. Scotsman Bill Smith, an expert motorcyclist at trials, scrambles and roadracing, arrived in 1956 as sales manager and

stayed on in that capacity until after the move south.

Hopwood's plan for Norton was to build up reserves of cash for a co-ordinated forward product plan to commence with a lightweight machine whose engine could form the basis of a modular range. He tried to do this by capitalizing on the company's assets of racing success for publicity value; by slimming down the workforce and rationalizing production; by sorting out the role of the potentially profitable R. T. Shelley associate company, and by quickly enlarging the range with a 250. His prime aim was increasing income, particularly by developing the US market. This was especially important since the company's twins in particular were not competitively priced, and because the company was not allowed an overdraft. When circumstances permitted it, another obvious necessity was a move into newer and more suitable premises. Unfortunately the parent AMC company was to prevent the move, erode the income, interfere with the 250 and provide no help with the export side.

As instructed, Hopwood mostly involved himself on the commercial front. One example of rationalization was his immediate rejection of the complicated and unnecessary AMC production control system, abandoning which instantly cut £5,000 off the annual bills on stationery alone! The R. T. Shelley company was making components for the motor cycle side (for instance, all the large clutches for both AMC and Norton— the former at a heavy loss since Plumstead had fixed the prices at a low level, and later reduced them still further) but Hopwood felt that Shelleys should concentrate more on their engineering work, and market a brand range of their own products, rather than the easily duplicated spanners, jacks and contract work they had been undertaking. He eventually succeeded in achieving this and Shelleys secured a profitable contract producing the original equipment 'Rollalift' jacks for Austin Mini cars.

On the publicity side he initiated a scheme whereby the 100 TT Silver replica trophies that

Far left *One of Norton's post-war aces Bob McIntyre aviates his 350 at Ballaugh Bridge in the 1958 Junior.*

Left *Bert Hopwood, Norton MD from 1957, in the hot seat at Bracebridge Street.*

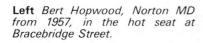

Right *Racing went on, thanks to the Manx. A good shot of the determined R. Anderson in 1958.*

Norton had earned were loaned to selected dealers for show, together with blown-up photographic reproductions of famous race scenes. This led to big displays of the roadsters 'Built in the light of racing experience', which was true of their Featherbed frames, at any rate. The racing side itself was kept modest; only Norton reliability meant that the Manx models, as the 30M and 40M production racers available to the public were known, continued as a force in the sport. They were the most successful standard production racing machines in the world, and there were still flashes of the old GP glory such as John Surtees' outing at Silverstone in 1955 on a works Norton. In the words of an *MCS* writer, Surtees 'whipped Duke on the all-conquering Gilera in the finest demonstration of calculated fury that I have ever seen.' And as late as 1961 the young Mike Hailwood was to win the Senior TT on a privately-entered single.

Around eighty Manx machines were produced each year until the end of 1962, with Doug Hele masterminding further developments. These included for 1958 shorter-stroke engines, the 500 a 93 mm bore variant with an eccentric crankpin sleeve, as well as the 'BBC' (big bearing crankcase) engine, and for 1959 an experimental desmodromic valve machine, plus the later use of five- and six-speed gear clusters and lighter pistons. There was no works team but selected riders were loaned the previous year's experimental racing prototypes. The £20,000 paid annually since 1956 by various suppliers for the publicity value of even privately sponsored riders' successes was a useful compensation (a major contributor was Slazenger in 1957 whose support permitted the building of several special engines).

But Hopwood's fundamental thrust was towards viability for the company rather than the old glory on the tracks. The sole exception he would make was if racing was the only method of securing a viable share of the world market.

Hopwood realized that enlarging the range with smaller capacity machines was essential, and in 1957 he sketched designs for two engines, a 125 cc single and a 250 twin, with 90 per cent commonality of parts between them. Both were novel in featuring a one-piece cylinder head, barrel and rocker box, and it was this feature that was seized on with ridicule by the AMC brass and used as an excuse to reject the project. No doubt the recent launch of AMC's range of own-brand two-strokes including 150s and 250s influenced their decision.

Instead Hopwood was forced by financial constraints to design and produce the Jubilee 250

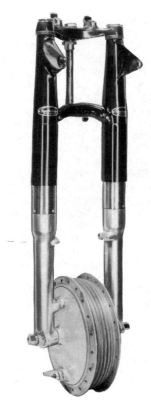

at the end of 1958, to celebrate the sixty years since Pa Norton had set up on his own. With several frame, fork, and electrical components in common with a brother AMC subsidiary, Francis-Barnett, the Jubilee was both more conventional and more trouble-prone than the original had given promise of being. One plus point, however, was the built-in capability to expand to a 350 capacity machine. This appeared for 1960 as the excellent Navigator, with Roadholder forks, and if the reader detects a note of personal enthusiasm, he is correct, as this was the author's first motor cycle and never once unseated him during all the early days of fumbling and uncertainty.

Meanwhile, even before the contract with the current US importer had expired, Hopwood had addressed himself to the problem of distribution in the States. At first it appeared that the Group umbrella would take care of this, for AMC boss Heather had bought the Indian Sales Corporation name from Brockhouse on 1 September 1959, and used it as an American subsidiary for marketing from then on. Hopwood was amazed and disgusted to find that Heather was not going to allow Norton to export their machines through the Indian Sales Corp or benefit from the trading arrangements, which were to be for the AJS/Matchless parent company only. (Initially not even that was true, since due to an outstanding previous contract between Indian Sales Corp and Royal Enfield, they had to sell 500 Enfield Constellation 700 cc twins!) Since AMC were helping themselves directly to Norton profits, this jealous attitude on their part was like a dog gnawing off its own tail. Hopwood proceeded to make his own distribution deal with the sharp but dynamic New Jersey-based Joe Berliner and his brother Michael.

He admits this 'may not have been the ideal arrangement'; Norton had no stake in Berliner's ready-made distributor organization, and no share in their profits, they simply sold motor cycles to him. But on the other hand, Norton were paid on the nose by Tozer Kemsley, a City finance house, and did not become embroiled, as AMC, BSA and NVT were to do, in costly overheads and warranty claims. On balance, for a smaller company, it was probably the more sensible course. There was also good feedback from Berliner himself, who helped with the initial development of the 650 Manxman, the name echoing the Domiracer's current success on the Island. The Manxman was a US-styled version of the Dominator, launched in the presence of the US consul and available in the

States for 1961. With capacity boosted to 650 cc, it was the direct forerunner of the mighty Dominator 650SS. The new marketing arrangements put Norton modestly in contention with BSA/Triumph, who were seeing big profits from US sales. This and other export markets also facilitated a steadier rate of production, one of Hopwood's targets, allowing stock to build up for the various selling seasons.

Norton made a profit of £300,000 for 1958. The factory was happy, the big twins were very fine machines indeed and selling well, but the firm continued to run on under the old limitations, such as belt-driven machinery. Even the primitive production methods were flawed, since as tester John Gill recalled, 'usually there was a steady stream of bikes coming off the 'track', but due to problems with our suppliers they were usually minus something. This didn't bother the boys on the track as they were still paid for each bike. However we [the testers] had to finish the job for them' (with 'slave' exhaust pipes, silencers, seats, and sometimes tanks), 'and as we were also paid so much per bike tested, it meant we were always on the losing end.' Under the circumstances it is not surprising that Gill was soon introduced to the 'fiddling stick', 'a piece of wire hooked at one end and soldered into an old needle jet', which was then inserted in the appropriate place and with 'a few flicks, the bike

Left *One part of Norton supremacy—the 'short' roadholder front fork for Featherbed-framed roadsters.*

Right *Export sales went well in the late '50s and early '60s. Somewhere in North Africa they rode slimline Featherbed singles.*

soon had the requisite number of miles on the clock.'

Not an ideal situation, and Hopwood had his own experience of unsatisfactory testing with the much more stringent rides given in wild Wales to the prototype Jubilees, which still failed to reveal their faults. Another unsatisfactory area of operation I can testify to personally was the standard of finish at that time, on the light twins at least. (Bracebridge Street housed its own enamelling plant.) I well remember the speed with which paint wore through to the bare metal, and wondering whether this was the normal state of affairs with all motor cycles.

All these production problems had their origins in the antiquated Bracebridge Street premises. By the spring of 1960, Norton had a pre-tax profit of £140,000. Orders won by export manager Reg Weeks for the new Featherbed-framed versions of the pushrod singles were coming in, including a three-year deal from 1958 to sell ES2s to Czechoslovakia. There were also fleet orders to the RAC and to foreign armed forces. So Hopwood felt the time was ripe for a move. With the parent board's approval, he located a comparatively modern factory within half a mile of Bracebridge Street for sale for £250,000. But just before finalizing the deal, a summons to head office was followed by a demand for the £250,000 cheque to meet 'a minor cash crisis'.

This was one of the last of Heather's strokes; the state of the company was finally revealing his unbusinesslike methods, and discontent was growing among the shareholders as well as among Hopwood's opposite numbers at James and Francis-Barnett. The situation had become critical because 1960 was a watershed year for the industry and the home market, and only those who had built up both reserves and exports would weather it successfully. AMC could not expect to; with the exception of the Norton twins, their products were largely dated and unsuitable, and their affairs in disarray. Too late a shareholders' committee was formed, but despite their anger at the AGM of late 1960, the move to oust Heather and his associates John Kelleher and Alfred Sugar was not co-ordinated enough to be successful. Kelleher was a butcher by trade who knew nothing of motor cycles and had arrived on the AMC board by marrying one of the Colliers' daughters; Sugar was a bureaucrat who had instituted the war-time 'flow' system. Heather had retired as MD in August of that year but had been replaced by Kelleher and Sugar as joint MDs, and he retained his seat as chairman of the board. A more concentrated effort by a body of the

shareholders to remove them in May 1961, sadly, could only give, as 'conclusive evidence' of the malaise besetting the group, the resignation of Bert Hopwood from Norton the month before. Alec Skinner, the company secretary, took over as managing director.

Contraction began apace. One of AMC's few remaining assets, sales manager Jock West, also left during 1961, and in October his place was taken by his Norton opposite number Bill Smith. Heather survived the 1961 extraordinary general meeting calling for his resignation, but in February 1962 was finally replaced as chairman. Ironically with the debacle of the Indian Sales Corporation, US sales of AMC machines were to be handed over to none other than Joe Berliner. And now that he was calling the tune, in the opinion of some at Plumstead, the factory was forced to sell their output to him for less than it cost to produce, with ruinous consequences.

The relevance of all this to the Norton story became clear in July 1962 when, following the move of Francis-Barnett to the James factory at Greet, a shock ran through the motor cycle world with the announcement that Bracebridge Street was to be closed and Norton Motors moved south to join the parent company at Plumstead. The R. T. Shelley business was moved to the James works at Greet, and Alec Skinner resigned his joint managing directorships of both.

In the meantime there had been a last burst of racing glory, together with some promising achievements for the future. In 1961 Mike Hailwood's father Stan had persuaded top tuner Bill Lacey (who had been involved with Norton singles for forty years) to forget their previous differences, and prepare one last brace of Manx models for Hailwood Jr to ride in that year's TT. The reliability of Lacey's work (as well as the pull-out of the Italian factories) allowed Mike to take three out of four of the main solo events, including the Senior where he kept the pressure on front-runner Gary Hocking's MV four until it expired. He won at over 100 mph, the first and only time this average race speed was achieved on a winning single.

It was a magnificent victory; but so was Tom Phillis' achievement in taking third place on a 500 cc Domiracer pushrod twin, the works entry. Doug Hele stayed on at Bracebridge Street for fifteen months after Hopwood had left, and his touch could be readily discerned in the Domiracers, tuned, lightened and extensively modified machines originally conceived for Daytona. They were being developed as the successor to the cammy singles, and had already reached the latter's output levels, while being 35 lb lighter. Phillis' best lap speed was 100.36 mph. Not until 1969 was another pushrod machine to better that, and then it was a 750.

Sadly this was something of a swansong, as the Domiracer and the Manx were to be abandoned by AMC in the stringent rationalization from 1962 onwards. Despite further successes by Derek Minter in 1962 on a one-off 650 which the factory built specially for him, the Domiracer never went into production, the components being sold at the end of the year to tuner Paul Dunstall. Dunstall kept the Norton name prominent throughout the '60s in the production endurance racing field. Successes in this area had come since the first victory-in-class for a Dominator 88 at the 1960 Thruxton 500-miler, as well as in the Formula One TT category (started in 1959 for standard production racers). These wins were a good selling point for the big twins to the café-racer rockers, but a high comparative price continued to present problems in the market place. For 1963 a Norton Dominator 650 cc cost £351, against £320 for a Triumph T120 650 Bonneville, and that £30 difference in price could represent nearly three weeks' wages at the time; secondhand values accentuated the gap due to the fact that Nortons were scarce. With rates of production continuing low, Norton twins, as I can well remember, were always thin on the ground and difficult to buy in the UK. Small wonder that many of the greasers imitated another of their heroes, successful endurance racer Dave Degens of Dresda Autos, and would cannibalize a Featherbed machine, fitting it with a Triumph pre-unit powerplant to create the café-racer supreme, the Triton.

The Manx models ceased to be catalogued after 1962, though about forty more were put together during 1963. The rights and stocks in 1966 were sold off to racer and frame-builder Colin Seeley, as were the equivalent rights on the AMC racing singles. Seeley eventually concentrated on the latter, selling the remaining Manx equipment to fellow sidecar specialist John Tickle, who used the engines in his own-framed T5 machines. The Manx name and tooling eventually passed to exhaust specialists Unity Equipe. Today (1996) with the help of components from Summerfield Engineering of Derbyshire and others, Bernie Allen of Marlborough can provide complete new replica Manxes.

It was fitting that both the Manx and Bracebridge Street should go down together in the same year, as in a sense both *were* Norton.

The cammy engines had excelled not just in road-racing, but in every brand of the sport, both solo and sidecar. In addition in the late 1940s and early '50s these engines were featured in small Formula 3 racing cars. From Arthur Carroll on, the cammy engines were the creations of an exceptionally dedicated team of rider-engineers, from the fanatically concentrated Joe Craig to the dedicated Gilbert Smith, who missed only one TT between 1920 and 1958, spent his holidays talent-spotting for the company, and knew every Norton dealer both at home and abroad in person. Men and machines, whatever the results for the company, had boosted the prestige of British motor cycles in a way that would have gratified the heart of Pa Norton himself.

The move to Plumstead was a more complete break than many realize. In February 1963 only five of the nearly five hundred Birmingham personnel accompanied the tooling southwards – sales manager Bill Smith, draughtsman Dennis Bourne, technical writer and service man John Hudson, and two apprentices, one of them Dave Bean, who fifteen years later was to be project leader on the Hesketh V1000. Only Hudson was to stay for long. As a recent *Classic Bike* profile revealed, he was not happy with the lack of development testing at Plumstead (one development rider against Bracebridge Street's four) or his new factory's quality control (one machine was sent to America with con-rods of unequal length), or with some lapses in production standards (Bracebridge Street's own-produced dull-chrome plated nuts, bolts and washers gave way to Woolwich cadmium plating). Ironically the lack of seasoned Norton hands was a severe handicap, because much of the production equipment was sufficiently old and worn-out that it could only be operated accurately by those familiar with its ways. Also, the Birmingham men, seeing the machines being moved out and their jobs lost, had very probably bundled them on to the lorries without being over-careful about any damage they might sustain.

But none of this applied to the Featherbed frames, which continued, in the Slimline format adopted for reasons of policy and of rider comfort in 1960, to be produced in Birmingham at Reynolds as they always had been. The Jubilee, as well as the big twins, was a welcome addition to the Plumstead line-up, since the 250 class had assumed new prominence with the restriction of learners to that capacity during 1960; and AMC's own 250 four-stroke and two-stroke singles had not been a sales success. But the Jubilee never achieved either the cachet of the fast Royal Enfield or the popularity of BSA's cheap and cheerful C15.

From February 1964 a bored-out version of the Dominator, the mighty 750 Atlas, after two years in production for export, became available for the home market. It had been laid out in Birmingham by Doug Hele in response to requests from America for a powerful engine flexible enough to accelerate from 20 to 100 mph in top gear. At Plumstead it was developed further by AMC's design department chief ex-Velocette man Charles Udall, the man who had co-designed the original underpowered and underlubricated Velocette LE. Wally Wyatt, expert AMC development engineer, was to say of Udall that he 'always resisted change', and it was Wyatt who did much of the successful Atlas development work. Udall's own work, on the lubrication system and on the bearings, was to have less happy results. But the engine was to be a fitting basis for remaining Norton glory. AMC's own-brand 750 had been withdrawn after only a few were completed and sold (machining out the 650 crankcase had left insufficient meat to take an adequate gasket). After that the Atlas engine, modified with an AMC primary chaincase and wider rear chain, was used in AMC cycle parts to create the Matchless G15/AJS Model 33 and their several derivatives. There were other signs of Norton influence as the Plumstead ranges shrank and were rationalized; for 1964 the Norton gear-

type oil pump was adapted for the AMC singles, and on all models but the 250s, Norton wheels, brakes and Roadholder forks were adopted. Though superior components, this didn't really please fans of any of the marques. Worse was to follow for 1965, with an ill-judged attempt to cash in on the name by sticking Norton badges on AJS/Matchless 350 and 500 singles (the all-Norton roadster Featherbed singles had got the chop after 1963), and calling the result the Norton Model 50 Mk II and ES2 Mk II.

In August 1966 the crunch came for AMC, with a statement issued to the effect that Britain's current financial troubles had stopped negotiations for working capital from US sources (in fact, Joe Berliner, their importer) and the directors had asked the company's bank to appoint a receiver and manager. Shortly afterwards, on 2 September, AMC was acquired, lock, stock and Norton, by Manganese Bronze Holdings (MBH), parent company of a group of engineering and metal firms. Their chairman, Dennis Poore, had apparently been planning this move since 1962, and pulling it off just after the receiver had been appointed meant no benefit from the takeover for the long-suffering AMC shareholders.

Though motor cycles were initially something of a hobby with Dennis Poore, MBH's ambitions seemed large. They had taken over Villiers the year before, and the new motor cycle division was soon dubbed Norton-Villiers. In March 1967 it was

An apotheosis. Norton 650 SS, seen here in 1968 guise, was really unapproachable.

An AMC abortion, the 350 'Model 50 Mk II' was really a Matchless G3.

announced that they had also acquired Royal Enfield's share capital (though not their spares, service obligations or remaining factories). In turn the Enfield acquisition also involved a stake in the Indian Enfield venture. All this meant that outside the ailing independent Velocette, virtually the entire surviving British motor cycle industry other than the BSA group was owned by Poore's MBH. The control was shortly enforced in July 1968 by cutting off the supply of Villiers engines to remaining small producers such as Cotton, DMW and Greeves. The AJS name was to be the repository of the last developments of Villiers power, the Starmaker, 37A Trials and Y4 moto-cross 250, and the Y5 370 and 410 scrambles engines. Otherwise there was, not before time, ruthless pruning; Francis-Barnett and James went, and Plumstead housed Norton-Matchless Ltd. For the next three years they produced, apart from around 100 Matchless G85CS scrambler singles, only Norton and Norton-engined roadsters, most firmly aimed at the USA.

Roger Dennistoun Poore became chairman of the new Norton-Villiers company as well as of MBH, and was to interest himself personally in its fortunes, becoming managing director as well in 1970. Fifty years old at the time of the takeover, this Eton and Cambridge man was also chairman of two finance companies, a director of another, and a member of Lloyds. Further, he was a man of action with an automotive background; he had served in the RAF in wartime and in 1950 had been British Champion of car hill-climbs, as well as being a motor cyclist. All this was hopeful for the motor cycle industry; but the City credentials were the significant ones. Dennis Poore was to prove first and foremost a businessman, and his priorities were commercial ones.

The move into the motor cycle trade made sound business sense at this time for despite the sad state of the home market, by April 1965 motor cycle export figures to America had exactly tripled over the previous three years, and it was predicted that America would be buying three-quarters of a million new bikes a year by 1967. Norton-Villiers were to reflect this pattern; by 1972 95 per cent of their product was going abroad, and 60 per cent of that to America.

It was Poore who chaired a meeting late in 1966 getting together executives from both the Wolverhampton Villiers plant and Norton-Matchless at Plumstead. Their purpose was to come up with a flagship for the new concern, a big bike primarily aimed at the US market, to replace the Atlas. They decided to resurrect a five-year-old design executed at Plumstead by Charles Udall, an 800 cc dohc parallel twin with unit-construction four-speed gearbox. This heavy engine was housed, inclined forward, in a modified Featherbed frame decked out with many AMC cycle parts and topped by a tank bearing the traditional Norton name. The project was dubbed P10.

Bernard Hooper, who had been with Villiers from 1958 to 1965, was designated the project's chief designer. Hooper was an experienced development engineer who, while at BSA, had already been responsible, with Hermann Meier, for taking the 125 cc Bantam to 150 cc, and for the experimental Sunbeam S10. Then, as a freelance, he had worked very slightly on the racing 344 cc Scott, and with John Favill at Villiers had developed their all-original 25 bhp 250 cc twin-carb two-stroke single, the Starmaker, which was to become the basis of some quite successful road racers. He had left late in 1965 to

New guv'nor meets old. Norton's new MD, Dennis Poore, expounding the joys of the new Commando to '30s' racer Freddie Frith OBE at a 1968 press reception.

go independent, rejoining NV late in 1966. (Later Hooper and Favill were to collaborate again, at first for NVT, on an idea they had initiated in the '65 freelance days, the revolutionary two-stroke stepped-piston SPX Wulf design.)

Hooper was quickly disillusioned with the P10, one of whose chief features was an inordinate length of cam-chain—88 to 90 links, as long as a conventional drive chain, run through a series of teflon-lined tubes that gave the superficial appearance of inclined pushrod tubes and made the bike, seen broadside from the right, resemble a stubby Vincent Comet. It was backlash from the long chain which probably necessitated the engine's drilled and threaded bosses on the end of the camshafts, with sprockets indexed with a dozen or so holes to give infinitely variable valve timing. The team's attempts to further modernize the cylinder head were rather undercut by the knowledge that Wally Wyatt, the seasoned Plumstead-based development engineer, had modified the Atlas engine to produce more power than the P10 looked capable of.

Another minus point was vibration, and this was of particular concern since the team had now been joined by the new overall Norton-Villiers director of engineering, the late Dr Stefan Bauer who arrived early in 1967. He came from Rolls Royce and previously the atomic industry. He was not a motor cyclist, and possibly it was these illustrious industrial antecedents that made his

methods seem abrupt and high-handed in a field best summed up by a statement about Doug Hele's highly successful Triumph Development Department—'There are no gaffers in a technical discussion'. Bauer was emphatic from the first that vibration would not be tolerated. He also endorsed Poore in insisting that come what may, the new flagship had to be ready very quickly indeed, in time for the Earl's Court Show in September 1967.

One report (*MCN*, 12 December 1983) suggests that it was Poore riding the P10 himself that put a stop to the bike which would have been the 800 SS. At that point there were around three months to go to the show. It was Hooper who provided the idea, during further discussions at Plumstead, of using the Atlas engine in something like the new-type frame with a single top tube that Bauer was also insisting on for the P10, despite the Featherbed's excellent reputation; and in this frame, vibration would be eliminated by hanging the engine, gearbox and rear swinging arm in rubber bushes, isolated from both the main frame and the rider (hence the 'Isolastic' tag for this system).

So a frame of the kind outlined by Bauer and Hooper was devised, but with not merely a single top tube but a 2.25 in diameter main spine, twin front downtubes and a triangulated rear section. While light (just 24 lb, some 11 lb lighter than its predecessor), the spine frame was to be something of a mixed blessing; after initial problems of fracturing had been cleared up by Ken Sprayson of Reynolds, it handled well enough, but in conjunction with the Isolastic system and with the continued use of a modified version of the old Roadholder front fork which economy dictated, it was never to provide the absolutely predictable standard of handling of the Featherbed.

Hooper and his development engineer Bob Trigg began work on the train back to Wolverhampton after the meeting with Poore. A recent article in *Classic Bike* (November 1982) provided details of their rapid progress. A rubber company was approached about the Isolastics, but when they said two years development would be needed, the team went ahead on their own, and after several experiments (an important one, cutting the rubber bushes in half, was suggested by Dr Bauer) they had eliminated vibration transmitted to the rider above 1,800 rpm. It was also vital that the machine should be styled to emphasize it as a breakaway concept from its parallel twin forebears. To this end Wolf Ohlins, an advertising agency, were employed as consultants. Using outside consultants in the motor cycle field has not always paid off in other cases, but though Wolf Ohlins had no previous experience with bikes, Hooper says 'some of their suggestions made us laugh, but others were good.'

The result was the Commando, reviving a name whose aggressiveness suited the styling but which had once been possessed by AMC's James two-stroke scramblers. The modified Atlas engine was inclined forward and a pleasingly straight line, echoed elsewhere, extended through the tank and the base of the seat, which was married to the tank by a non-functional but distinctive pair of 'ears' extending forward from the seat's front end. A lean machine at 430 lb kerb weight, it lived up to the Norton desiderata of a motor cycle that 'should look as if it's doing a hundred miles an hour when it's standing still'.

Personally I prefer the looks of the later Roadsters, but for some the Fastback, so called for its racing-style rear end, was to be the most attractive variation of them all. The Commando prototype, resplendent with silver frame and tank plus orange seat, was the sensation of the 1967 Show. One further contribution from Wolf Ohlins was the 'green spot' NV corporate symbol; in view of the rapidly increasing Japanese penetration at the time, some wags queried whether this wasn't simply a sick parody of the Rising Sun. (Symbols were to be a headache for

Bernard Hooper, one of the Commando developers, points to an Isolastic mounting during the Castrol design award ceremony which he won in 1970.

the company; in 1973 they offered a £25 prize for a logo for the new Norton-Villiers-Triumph [NVT] setup, which prompted a suggestion for a symbol depicting infinity, since Atlas crankcases seemed to be infinitely unobtainable. . .)

This wisecrack leads us back to the situation for Norton for the three years following the takeover, which was an uncomfortable interim period. Factory spares and service facilities at Plumstead were discontinued by Norton-Villiers, leaving local dealers to cover these and warranty requirements, a frequently unsatisfactory situation for the Norton owner. The exception was veteran Norton man John Hudson, who went to extraordinary lengths to honour the commitments made in the company's name. He would come to owners' homes, usually on his own time, to repair and service their machines under warranty, sometimes sleeping in workshops while he did so.

As to the machines produced, the object was to clear remaining stocks from Plumstead while taking advantage of the booming US market. The result was a number of Norton and Norton-Matchless big twin hybrids. Typical of these were the P11 'desert sleds', basically a modified Atlas engine shoe-horned into the new G85CS Matchless scrambler frame and forks. The idea had come from America, with two prototypes built up by Bob Blair of 2DS Motors, the Norton

West Coast distributor and a representative of Berliner; Blair then shipped one back to Plumstead. In addition to the regular Norton 650SS and Atlas models, there was a single carb 650, the Mercury and the N15CS, a Roadholder-forked P11, and the various Matchless G15 variants. Handsome brutes, the P11, the later P11A, the Ranger, the N15CS and earlier, the Nomad, were well received on the West Coast both as street scramblers and highly successful desert racers in the Mojave, taking the No 1 plate for a couple of years. But it was confusing for the home market, and the hybrids virtually ended when Woolwich ceased to produce in 1969, leaving a few cancelled export orders to be had cheaply on this side of the pond. It was as well that the presence of the Commando, produced at Plumstead for a year and a half, with the frames made by Reynolds, provided a clear direction to the company's endeavours.

The absence of service provided an indication of something that was to be another Norton-Villiers characteristic, namely unwillingness to spend money. There was no way that the motor cycle side could show a large profit at this stage, but there seemed a disparity between MBH's ambitions and the amount of cash they were prepared to invest in maintaining engineering standards, forward planning, and a viable industry while achieving them. An example was quickly

Left *Goodbye Woolwich. July 1969, and the gang at the old Matchless factory in Plumstead with the last machine built there, a 750 Commando 'S' model.*

Right *Hello Andover. 1970, and Commando production racers are created prior to despatch at the new assembly plant.*

provided with the new hope, the Commando. In addition to the use of the old forks and engine, even the Isolastic system was skimped. Hooper and Trigg had devised and patented an instant vernier system of adjustment for the rubber mountings (they were to receive a £1,000 Castrol design award for the system as a whole in 1970). But an alternative adjustment system with shims and polyurethane thrust washers had been employed on prototypes, and since it was cheaper to produce, this was what Commando owners were lumbered with until 1975. It meant a long and absolutely necessary piece of servicing every 5,000 miles that was beyond most riders and many dealers to perform, and had detrimental and sometimes dangerous effects—at least one coroner's court suggested that a fatal crash might have been due to instability arising from Isolastics on a second-hand Commando that had got too loose through lack of attention.

This parsimony on the part of the company also led to a lack of centering for its operations. The way in which they appeared to juggle, from the head office at 1 Love Lane in the City, existing products and company names, was reinforced by the absence of an identifiable base for operations. The Woolwich factory was due for demolition and sale of site by compulsory purchase to the GLC. Plumstead, the home of Matchless Motorcycles since 1912, entered its final run-down period in 1969, with the last Woolwich-built Commando leaving the plant on 25 July, though the building was not in fact demolished until 1971. The Wolverhampton works at Marston Road, antiquated as they were, were very extensive and could have provided a new base for Norton-Villiers. Instead it was decided to take advantage of a government-assisted development area at Andover in Hampshire, and establish the assembly plant, on North Way, Walworth, in an industrial estate, at the same time creating a test department for Commandos there.

But Commando *engines* were to be assembled 120 miles away in Wolverhampton. They were then brought down overnight, with rear engine plates and gearboxes attached, by Samuels Road Transport, whose lorries were often waiting to unload when the Andover factory opened up in the morning. The disadvantages of this scheme are obvious.

Already, lines familiar to the observer of the British motor cycle industry were being drawn, between the genuine motor cycle engineers, and the executives. A recruit from the latter to the motor cycle camp was Bill Colquhoun, whose father John was an MBH director and former

chairman. Initially Colquhoun Jr took over at Woolwich, but in 1969 he took charge of the new Norton-Villiers Corporation at Long Beach, California, with the Norton franchise for the seven western states formerly held by the Berliner Motor Corporation, who continued to handle Nortons elsewhere in the USA; Bob Blair of 2DS in California was understandably not pleased about this. Bill Colquhoun was to become friends with the legendary Neale Shilton, hard rider and ex-Triumph Police fleet boss. Shilton had been recruited in November 1968 by Poore himself, to create a Police Norton and win fleet orders for it. Shilton tells the story in his autobiography *A Million Miles Ago* (his actual mileage on two wheels in the service of the industry). One who collaborated with him later characterized him as 'very authoritarian, but OK to work with.' He pursued the Interpol goal single-mindedly, and it was eventually to profit the company considerably. He bonded with Bill Colquhoun through yearly participation in the tough Circuit des Pyrénées road rally event. Mike Jackson, an ex-scrambler who had come to the sales side of NV from Greeves, a frenetic individual giving the impression of perpetual motion, was another Circuit des Pyrénées competitor.

But unfortunately at the start of Shilton's period with NV he ran up against the man who replaced Colquhoun when the latter left Plumstead. This was NV's future director of

marketing and Poore's right-hand man, Hugh Palin MBE. A rider and chairman of the Cycle and Motor Cycle Association, Palin was a man with a dry manner either dignified or pompous according to interpretation. His future with NV was to include many unpleasant tasks in the field of industrial relations. In this instance, according to Shilton, when the latter arrived at Woolwich at the start of 1969 Palin simply told him to go home and wait until he was called. The pugnacious Shilton restrained himself from reacting to what he reckoned was deliberate provocation, and though the feud continued, he simply went to work with Wally Wyatt, the Atlas development engineer and another genuine motor cycle man, until transferring to Andover with several other members of the Woolwich workforce. They did not include Wyatt, whom Shilton says was offered an insultingly minor job and left to work for the Rickman brothers. Poore was later to offer him a job again, but it was in Wolverhampton not Andover, and too late. Luckily, at least one top-line rider of the old school remained; this was Bob Manns, long-distance road racer and winner of seven Golds in the ISDT, all but one for AMC. Initially on the sales side, Manns became from 1973 Poore's 'chief test pilot' and a valuable development engineer for the Commando.

But the diffuse nature of the production set-up inevitably fostered self-interest among the various separate groups at Wolverhampton and Andover.

Shilton records opposition to the Police bike from Bob Trigg at the Wolverhampton design department, after Shilton had gone ahead on his own authority and commissioned the steel tanks for the machines required (current production Commandos were fitting fibreglass tanks). But in this instance Poore backed Shilton, saying steel tanks would be needed for the US (and from 1973 they were to be a legal requirement in the UK also). Shilton was also refused the use of the Andover assembly line for his first production batch and records that John Pedley, the Wolverhampton works director (and from 1970 a member of the Norton-Villiers board) called Police business 'a nuisance' which must not interfere with normal production, and told him that the USA could take all of their output for a long time. This was to prove a short-sighted attitude, for while Police fleet business was not notoriously profitable, as Shilton points out, the time would come when Police machines were the only ones being built for which orders were in hand.

Poore was a rider, and commanded the respect of some of his experienced employees, but there were factors that often denied them access to him. One of these appears to have been Dr Stefan Bauer. In a *Penthouse* article by Ronnie Mutch, Clive Stokes, who worked in the experimental department of NVT, states baldly: 'Bauer was partly responsible for the demise of NVT—he filtered all the information that came up to the chairman [Poore] from the factory, and so the chairman was making decisions on distorted information.' Bauer left NV in February 1969 to go to BSA, but by 1972 was accepted back by Poore as technical director and stayed until he retired in 1975. Stokes gives an example of the problems this created.

'The chairman on one occasion asked me to prepare a report on the possibility of using electronic tachometers. I made the report and passed it on. The next thing I knew, Dr Bauer came in, flung the report on my desk and asked me what it was all about, telling me that I must send reports through him and not to the chairman direct, because he would decide whether the chairman would see it or not. So I was in the position where the chairman was telling me to do one thing, and the technical director was telling me to do another.'

However for the moment, in 1969, Norton was looking good. The Commando had been hailed as an instant classic in North America, where its brutal good looks, novelty, excellent performance and new standards of long-distance rider comfort (riding position excluded) had secured good reputation and sales. In Europe, too, having got in ahead of both the BSA/Triumph triple and the Honda 4, the Commando became something of a cult bike, having been voted, for what it was worth, the *MCN* Machine of the Year for 1968, the first of five consecutive awards. Though there was to be a slump in new machine sales in the UK for 1969, the motor cycle scene in the US was booming, and by October Norton-Villiers' total sales there for the year were up 25 per cent on the preceding year, with demand having exceeded supply for February/March 1969. This was as well, since the relocation in Andover was claimed to have involved a half-million pound investment by MBH. Production at Andover started modestly with thirty machines a day, but shortly increased, and after expansion into an ex-steel works in Central Way on the estate, production rose to 300 a week in 1973.

The Norton test department was initially an unheated aircraft hangar on nearby Thruxton airfield. The location in Thruxton with its road race circuit began to seem less coincidental in February 1970, when after a win by Mick Andrews in the 1969 Hutchinson 100 race on a Commando and a second position by Paul Smart in the 750 Production TT event (run on the Isle of Man since 1967 and won by Ray Pickrell on a Dunstall Norton in 1968), it was announced that tuned, disc-braked production racers would become available to the public. Norton-Villiers were opening a performance shop to produce special

machines and racing custom equipment. These were to be brand-named Norvil, with the shop under the management of former road-racer and development engineer of the Villiers Starmaker, Peter Inchley, who was also executive in charge of the AJS effort.

Top flight GP racing was by now completely divorced from everyday roadster machines, and this production racing offered a way of providing spectator identification with the machinery on the track. With Nortons, South London dealer Gus Kuhn had already entered this field with a racing team and custom goodies. Paul Dunstall, the leading Norton twin exponent on the tracks since 1958 (who it will be recalled had bought the Domiracer and its components) was also running his own-framed Commando racer, with Ray Pickrell taking records on it at Monza in 1970; and he too offered custom racing parts for the bike. So factory involvement was nothing but logical, since from the first Norton-Villiers had been offering a series of tuning kits devised in conjunction with Dunstall. It was also in line with the Norton tradition, and it pleased the sporting chairman. It was to lead to still greater involvement shortly in the new Formula 750 category. Whether for top class road racing a machine with the ageing pushrod parallel twin engine at its centre was really desirable remained to be seen. Some cynically considered that the Formula 750 class had been instituted solely to

Above left *Hugh Palin MBE, Norton Director of Marketing in 1970, with that year's production racer.*

Right *Driving force. Peter Williams on Commando racer, 1970.*

publicize and benefit what the British manufacturers were stuck with making.

A good deal of this renewed interest in racing was due to the arrival on the development team at Andover of Peter Williams, a man in the Norton engineer/rider tradition. Son of AMC's 7R-developer Jack Williams, and already a skilled exponent on his Arter G50 Matchless, Williams was to combine technical ingenuity with top-class riding skills, especially on the TT circuit, to produce a last intermittent burst of Norton racing glory.

But if it was to be disadvantaged on the track, nevertheless it must here be acknowledged that the Commando was in many ways an excellent compromise between the old and the new. It is dealt with in detail in its own section, but here it can be said that the machine which single-handedly carried the Norton name for some ten years had an engine that had made a better and stronger job of the expansion to 750 cc than the other British parallel twin four-strokes. This plus the Isolastic innovation made fast motorway cruising a real possibility, while providing the basis of a 'real motor cycle', ie, one that looked, sounded and handled itself on twisting A-roads in a satisfying manner, and (Isolastics excluded) could be looked after reasonably easily by mechanically minded owners. In addition, it was to form the basis of sprinters and drag racers, record breaking machines, road racers and world-beating sidecar moto-cross outfits. It was well up to all these functions when judiciously tuned and, above all, carefully assembled.

This last point is most important, because it explains the increasing shadow that began to fall on the Commando name from around 1970. Tales of electrical problems, trouble with piston rings, porous castings and above all main-bearing failure, began to circulate among riders, a suspicious fraternity, and many of the rumours were substantiated in fact. Admittedly an ageing model by 1970, it must be said that the Commando's deficiencies were almost all attributable to management and production foul-ups rather that the basic design. The heart of the problem was Wolverhampton, where in the 17½-acre site dating back to World War I, the engines and gearboxes were now made.

The attitude at the top there was, as Neale Shilton put it, 'quality being seconded to quantity production—primarily for export'. Shilton wrote feelingly on this, as his demonstrator Interpol nearly killed him when at 80 mph its alternator rotor seized on the stator—due to main bearing wear. Since 1969 he had observed that 'if Wolverhampton could have reproduced the

The most exciting pin-up of the year.

Sales drive. Aimed at the New World and spearheaded by the Commando, Norton publicity for the 1970s became quite flamboyant.

quality of the Woolwich-built [Atlas] engine, there would have been no need for the Isolastic system.' As a hard, seasoned rider since the pre-war days of unsprung machines, he probably underestimated the importance both in terms of comfort and, as a selling-point, of the Isolastics (or 'knickerlastics' as they were soon rendered in the vernacular). But he has a point when he says that 'unfortunately as time went by [the Isolastic system] was expected to take care of inherent defects in engine quality.'

Defects arose in large part from Wolverhampton's deficiencies in quality control and poor standards of finish, which were a factory responsibility. Poore himself became exasperated with the place. 'We don't solve problems here, we create them', he is reported to have said to Wally Wyatt while attempting to recruit him to help. But they also came from the archaic production methods dictated by NV management's already-noted unwillingness to spend money, in this case to invest in modern plant. Some of the results were related in a *Which Bike?* article on the modified Commando of 'chief test pilot' Bob Manns. Of Wolverhampton Manns says:

'Everywhere you looked there were funny things going on. Tolerances were always generous, making motors noisy—unlike the fine tolerances on the Jap bikes. When I selected timing and crank pinions for my bike, I went and selected some that had been made oversize. It transformed the engine.

'Every big end was out of true . . . I put the crank together (on my own machine) really carefully. The trouble was that the cranks came in as a casting, the big end journals etc were machined, and then the whole thing split. Now here's the rub. The machine splitting the shafts could be out by a few thou, and certainly not consistently so. Afterwards the halves were put in separate bins—never matched up. [Cylinder] barrels too could easily be bored out of alignment—it was all pretty heart-breaking stuff. Swarf and sand from blasting would be all over the place during the assembly stages, that's why I put my engine up myself.'

A letter to *MCS* from Tim Stevens, who was working under the quality manager at Wolverhampton, also pointed out that critics of British quality control often overlook the fact that the problem lay deeper than that; since 'because of lack of development and drawing office personnel, many of the finer points of machine detail simply are not decided and put on paper. There are, for instance, no diagrams of how the wiring harness and control cables should be laid to the frame. . . Thus the quality engineer has no chance of saying 'This is right, and this is wrong', and therefore production urgencies ensure that the cables are laid the most expedient way for speed of production.' On Commandos (other than the 850 Mk III) this presents one, for instance, with a choice of routing the wires to the ignition switch down by the left hand side panel either between frame and panel, where they can be chafed and short out, or stretched round inside the frame, where they can pull clear of the connectors on the switch itself. I know; my own Commando has ground to a halt for both those reasons.

A final note may be supplied by a letter to the papers from a Wolverhampton worker after Poore had complained publicly about low levels of production by the Wolverhampton workforce. The correspondent maintained, 'the workers are willing and able but the system and tools are sadly lacking.' He instanced as evidence of this the necessity of hand-tapping the threads on the petrol tanks (most of the civilian machines' steel tanks were Italian made) and concluded by claiming that Norton-Villiers was making 'a consistent loss'. This is confirmed by Shilton; on machine price alone, the 750 Commandos, at around £650 for 1972 and 1973, were according to him making well under £170 profit, much less than the ideal one third profit a producer generally expects to see returned on manufactured goods. This was despite the fact that they had always been £100-150 more expensive than the list price for the equivalent BSA and Triumph twins (though both the latter were heavily discounted for 1972 and 1973).

Initially though, despite all this, the NV company appeared to prosper and an overall export figure of £10 million for the industry (now virtually BSA-Triumph and Norton-Villiers) was recorded for the first half of the financial year of 1970. Surprisingly, only £2.75 million of this was from the USA and Canada; there had been good returns from Europe. For Norton-Villiers this may well have had to do with the low levels of profit from Berliner. By 1971 Norton were also involved in Australia with the Norton Villiers Pty Ltd, based at Ballarat, Victoria, and around 20 per cent of export production was going to Australasia. 1970 had seen yet another of the confusingly proliferating associated companies, Norton Villiers Europe, formed to distribute to the UK and the Continent under Hugh Palin, with offices at 54 rue Rouget de l'Isle, Paris.

In Europe the flow of goods was not to be all one way, as the management discovered the competitive prices on components offered by the Italian industry, which was thriving behind a system of protective tariffs and a ban on the import of foreign lightweights. This was the start for Norton-Villiers of the route that would lead to the Easy Rider, but it began with equipment for the production racers (Tomaselli levers, Campagnola racing hubs). In addition to some of the steel petrol tanks, Shilton says that the later models' steel mudguards were from Paoili, and that 'all the frames' came from Italy; but the Press in the late '60s and early '70s attributed them to Reynolds, and John Hudson confirms that only from about 1972 or 1973 did they come from Italy, with a distinguishing mark to identify them on the front petrol tank platform. None of this was

Sempre all'Avanguardia....

Prima la Sprinter...

ora la Strider per le lunghe distance

The Italian connection. How many of these frames were made there?

mentioned at the time by the publicly patriotic chairman.

The next year, 1971, also seemed to be a good one, with Norton-Villiers announcing £5,556,000 from the sale of motor cycles to July 1972, a twelvefold growth in the five years since 1967; though during 1972 the dollar was devalued cutting into the US earnings. The relationship with Europe in those pre-Common Market days was also evidently not without its problems. Poore's own report to the shareholders at the end of 1972 mentioned 'a disappointing performance', with 'the difficulties of trading in Europe facing British companies compared to the relative ease of trading in the US and the Commonwealth where the British commercial tradition prevails.'

There were, of course, men aboard Norton-Villiers who could have helped on overseas commercial transactions, in particular Neale Shilton, whose personal touch with Police sales had generated orders from France and Yugoslavia,

and had led to Commandos being built under licence in Greece. Shilton also, among several other export markets including Argentina, had negotiated a substantial contract with the security forces in Nigeria. By using an established company with a base in Lagos to handle the financial side, he avoided getting his fingers burned as someone else in Norton-Villiers had earlier, and someone at Triumph was to do shortly, when machines were supplied and not paid for. But presumably since Hugh Palin was at the head of Norton-Villiers Europe, Shilton simply let him get on with it.

In his annual report for 1972 Poore went on to add that 'demand for motor cycles in Europe shows every sign of repeating the trend which began in America a few years ago, but clearly the company has much to learn about European needs and procedures.' There had been an increase in home sales from £290,000 to £1,578,000, and the fifth and last accolade of the *MCN* machine of the year for the Commando. For 1972 Norton-Villiers declared a modest profit of £372,000. But losses could be hidden in the group's finance companies, and in fact the situation for the company was deteriorating fast, with profits falling £236,000 for the first half of the 1972-73 trading period; and by January 1974 Norton showed a pre-tax loss of £163,757.

The reasons were fairly clear. The Japanese were underpricing and outgunning the ageing Commando, there was no replacement machine planned, and the steps taken to remedy the situation for the big twin made things worse. Then the step Poore took to remedy *that* situation turned into a disaster.

The four cylinder overhead cam Honda CB 750, launched in the States in October 1978 and in Britain in April 1979, really was the one-bike start of a new era for roadsters. It was the basis of the smaller Honda Fours, and unchallenged until Kawasaki leapfrogged them with the Z1. The bottom line was not the CB's disc brake, electric start, quietness, smoothness or high level of equipment; it was the 67 bhp which the untuned model pushed out. To their credit, Norton, in collaboration with Lockheed, after some initial problems produced a good disc brake, they fitted trafficators and smartened up the instruments, they (in the person of John Favill) collaborated with Roe and Thorpe at Birmingham University to produce quiet but effective annular discharge 'black cap' silencers, and for 1975 there was even an (unsatisfactory) electric foot. Some riders preferred the torque of the big twins to the buzziness of the Japanese motors, they were easier to maintain, and Nortons still out-handled the 750 Fours.

But they fell down on reliability. Shilton recalls the Thruxton hangars crowded with ranks of bikes rejected by the experienced ex-Woolwich testers for porous crankcases, rotating main bearings, etc. One Police bike at the time got through rear wheel bearings at 200 and 3,000 miles. The factory replacement bearings had 'MADE IN JAPAN' stamped on them, but Japanese engineering was not the culprit; at Wolverhampton no grease had been applied to them. One high mileage rider at the time, who reckoned to put in 15,000 miles a year and was experiencing a stream of troubles with his new 1972 Commando, was finally quietly and despairingly told by service man John Hudson that anyone who was serious about motorcycling should now be riding Japanese.

However, what Norton were up against at base was brute power, of two kinds. Following that inexorable logic which Joe Craig and the racing Nortons had discovered the hard way many years ago, the output of a 750 with four cylinders was automatically greater than a 750 with two cylinders. Standard production Commandos claimed 59 bhp, and the very best engine built by the Norton racing shop put out 75 bhp; even a late experimental four-valve head, initially developed by Piper Engineering in 1972, and then worked on by Douge Hele at the NVT Development shop at Kitts Green in 1976, failed to lift the yield to 80 bhp. Whereas the completely standard CB 750 was producing 67 bhp, and the Four in the lightest state of tune among several factory entries, with which Dick Mann won at Daytona in 1970, put out 90 bhp. In roadster terms this made the CB 750 a genuine 120 mph motor cycle, with acceleration to match. The Norton was no slouch either, average top speeds on the 750 being around the 115 mph mark, with standing quarters in the low 13s, but trying to maintain those levels of performance for extended periods rapidly led to grief, which was not the case for the 750 Four. Word of this inevitably spread.

The other application of power was the efficiency and sheer volume of Japanese production and marketing. Between their launch and the end of 1974, over 390,000 CB 750s were built, an annual average of 65,000. By contrast in Norton's best year only around 17,000 Commandos were made, and in the end the total was less than 70,000. This disparity in production levels was reflected in price. By 1971 in the USA, the main arena, the Commando was selling at

$1,495, against the infinitely more sophisticated Honda Four at $1,490.

Something had to be done, and the Commando was the only thing on offer. Despite some works' successes, commercially the AJS Competition two-strokes were to prove an expensive dead-end, and that side was sold off in September 1974 to ex-employee Fluff Brown to develop and produce in small quantities as his own FB-AJS machines. For 1972 moves were made to strengthen the 750 Commandos and increase its output, prior to another boring-out job, which would raise the engine's capacity to 828 cc. In practice these strengthening measures had an adverse effect on the engine's reliability.

But worse was to come. Since 1970, in addition to batches of production racers, there had been a high-performance Combat option of the 750 engine. It had been hoped that this would raise output to 69 bhp, exceeding the Honda's magic 67, but actual results settled for a claimed 65. For 1972 this continued as an option for most of the range but was now supplied as standard for a new big-tank model, the Interstate, which also fitted the front disc brake developed for the racers.

Racing had taken on a new prominence with the announcement at the end of 1971 that Norton were once again to field a road racing team. This was to be under the management of Frank Perris and sponsored by the John Player cigarette company, as John Player Norton. Top riders for JPN, including Phil Read and Mick Grant, were to be part of the effort at different times, but the backbone was the talented Peter Williams, who doubled as designer and developer, backed by Dave 'Crasher' Croxford, an exuberant ex-poodle clipper with, nevertheless, twelve City and Guilds and a string of other qualifications to his name. In fact, all the fourteen-man team out at Thruxton turned their hand to everything, including ex-Rickman frame builder and mechanic Peter Pykett, today an ace restorer of AMC singles. Their resources were the detritus of the industry. Their dynamometer was the one on which the last works AJS racer had been run up in 1956, the cylinder-honing machine had been sold for scrap in 1966 for a fiver, bought back for £80, and the chuck had 35 thou play in it, while the bed on their milling machine had to be levelled up with alloy blocks. With the exception of the flash JPN Dodge transporter, it was a very undergunned endeavour in GP terms, in everything except effort, which was on the heroic, and ultimately the tragic, scale.

The presence of the professional publicists was also evident from the start, with everyone

The JPN team with, from the left, Team Manager Frank Perris, Dave 'Crasher' Croxford, John Cooper and Peter Williams, in 1973, their best year.

involved, from Poore downwards, sporting spiffy paddock-jackets in the JPN colours, which were a patriotic red, white and blue. The abrasive Phil Read took a less than charitable view of it all when he quit the team after 1972. 'I did not like the red tape that surrounded the JPN set up,' he told *MCN*. 'There were too many hangers-on involved, which rather detracted from the racing. Instead of concentrating on that, we were getting fittings for jackets, trousers and T-shirts.' The team did not prosper that year at Daytona or the TT, though Williams did achieve a second place on the Island, and Croxford and Grant won the Thruxton 500. Gearbox problems were prominent, the transmission becoming the weak link as the engine's power was boosted.

Meanwhile, for the road bikes, the situation became much blacker. According to Shilton, Poore was personally aware of and involved in a fateful decision. This was to switch all Commando production to the overstressed Combat-engined version, linked, on the Interstate specification, to the disc brake, something most riders wanted. Shilton writes that he was not slow in pointing out that what was appreciated by Police motor cyclists particularly was reliability rather than brute power, and that he took the opportunity to let the chairman know ('apparently it was news to him') of the many engine and gearbox failures that were already occurring. There had also been a change of works manager at Wolverhampton, and the new man admitted to Shilton he knew

nothing of motor cycles and asked for his help. Of Poore's decision Shilton observed, 'nobody ever stopped RDP [Poore] from doing what he had decided, except the Meriden factory pickets.' Indeed, Poore's abrupt moves were beginning to look more like impulsiveness than decisiveness, and once made were stubbornly adhered to.

The Combat engine, however, was a disaster that could not be ignored for long. From July 1972 it was announced as the only option available for most of the range. In conjunction with that year's lowered gearing, this made it all too easy to over-rev the flexible engines causing the corners of the new timing-side roller bearings to dig in when thus overstressed. In addition the ignition often jammed on full advance. Mains were often well on the way out by the end of 3,000 miles.

Thousands of Combat engines were built— Norton at this time were actually reducing their prices because, they said, of increased production levels and although matching the price-cuts by BSA-Triumph was a more likely explanation for the cost-cutting, production did indeed increase. As opposed to the 25,000 Commando 750s built in the four years up until the end of 1971, 30,000 more 750s were to be made between then and the end in late 1973. The Combat, as Shilton wrote, was 'a major disaster, not only financially because of the avalanche of warranty claims, but [because] it did great harm to the name of Norton.' The Commando's reputation on the street at the time never really recovered. Even *Bike*'s Ogri, the cult rocker cartoon hero, made a lightly veiled throw at them ('Not one of *those*, Malcolm.' 'But it was Machine of the Year!'). On the warranty claim front in Europe, John Hudson recalls, 'The German distributor in Darmstadt sold some 200 Commandos in '72—and had them nearly all back under warranty, and then they "axed" him and transferred the distributorship to the BSA distributor at Oberhausen. . . I don't think he ever sold a bike . . . [the Norton management] did their best to destroy whatever there was of [the European market] after 1972.'

Error was then compounded by error. The Combat engine's 10:1 compression had been achieved cheaply, by using a standard piston but machining down the joint face on the cylinder head. Wolverhampton now decided to go back to the original lower ratio by the cost-cutting use of an alloy head gasket with the Combat heads. But according to Shilton, who only discovered this after two batches of Police machines abroad had been seriously damaged, the alloy gasket material deteriorated through burning, causing the cylinder head joint to leak, resulting in weak mixture and thus overheating of the valves and valve seats. In Shilton's view the Wolverhampton engineers must have known about the effect the gasket would have, and it was, like the Combat itself, a result of 'individuals unwilling to risk their

position by challenging a high level mistake.'

Shilton watched a thousand Combat-engined machines go down the Andover assembly line for the second time, so that the engines could be removed and trucked back to Wolverhampton to have the gaskets fitted, then returned to Andover for a third go. Eventually the situation was sorted out in February 1973 with the Mk V, the last and most satisfactory 750, using the eyeletted composition gasket, raised gearing, a more securely anchored and strong auto-advance mechanism, improved oil filters and above all, the FAG and other Superblend main bearings, which successfully turned the trick for the bottom end. The laudable decision to fit these bearings on all existing engines meant yet another pass down the assembly line for thousands of machines.

Production was severely disrupted by both the initial errors and these frantic attempts to correct them, and profit suffered accordingly. The other step, the announcement in March 1973 of the 850 variants, was also to prove expensive (£297,000 had been spent by Norton in 1972 on plant etc, mainly on the 850 project), as the engine internals shared little more than the camshafts and connecting rods with the 750. The latter was phased out from July 1973, production ceasing in October. Another direction was the 300 short-stroke racing engines produced for homologation purposes.

For the JPN machines Peter Williams had

Frank Perris at work on the Barcelona 24-hour bike for 1973.

devised a steel monocoque frame, of double skin section, with built-in pannier fuel tanks and cast alloy swinging fork. 1973 turned into the JPN racing team's best year, as Williams (together with Suzuki's Barry Sheene) set a new lap record at Brand's Hatch in May on the Mk III JPN racer. On the Island he knew this was perhaps his last chance to win a TT, and announced his intention to win the Formula 750 race 'at the slowest speed possible'. In the event, after the customary gearbox breakage had put him out of the Production race while he was leading by 24 seconds, in the Formula 750 where the rules permitted stiffening the gearbox, Williams won with a best lap of 107.27, not very far behind Hailwood's 1967 lap record of 108 mph; and Mick Grant, Norton's second rider after Croxford in the Production race had crashed at Bungalow Bridge, came second. They were presented with free Commando road bikes. It was to be Norton's last burst of glory on the Island where so much of their name's reputation had been forged — until 1992.

It also contributed to an impression of health, or at least high levels of activity, on the part of the company, and this was extremely important at the time. For since mid-1972 Dennis Poore had embarked on his final expansionist gamble in the world of the British motor cycle industry. During that year BSA-Triumph had been convulsed by economic troubles (See 'BSA' book). BSA motor cycle production had virtually ceased at Small Heath and a managerial team under Lord Shawcross and including Bert Hopwood at Meriden Triumph, were struggling to keep continuity of motor cycle production and to claw back the £11 million debt that previous bad management had accumulated, while bringing an entirely new range of modular motor cycles to production as rapidly as possible. In eighteen months Shawcross's team did in fact wipe out half the debt, but unfortunately a number of factors combined to slow the recovery.

These included disastrous industrial unrest at Meriden and elsewhere, against a background of the miners, and the trade union movement in general, taking on the Heath government with strikes and 'Days of Action', culminating in the three-day week at the end of 1973. In this uncertain climate Shawcross's gradual progress was criticized as feet-dragging, and further group losses of £½ million for 1972 could not be denied. So to the Tory government a man of Poore's background, with what was on the face of it in mid-1972 a modestly successful motor cycle company, was looked on with favour. Quite clearly now the industry needed a big injection of capital to stay in the ring with the government-assisted Japanese, and by the time BSA approached the Department of Trade and Industry (DTI) in July 1972 with requests for help, it was

A happy Peter Williams with Dave Croxford on the road bikes they were given for winning the 1973 Formula 750.

evident to Bert Hopwood at least that the government had 'already reached a conclusion.'

By November it was clear that the DTI would provide capital, up to £20 million being spoken of, but only on condition that BSA and Norton should merge. As Bert Hopwood writes bluntly, 'It appears that [Norton] had intimated that BSA, unlike themselves, were "doing badly" and they [Norton] would be the continuing profitable partner, which would be exploited accordingly. The Norton balance sheet, which was not yet due, would prove this to be quite untrue for they were a sick enterprise with little achievement and less to offer for the future. The plain facts were that both companies were in need of government help.'

Curiously enough, verification of this comes indirectly from Poore himself. Fielding an *MCN* interviewer's question in January 1973 on the possibility of reviving Norton, he replied that 'given a feasible governmental climate, there is virtually no other problem.' Having looked at a few of the 'other problems' the company was facing, this sounds very like a covert admission of the need for government help.

From the government side, Bert Hopwood writes, 'it was quite obvious that no doubt ever existed. . . [that] Mr Poore was the man capable of saving the British motorcycle industry.' Who approached whom first must at this stage be a matter of conjecture. It would nevertheless be interesting, in the light of Mr Poore's subsequent blaming of the involvement of the politicians for his business problems, to know who made the first move, and whether Poore's account of being called to the DTI in autumn 1972 was not preceded by some less formal encounters. Mr Neville, MD of MBH, had for instance been a college friend of Laurie at the DTI, However, it is quite possible that Poore had greatness, as it were, thrust upon him, for Hopwood records a management meeting shortly after the formation of NVT at which Poore announced that he had been 'entrusted with the task of creating a viable British Industry', but that he 'did not know how this was going to be done' – scarcely the statement of a strategic forward planner.

In any event, by early 1973, as Hopwood puts it 'the DTI had concluded that their help would be forthcoming only if Mr Poore became the chairman of the merged companies.' This was interesting, because despite their losses, BSA-Triumph had between four and eight times the production capacity of Norton Villiers. But since the offer was presented on a take-it-or-leave-it basis, the BSA board got busy, in strictest secrecy, negotiating the most favourable terms possible. BSA were to technically acquire Norton-Villiers, whose parent Manganeze Bronze Holdings would take the considerable BSA non-motor cycle holdings. In February 1973 MBH issued 1.6 million shares at 25p, ostensibly planning to spend 'millions' retooling Wolverhampton. But on the brink of this agreement being finalized, a leak in the Stock Exchange led to BSA shares being wiped out, allowing Poore, with the government pledging £5 million in various ways, to pursue a much more advantageous deal. This was made public at the end of March, though details continued to be thrashed out until August. For the full story, see 'BSA', p49, but here all that need be mentioned is that the Norton parent MBH company acquired some very desirable assets, which were kept strictly separate from the motor cycle operation and must have gone some way to compensating them for the risks involved in taking on BSA and its debts. Nevertheless, the stigma on motor cycles in the City was now sufficiently great to mean that MBH shares went into a steady decline from then on.

Why did Poore, a clever man, after the previous year's troubles with Norton-Villiers, venture so much deeper into the motor cycle field? Some contemporary statistics go part of the way to explaining it. BSA had managed to rally to some extent in 1972 thanks to unprecedented levels of demand for motor cycles in the United States, and British bike exports had soared a further 40 per cent in the first two months of 1973, which was to grow to a £2.75 million increase in motor cycle exports for the first half of that year. The government seemed disposed to be helpful, and the prospect of major profit tantalizingly close. There was also the possibility, cited by NVT's own apologia, *Meriden: a historical summary 1972–1974*, that if Poore had declined the merger, the DTI would have gone ahead and rescued BSA alone, thus creating a government-subsidized competitor for Norton-Villiers. And if the DTI had let BSA go under, Norton-Villiers as a small company would have probably encountered difficulties in maintaining the supply of motor cycle components from outside sources. Then on the positive side there were the acquisitions of the BSA non-motor cycle assets.

Then again, Poore did have some forward plans, though they were a long way from Hopwood's carefully formulated and technically innovative new modular range, which had been achingly close to the production prototype stage just as the merger had occured, and which would

44

get no further under NV. Poore's vision of the
future had originated firstly in the course of the
racing involvement, when the possibility arose of
reversing the former use of Manx Norton engines
in Formula 3 car racing, and using a modified
version of the Cosworth Formula 1 car technology
to build a twin cylinder water-cooled racing motor
cycle, which could then hopefully be adapted to a
roadster. In the opinion of Bert Hopwood, this
was a spin-off from Poore's hobby-like interest in
motor cycle sport rather than real business
thinking. Interestingly, from his insider's stance,
Hopwood is able to confirm that there were
tentative plans for a four-cylinder machine also.
The link with Cosworth was announced at the
beginning of September 1973.

There was another Norton Villiers project
already under way; Hooper and Favill's SPX Wulf
500 twin. A prototype was built at
Wolverhampton in 1973 with the stepped-piston
engine housed in a pressed steel monocoque
frame said to be the brainchild of Sir Alex
Issigonis, the inventor of the Mini, who had
become associated with NVT as a consultant in
1970. The project relied heavily on financial
support from the National Research Development
Corporation, and thus was halted in June 1974
when the [Conservative] Minister of
State for Industry, Christopher Chataway,
declined to renew its NRDC grant. According to
Meriden: A Historical Summary, this veto
continued under the following Labour
government, their Secretary of State saying
explicitly in the summer of 1974 that this was a
bargaining counter with Poore over the setting up
of the Meriden co-operative. By November 1974
Poore had decided against the Wulf in favour of
the Wankel project inherited from BSA, and
Hooper and Favill were left to go it alone.

It was at the beginning of 1974 that Poore's
own second string had emerged, with the first
mention of the possibility, bred of his Italian
connections for Commando components, of
importing small-capacity foreign engines, or
complete motor cycles, for Norton-Villiers
Triumph, or NVT, as the new joint company was
called. (The name and fortunes of Norton from
this point are inextricably bound up with NVT, so
some events which concern Norton only indirectly
will be dealt with from here on.)

There were several flaws to these forward
plans, and an underlying flaw of attitude. For a
start, British bikes were genuinely unfashionable
at that point in Europe and at home. Only later,
when the industry had effectively collapsed,
would the cult of the British bike make these

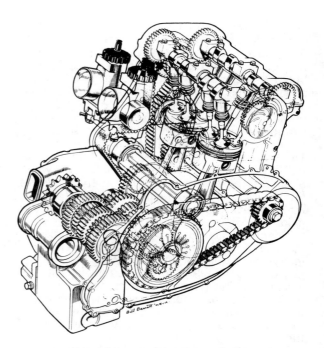

machines highly valued in Italy, Germany, Holland
and to a lesser extent at home.

In America, the British market share had fallen
from 66 per cent in 1968 to a mere 14 per cent in
1973. But the number of models sold had
remained constant at around 35,000; though the
Boston Group's report would emphasize how
sales had fallen to 20,000 in the freak year of 1974,
which made a neat but irrelevant contrast with
Japanese sales of two million. The Americans
would absorb our product, but it had to be
technically competitive, in line with their
legislation, to be in their showrooms punctually
for the selling season, and with a good spares
backup. And to take any kind of proper and
progressive advantage of the market, new models
were going to be required very shortly, in view of
Japanese progress. NVT were to try hard on the
former requirements, expanding their own West
Coast organization into the Norton Triumph
Corporation, based at Duarte, California. In 1973
this outfit employed 300 people. Then for 1975
NVT produced the quietened, left-hand shift
Commandos and Tridents with improved
emissions, as US regulations required.

But as for the need for new designs, Poore's
forward product plans were neither decisive nor
realistic. There were many problems, both
technical and in the field of marketing, with the
Wankel project which he had inherited from BSA.

Left and right *A new direction that never happened. Cosworth challenge on a rare outing during 1975, and the depiction of the engine in MCN.*

The Cosworth engine, even had it been suitable (which it was not), could be expected to take at least two to three years, after race-proving in 1975, to develop and get into volume production as a roadster, which left a fatally long interim period.

In the event, industrial and political troubles soon swamped the regular supply of existing machines and spares. The main factor was of course NVT's confrontation with the workers at Meriden Triumph, which will be dealt with in the appropriate section of another volume.

When NVT later did become involved in importing and assembling foreign-engined machines, in the absence of the motor cycling tradition they had helped to dismantle, they had to rely on nothing but quality and competitive prices, without benefit of any traditional loyalty to British brands and, head on with the Japanese, this was not to be a successful or profitable enterprise.

The failure to interpret the political climate wisely was evident soon after the takeover. The militancy of the late 1960s was still very much in the air, and the labour movement had not yet suffered the bodyblows of the post-industrial period, recession and the new technology. So when, at the end of April 1973, Poore announced that a hundred men were to lose their jobs at the Andover assembly plant, since the work was to be transferred to Wolverhampton, there was a rapid

sit-in by shopfloor workers in protest. Poore's explanation was that Norton-Villiers' workforce varied by as much as a hundred in any given month, and that in the context of the numbers employed by the company, a hundred 'was neither here nor there'. This was an unfortunate turn of phrase (particularly if you were one of the hundred), and rather begged the question that less than four years previously in order to work for Norton-Villiers most of these men had moved from homes in Woolwich to sub-standard housing in the Andover industrial estate.

The workers' ten-day occupation of the factory received full press and TV coverage, which did nothing for Mr Poore's image. Following union negotiations, there were successful demands for very substantial redundancy payments. Andover stayed open as headquarters for the newly formed subsidiary Norton-Villiers Europe Ltd (shortly Norton Triumph Ltd) under Bill Colquhoun, with Shilton as a director. Hugh Palin was moved from sales to become Poore's 'Special Assistant', which mostly meant the unpleasant work of industrial confrontation. Poore's abruptness and his underestimation of the unions on this occasion provided a demonstration in miniature of the troubles to come at Meriden.

These began, soon enough, in September 1973, when Poore, without prior consultation with the unions, announced the closure of the

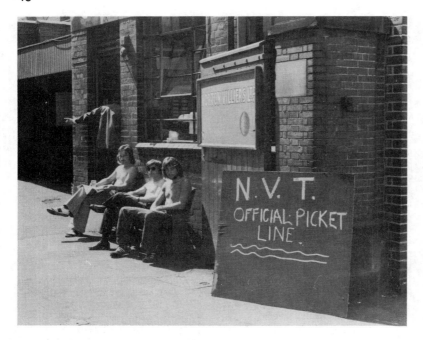

Troubled times had begun. Pickets outside the Wolverhampton works after the 1975 summer crisis.

factory. From then on the affairs of NVT were inevitably in disarray, and soon the Norton story was directly involved. It is difficult to pinpoint the moment when the much-quoted 'two-factory plan', ie, 'NVT = Small Heath + Wolverhampton', which Poore said had been agreed on with the Tory DTI prior to the formation of NVT, was modified to a 'one-factory plan'.

As early as October 1973 Poore had made remarks in the interview indicating disappointment at Wolverhampton's production performance. According to the *Historical Summary*, since the Triumph trouble the shop stewards at Wolverhampton 'had not' (unlike their Small Heath counterparts), 'felt directly involved, and, in general, were supporting the principle of the co-operative' (ie, NVT management was now locked in battle with Meriden, and considered Wolverhampton was on the co-op's side). It goes on: 'They were persuaded that, if anything, the empty spaces at the Small Heath factory were more of a threat than Meriden lest they absorbed their factory's production too. Such an idea was, of course, wholly at variance with any company plan. . .' But Tony Griffin, then production planning controller at Small Heath, has told me that during 1974 a plan did exist, known only to the Norton board, and half a dozen others, to shift Interpol production to Small Heath in the event of Wolverhampton closing. Neale Shilton had been

at Small Heath trying to find alternatives to Wolverhampton parts among components in stock at BSA.

With the Meriden dispute costing NVT an estimated £20,000 a week, disrupting Small Heath's Trident production to the tune of £½ million and immobilizing a £7 million asset, the company failed to prosper during 1974. For the Norton end, though the serious problems had been largely overcome with the 850s, the '74 models were 30 lb heavier than the 750s, and though the good mid-range torque remained, they ran out of puff at the top end. Another thing that ran out was demand for this biggest of parallel twins, and unsold Commandos began to pile up in the Andover warehouse. This was a pity as the experimental department in Wolverhampton had worked tirelessly and after nine months, produced in the Mk IIA a particularly well-silenced model.

Apart from Dave Rawlins' 12 second quarter mile at MIRA on a lightly modified Mk IIA, sporting events had not gone so well for Norton. In autumn 1974 there was an attempt, co-sponsored with Gulf, at the World Land Speed record at Bonneville in a double-engined 850 projectile, justified by the chairman on patriotic grounds ('We want to bring some old-fashioned glory back to Britain. We belong to the old world of endeavour, of the burning desire to do better— the stuff that made our country great,' etc,). But even a best run of 271 mph couldn't cut Don Vesco's Yamaha. However double-engined Norton dragsters like T. C. Christensen's *Hogslayer* and Chinn/Messenger's *Pegasus* did well on the strips.

Another US-oriented sports project was the very popular flat-track racing, which Norton contested for 1975 with a three-man team that did so badly they had to withdraw in mid-season. Ironically this was in a year when Norton-mounted Alex Jorgenson became West Coast dirt track overall champion. But he was aboard a Ron Wood Norton; Wood, a wealthy lampshade manufacturer and meticulous craftsman, while considering the Norton twin 'archaic', had selected the engine for its good head flow characteristics, and with the help of top tuner C. R. Axtell, extracted no less than 81 bhp from the 750, better than Norton's own race shop ever achieved. Though he dominated his local Ascot Park track from 1974 to 1976, Wood received little factory help and no acknowledgement, and on his later machines the name of Dellorto carburettors featured larger than the Norton name on the tank! A final sporting footnote was provided by the use of the Commando engine in Jawa-framed pacing machines for indoor bicycle racing; these single speed belt-driven machines echoed the very earliest function of the motor-bicycle in its pioneer days.

The JPN race effort continued, reverting for 1974 from the monocoque to light and intricate tubular 'space' frame built by team member Robin Clyst. But the unequal struggle took its toll. Mechanic Peter Pykett, for instance, found the strain too much and was released to work on the machines in the factory, explaining that 'the job started to get on top of me. The bikes were too old and just not quick enough and the stress on them was terrific.' The season's only real successes were wins in the wet at Brands in the Hutchinson 100 and other events, and in August tragedy struck. Peter Williams crashed badly at Oulton Park, with photographic evidence apparently indicating that he had fallen when the seat became detached from his machine due to inadequate preparation. Both arms were broken, both his lungs punctured, he died technically and was resuscitated. Both he and Frank Perris remained very loyal to Poore, Perris writing that he had 'rarely come across someone with greater enthusiasm or grasp of the fundamentals of the trade and sport', but Williams had to resort to a lawsuit to obtain compensation for the crash from NVT. He never raced again.

John Player withdrew their sponsorship in November, and Poore was uncertain whether they could go on. The postscript to the JPN story came the following year in 1975, when there was sporadic activity by Croxford on Commando-engined machines, but all hopes were pinned on the water-cooled Cosworth 750 twin. This was by then also important as a demonstration of NVT's viability and potential, and had been announced as costing them £100,000 already. But both the race and roadster versions of the engine were heavy (Norton claimed 155 and 175 lb; Cosworth drawings, according to historian Roy Bacon, show both at 195 lb).

In an all-new frame, the Cosworth Challenge made its debut at Brands only to be dropped by Croxford at a first corner pile-up; Alex George had better luck the following day, until the radiator ran dry. The Challenge was disappointingly underpowered, and many questioned the necessity of the whole enterprise when the group owned and had just begun again to produce an outstanding proven road racer, at least at production level, in the Trident, works versions of which had produced 87 bhp as long ago as 1971. Perhaps the association of the Triumph name with Meriden was enough to disqualify it. With Norton-Villiers Wolverhampton by now in receivership, there was no chance of continuing with the Cosworth. Ex-JPN rider Phil Read made preliminary moves to take over the project as his own equipe, but this foundered for what some said was also the reason for the Challenge's lacklustre showing for Norton — the engine concern's unwillingness to release their full-works' specs for the 25 units ordered so far, which for them compared to the lucrative world of GP car racing was an unimportant sideshow. And that was the end of the mighty Norton name in GP road racing until the 1987 rotaries. With the company's fortunes having been so shaky, Hopwood's judgement that the David and Goliath effort had been 'a luxury' probably had it about right.

To return to 1974, none of that year's sporting endeavours helped the company's fortunes. The year began with the three-day week caused by the miners' strike, followed immediately by the energy crisis as the Arabs flexed their oil muscles. Inflation hit production costs in a way that was, in Palin's words, 'frightening'. Commando prices rose £60 immediately, and production was curtailed. Then February saw a general election, and a minority Labour government was returned.

Poore had had a rocky road already with the Conservative minister who had forbidden him to get tough with Meriden at such a politically sensitive moment. Now Labour was in, and the

Secretary of State for Industry was left-winger Tony Benn. The latter's belief in the ideology of the Meriden Co-op not unnaturally changed the situation, which was further complicated by the opposition of the Department's civil servants to the whole idea. While NVT got a badly-needed £8 million of export credit guarantees by early November (ie, they were to be paid as soon as export orders were shipped off, without having to wait for the foreign buyers to pay up), a month later Benn confirmed to the Commons that a £5 million loan was to go to Meriden. This sum was the maximum the industry could get from the government under the Industry Act without a debate in Parliament, and was also desperately needed by NVT. So Poore at this point told Benn, 'either to take NVT into public ownership or tell the Meriden men to go home. We cannot operate without a very much larger investment from the government if Small Heath are to make motor cycles as well as Meriden.' Interestingly, there is no mention of Wolverhampton, and as we have seen, some evidence that behind the scenes contingency plans were already being made to shift Commando production to Small Heath. Despite NVT's protestations, the Commons passed the £5 million for Meriden on 6 March 1975.

Meanwhile, the Commando saga carried on, after some aggressive marketing in 1974 with a 'British Bike Bonanza' campaign and competition. This featured advertisements depicting little Japanese people clustered in envious admiration round a Trident and Commando to the slogan 'Bike British. You've Arrived'. Presumably the irony was intentional. Then came the launch in January 1975 at the Anaheim Show in California (it was March for England) of the new 850 Mk III Commando, together with the Small Heath-built Trident T160. Both sported gearshifts on the left side, in line with the Japanese as US legislation now required, and electric starters. The Mk III Commando's starter was a bad joke, once again it was over 30 lb heavier than its 850 predecessor at 490 lb kerbweight, and the combination of this and the silencing and emission restrictions made it well down on top speed and power from previous models. The same thing had happened as with the raised and rubber-bumpered MGB sports car; US regulations had done for its original character. It was also dramatically more expensive than even the Mk IIA models, which themselves had jumped to £928.80; the Mk III was a whopping £1,161. This had its effect. The same week in May 1975, that the Interpol Mk III was launched in the UK, Avon County Police ordered some of the first

BMW Police bikes.

The price was dictated both by inflation, which was to reach its highest level ever in 1975, and by the company's fortunes. In December 1974 NVT announced a trading loss of £3,670,000 for the year ended July 1974. At this point Benn, anxious to speed the setting up of the Meriden Co-op, withheld the £8 million export credit guarantees which in November he had granted in addition to NVT's existing £4 million export credits. Poore's public position was still that Meriden should 'go home', which he said would provide NVT with a further £4 million in compensation demands.

Even the loss figures were problematic, since Poore was quarrelling with his auditors, whom he had inherited from BSA. Counting only that part of NVT which was under the control of the management, the deficit would have been £5.8 million to the end of July. But for Manganeze Bronze Holdings itself the annual figures showed a £670,000 profit, and the ex-BSA auditors took the position that since MBH had benefited from the BSA non-motor cycle assets, the MBH group accounts should include the NVT loss figures, which would then show MBH trading at a £1,100,000 loss.

Poore had fired these auditors, and Palin explained to MBH shareholders that the company had been so structured that NVT were not part of the MBH group but 'investment was simply held in it', so that if NVT went broke, it would not affect the MBH shareholders. He blamed the trading loss on the hold-up of Trident production due to the Meriden blockade, and went on to explain that the £5.8 million deficit was actually less than the £6 million set aside for the takeover of BSA. The deficit figures, for instance, included a quarter of a million reserved for claims for which the company's insurers were disputing liability. 'In America,' as Palin put it, 'people love making these claims.' He confirmed that while none had to do with the failure to supply machines to dealers, there were some threatened lawsuits over the interrupted supply of spares; NVT were discovering, as BSA had before them, the pitfalls of owning their own distribution organization. These considerations (disputed claims, etc) presumably explain the lower (£3.67 million) loss figures announced by the company. The point that emerges clearly is the unwillingness on the part of the parent company to financially assist the motor cycle side.

Despite the encouraging words about everything being budgeted for, in reality the situation was deteriorating rapidly. Though £4 million of the export credits were shortly reinstated at the same time as Benn's £5 million went to the Meriden co-op in March 1975, the picture in America suddenly took a turn for the worse. There was an apparent slump in 1975 registrations, contrasting with the (transient) 1974 boom due to oil price panic. This unfortunately coincided with the compilation of a report, commissioned by Benn, from the Boston Consulting Group, which emphasized the downward trend. In fact, 1975 levels of demand had simply returned to the quite respectable 1973 statistics, but due to the Meriden troubles British output was low.

By the time this report was to hand, there had been a referendum on Britain's entry into the Common Market, and subsequently a Cabinet reshuffle which saw Tony Benn replaced as Industry Secretary by Eric Varley. Further to the right of his party than Benn, encouraged by his civil servants, armed with the Boston Group's report, and faced with Poore's current contention that £40 million, excluding export guarantees, would be necessary to build a viable industry, Varley in effect washed his hands of the whole situation. In the view of many, this amounted to reneging on a commitment, both implicit and, from Benn, explicit, by the government to the industry from 1972 on.

The means chosen was a speech in the House of Commons at the end of July 1975, wherein a renewal of export credits was refused. This action was justified by the statement that there were 13,000 unsold British motor cycles in warehouses all over the world, and that there was no market for them. There were also to be no further funds for the industry as a whole, which Varley claimed was too great a risk and had already absorbed £24 million of government money. Bromsgrove MP Hilary Miller was to point out that compared to other government rescue operations, the sum involved was 'peanuts'. Poore later described these events in Ronnie Mutch's *Penthouse* article in the following terms:

'Varley stood up in Parliament when he was justifying the Government's decision to take back a £4 million-pound loan which was going to cause the death of the Norton Commando, because we were going to have to sell off the tooling to pay back the money, and close the factory . . . We had sold every one of those 13,000 motor cycles without any trouble.' (However, this is in contrast with his reaction at the time, when he admitted that there were 3,500 more bikes than he would have liked in the USA, but pointed out that these comprised non-NVT machines such as 1,200 Rickman scramblers inherited from BSA, plus

Bonnevilles and other material recently released by Meriden.) 'Whoever fed Varley that ridiculous information was almost single-handedly responsible for the death of the British industry.'

At the time some people, such as the Coventry MP Leslie Huckfield, who had been a supporter of the Co-op from the first, took a different view, attributing the crucial loss of American sales and consequent stockpiling of the 13,000 bikes not to Benn, or the Co-op, but to Poore's procrastinations in signing agreements to cut his losses and clear up the Meriden situation. Poore later admitted that he had stalled, believing the sit-in would collapse. 'We never had any other object than that. We couldn't have. We hadn't got any money to have any other object. Unless we had the Triumph money to put into Small Heath, Small Heath couldn't work.'

He went on to Mutch: 'When Varley took over from Benn, it was glaringly obvious that he was told "Whatever Benn's done, do the opposite". The government could have had a healthy industry if they had waited the nine months we asked for before taking their four million back. The minute the receivers go in, millions of pounds go missing. Everything is sold at knockdown prices.' It is possible that Poore, like the Wolverhampton workers who were informed of all this shortly in advance, felt that Varley's speech was 'a charade', another move, like Benn's previous ones, to accelerate his secession of Triumph rights to the Co-op.

The 'nine months' which Poore refers to would have carried them through to the vital US selling season for 1976, when the bulk of the machines probably would have been sold. As it was, by October the price of Commandos and Tridents in the States had been slashed by £300, in response to similar price-cutting by the Japanese. Varley's announcement had been made on the day before Parliament went into summer recess, so there could be no further debate, despite a question tabled by Hall Green MP Ronald Eyre, asking for more help, and a telegram from Neale Shilton saying that on the outcome of this matter depended 'whether we abandon forever repeat forever all motor cycle business to Japan and Germany'. Within a week the NVT board had put all its 3,000 workers on a three-day week, and set in motion existing plans for liquidating the Norton-Villiers Wolverhampton operation.

Neale Shilton, by now thoroughly disenchanted with his fellow directors, took a jaundiced view of this, observing that 'the timing had been convenient for the management, which had been responsible for letting the situation deteriorate until it was interpreted into the prescribed formula for voluntary liquidation, though the word voluntary was hardly accurate.' After some last-ditch efforts to continue Interpol production, he resigned from the company in January 1976.

Later in 1975 a piece of the inter-company juggling so beloved by NVT had come unstuck. According to Louis and Currie's *Story of Triumph Motorcycles*, 'by September . . . it was apparent that, because of the joint buying programme under which materials had been ordered in the name of the Small Heath company (NVT Manufacturing Ltd), but for use at Wolverhampton without necessarily making that fact clear to suppliers, the Small Heath company could not avoid liquidation.' Whereas Wolverhampton and the Commando might have been expendable, the demise of Small Heath and the Trident (of which a 900 cc version was already well developed) had been no part of NVT management plans. According to Shilton, a creditor tired of waiting for a £23,000 payment issued an application to wind up NVT Manufacturing. Promises of an immediate cheque were then no good, because once the application had been made, it was irrevocable.

This meant, with the exception of Meriden, the end of the industry as it had been known. The names among the mass redundancies from NVT at the end of August emphasized the point. They included Norton men John Hudson (who had first read of it in the papers while on the Isle of Man),

the injured racer Peter Williams, and mechanic Peter Pykett, as well as 300 from Small Heath, the first of 1,200 over the next months. From another part of the NVT empire, the Norton Triumph experimental shop at Kitts Green, Birmingham, where many of the most talented men from Meriden had gone after the factory closure, among the sixty sacked by November were numbered designer Doug Hele; Les Williams, the builder of Slippery Sam; ex-Triumph and BSA publicity man, Ivor Davies; ex-BSA competition manager Brian Martin, Trident development engineer and sprinter Norman Hyde, and his engine specialist Jack Shemans. The latter wrote to *Bike* magazine something which provides an important insight into NVT's failure: 'We were never short of . . . ideas, or the enthusiasm to make them work . . . We made lots of different things, some good, some bad, but never with any guidance or definite plans from the hierarchy . . . we made balanced cylinder twins (Triumph and Norton) . . . but . . . it always ended up with the same cry, ''We can't afford to make it''.' The squandering of this talent and enthusiasm through tight-fistedness and lack of planning was probably NVT's most culpable error. Here near the end of story, the attitude of expediency that lay behind it stands in the strongest possible contrast to the idealism of the old company's founder James Lansdowne Norton, whose name this organization had chosen to lead with.

At Wolverhampton the 1,600 workers, who had

Left *Positive plans. Bernard Hooper (second from right) with Norton 76, the Wolverhampton action committee's handsome version of the Commando.*

Right *Nearing the end. One of the final builds of 850 Mk III Interpols at Wolverhampton late in 1975.*

been on full production of Mk IIIs since mid-1974, had returned in August from their summer holidays to find the liquidation a *fait accompli*, and no money available for the week's pay owed to them. The representatives of the unions at the works, which they claimed had had the least stoppages and lowest pay structure of the three NVT factories, had not until recently conceived the events at Meriden as a threat to their survival. They now rapidly became active. They advised the workers to lay themselves off temporarily, so that they could draw dole while the union men sought backers to finance continued production.

Distrust of the management was now complete. At a last-minute meeting at Kingswinford between NVT and the Small Heath unions and company representatives, the Wolverhampton men refused to discuss a phased rundown of their factory to extend production while reassuring creditors. From the time that the liquidation was announced on 7 August, a sit-in by 1,300 of the workers to prevent the removal of 500 part-built Commandos began. The unions, encouraged by local MPs, were active in several directions. They took legal advice on recovering £250,000 outstanding wages from NVT Manufacturing Ltd, since again the Wolverhampton employment contracts were with that company rather than Norton Villiers Ltd, the actual Wolverhampton operation. Backed by Hugh Scanlon's AEU, they formed an Action Committee, sought advice on profit sharing, and even asked the help of the dockers' unions in blocking two-wheel imports.

They had positive aims; the continued production of the 850 Commando, and the introduction of a 500 cc version of Hooper and Favill's stepped-piston two-stroke, the Wulf. NRDC money for this project had flowed again, and with Hooper and Favill on the Action Committee's side, an impressive 500 cc prototype Wulf was unveiled in September 1975; there were also plans for 350 and 750 cc versions and a Mk II featuring a stratified charge system. By January 1976, again from Hooper and Favill, there was a modified version of the 850 Commando, christened Norton 76 and displayed by ex-Norton agent Joe Berliner at the Daytona Show in Florida early that year. Handsomely restyled, the Norton 76 featured an SU carburettor to meet upcoming US emissions regulations and to aid economy, plus Italian front forks and brakes, to get round the fact that some of the tooling for the Commando, including that which produced Roadholder front forks, was owned by Mod Hire, yet another NVT group company, which was not in liquidation.

There were also negotiations initiated to find backers for continued Commando production and for the Wulf. These first involved interested parties from Iran, and US bankers, but by 1976 the firmest hope looked to be the British Norton Partnership, with Lord Hesketh lending his name, but the bulk of the £4 million necessary to buy the factory was to come from Australian financier Ron Titcombe.

Initially the Wolverhampton men were behind Meriden, and at the end of September 1975, Action Committee member Tom Potter rejected news of a fresh NVT scheme to safeguard 200 jobs because it was dependent on a two-factory company. The Meriden Co-op was obviously the Action Committee's inspiration, but by now there were important differences in the situation at the two factories. The bottom line was that there would be no government money for Wolverhampton, and this was confirmed unequivocally by December 1975. When the Norton Villiers men realized that it had been, after all, an 'either/or' situation in terms of government funds, they grew disenchanted with Meriden. Citing continued Police willingness to buy the Interpol, in contrast to the Forces' rejection of the Co-op's twins, they judged, rightly in the author's opinion, that in terms of actual machines, the Commando was the superior twin (though the Triumph name was probably a greater selling point in the civilian market).

Again, the NVT management took a much less equivocal line. As early as August Poore had stated, 'We will discontinue the Commando which will be superseded by the Challenge'. With Norton Villiers Ltd compulsorily wound up and facing claims in the High Court of £4,250,000 in early October, NVT management's only continuing interest was to dispose of the blockaded Commando stock as quickly and profitably as possible. Wolverhampton itself was the liquidator's pigeon now, but after the Meriden experience they were evidently not going to put any further NVT assets at risk. To this end, when Joe Berliner in 1976 was reported to have provisionally ordered 7,000 Norton 76s, Poore declared that 'the authorized channels for distribution of Nortons and Triumphs are the distributors and dealers we [NVT] have appointed throughout the world.' Berliner's interest ceased forthwith. When Peter Watson of *Bike* magazine spoke to Poore on the subject of Norton 76, the latter 'made it abundantly clear in two crisp sentences that he had no wish to have anything to do with the Commando or Norton 76.'

Another difference from Meriden was the depth of commitment by the workforce to the factory and the name. Until eight years previously Marston Road had been producing not Nortons but Villiers engines, so inevitably the fierce loyalty to the marque was lacking. By February 1976 the number of men involved had dropped to 800. All services had been cut off the moment liquidation was announced, and the men could not even clean the factory, let alone start work, until contracts for the sale of the factory had been signed and the liquidator gave the go-ahead; if they did, they would lose their unemployment pay, on which, unlike Meriden with its assistance from other local unions and NVT redundancy payments, they were forced to survive. But picketing continued in order to discourage possible buyers other than the Partnership for both the motorcycle and the industrial engine side.

Meanwhile, NVT's position had strengthened considerably. Following the petition in October 1975 to wind up NVT Manufacturing Ltd, the Small Heath operation, in November, the High Court was told that plans to resume parts of the operation had the provisional approval of the government. The assistance was to cost them nothing extra as it was given within the £8 million that had been agreed in the Commons to help NVT in March 1975. NVT Manufacturing Ltd's debts were both complicated and extensive. They were estimated by the receivers at around £5.5

million, plus another half a million if overdrafts of other companies in the group were claimed against them. The figures were only estimates, as access to the company accounts books and computer records had been denied due to the Wolverhampton sit-in.

There was a period of suspense while creditors considered the rescue scheme, and the government equivocated. Then in mid-December 1975, with just three hours to go before the High Court issued the winding-up order on NVT Manufacturing Ltd, the government finally stepped in to save part of its operation. In the month when they had just propped up Chrysler UK at massive expense, the total demise of NVT might have been a bit pointed.

NVT Engineering Ltd, the new company, was joint-financed by the government and Barclays Bank, with a £275,000 grant plus a guaranteed overdraft of £1,000,000. With a workforce reduced from 1,300 to 300, the new operation was to move from Small Heath to a smaller company-owned factory at Sparkbrook, Birmingham. The government announced that it was taking these steps 'to enable stocks of motor cycles held overseas under a government export credit guarantee to be disposed of in an orderly fashion, and to enable better service to be given to British motor cyclists throughout the world.' (Their number was estimated by NVT at over 200,000.) There was no commitment to NVT to help them continue producing motor cycles.

Spares were to be distributed shortly by a subsidiary company in the group not previously concerned with the bike business and now renamed NVT Motor Cycles Ltd. A trust fund for the creditors of NVT Manufacturing was also to be set up, which would offer them the best chance of eventual recovery. The Andover works (as opposed to the warehousing) was in its final rundown, with 600 Tridents and Mk III Commandos and 100 Interpols being assembled there. The Norton-Triumph warranty was still to fully cover newly bought Commandos, Tridents and Bonnevilles.

From this newly regularized position, in February 1976 Poore announced that NVT Motor Cycles had agreed to buy from the Wolverhampton liquidator all the partly built Commandos in the factory. The Action Committee, however, were still holding out for the purchase from the liquidator of the factory, plant, equipment, and work in progress, by the British Norton Partnership, for a sum now reduced to £2.8 million.

The deal was to be signed during the second

week of March 1976, when Ron Titcombe began to speak of 'a number of legalities still to be sorted out.' By mid-May he had broken off negotiations, citing the City's timidity, and the loss of the marketing season due to over-prolonged government deliberations—it was the first time possible government involvement had been mentioned. *Bike*'s Mark Williams speculated whether the Action Committee had ever bothered to check Titcombe's business record; in the most recent year available for inspection, Titcombe's company, Arunta International, on a turnover of £100,000 had made a profit of just £769.

That was effectively the end for the Action Committee's chances. Since March 1976 they had produced 100 Interpols which NVT had sold, and in June the blockade was quietly lifted as now thirty workers prepared the factory for production of industrial engines again. This was spoken of as 'a life-line' to produce finance to complete a further 500 Commandos; work on the latter got under way in June and was completed by August. By October a firm bid was made for the factory by Mark Scull and David Sankey, a well-known West Midlands businessman who later in the year paid £300,000 plus £200,000 of government money, and set up Wolverhampton Industrial Engines, initially employing around 200 men.

Meanwhile, in November 1976, 220 men at Wolverhampton got the go-ahead to build a final batch of 1,500 Mk III Commandos. The liquidator had signed an agreement with Dennis Poore to manufacture them as work in progress, with NVT doing the buying in. Poore had bought the Norton name and manufacturing rights from the liquidator, though he was still uninterested in the Commando's future ('I don't want to make outdated motor cycles'); and profits from this final build were shared between the two of them. The Action Committee fully co-operated in all this, for it was hoped that the bulk of the 220 workforce would be kept on by Sankey. The 1,500 machines were completed by September 1977. During 1978, a further thirty were assembled at Andover, and that was that for the Commando.

While the unions had continued efforts to go on with small-scale production of the Commando, Favill and Hooper, blaming government delays, already realized that it was too late for the Wulf in this context. But they continued development, and spoke of the possibility of putting the machine into limited production, perhaps in the US. Today, while John Favill has gone to America, Bernard Hooper operates his own Templewall Company, offering among other things SU carb conversions for British twins while

still promoting the SPX engine which continues development with the help of NRDC funds. The blue vans of Sankey's industrial engine concern,' now once again entitled Villiers Engines Ltd after the name had been bought back in 1980, can still be seen in the streets of Wolverhampton.

The broad outline of the resurrected NVT operation can be summarized as follows. The residue of BSA personnel went to Montgomery Street, where they carried on the general engineering contracts that Small Heath had subsisted on principally since 1972. It also housed an experimental laboratory where some work on the Wankel engine was carried out. The spares operation was run by what became, in summer 1977, Andover (Norton) Ltd; later they expanded into imported motor cycle accessories. Norvil was shut down in 1975 and Frank Perris' Thruxton-based performance and race shop ended up converting and marketing Cossack and Anglo-Russian sidecars, until they closed down in early 1977. The Norton Triumph Corporation in the

Poore's white hope, the 1976 Easy Rider moped with Italian motor, French frame, British lady rider.

western USA shrank from 300 to twelve people, but by 1979 had taken the title Manx Industries, and they too dealt with spares and accessories, employing between fifty and sixty people.

Actual motor cycle assembly took place at two further venues. NVT Motor Cycles Ltd operated from Bannerley Road, Garratts Green, Birmingham, under the leadership of Bill Colquhoun and ex-Velocette family man Bertie Goodman. The Easy Rider moped had been launched in March 1976, being assembled initially at the NVT plant in Shenstone, Staffordshire, with an output of 100 a week by August. With an Italian Franco-Morini engine and components, and a frame built in France, the four Easy Rider variants were scarcely a renaissance for the British industry, but they did represent an attempt to answer the long-felt absence of British lightweights.

They also answered a need. Ironically the disintegration of the British industry had taken place against a background of rising registrations at home: 1975 had been a record year, with 270,085 new registrations, a 40 per cent increase on 1974; and in 1976 British riders spent £58.4 million on 237,732 Japanese machines. The small capacity end of the market was particularly

White hope II. NVT's 125 cc Rambler trial bike with Yamaha engine for 1979.

buoyant in view of the energy crisis and rising fuel costs. Chairman Poore himself was reported to have taken a short run on an Easy Rider and returned with a pained expression declaring it had been misnamed. But Easy Rider sales, plus the sell-off of the remaining large four-strokes with few further production expenses, meant that by the end of 1976 NVT was able to pay back the government's £8 million export credit money.

The Easy Riders were joined in 1978 by Rambler trail bikes with 125 and 175 cc Yamaha DT two-stroke single cylinder engines, as the Japanese came to the end of that range. These never sold well in the UK, but have been the basis of another even more convoluted piece of sales practice, whereby 500 a year are produced for British Overseas Aid Programme workers, for whom our government specifies that all equipment supplied must come from a British company. In 1979, with the industry well dead, the Classic movement came on song, and NVT Motor Cycles took advantage of this to rename their operation BSA, out of the lucky dip of ex-NVT titles now held in trust. The name was applied to the Beaver, Brigand and the unrestricted Boxer, with four-speed versions of the same 50 cc Franco-Morini engine as the moped, but housed in a monoshock frame designed by Goodman and built in Italy.

Further work was provided in the shape of assembling the 1,600 Rotax-engined Canadian Can-Am Bombardier bikes selected by the British Army and featuring a 40 per cent British component content. It was never a Forces' favourite, and in 1984 the latest order for fresh Army mounts has gone to the Bolton-based Armstrong (ex-CCM) company. The Easy Riders were profitable for a time, NVT signing a £2 million export contract to sell 1,000 a month to Minnesota snowmobile manufacturers Scorpion, who marketed them in the US under the Scorpion name. By 1979 BSA were employing fifty people and had expanded into larger adjacent premises. But quality and dealer problems and the deepening recession meant disappointing sales performance afer that. Since 1981, 50 per cent of BSA has been owned by Colquhoun and Goodman, and after a peak production year of 5,000 machines, as Goodman admitted in *MCN*, attempts to secure a larger share of the UK market 'flopped'. In late 1983 Bannerley Road was vacated and after that they were located at Falkland Close, Charter Avenue Industrial Estate in Canley, outside Coventry, employing just twelve people. The bulk of the business was either the supply of machines CKD, or as in the case of Bangalore, India, supplying the expertise to establish assembly points for their machines in Third World countries.

All this commercial activity was complicated but initially successful. NVT profits for 1978 were £160,000, for 1979 £200,000, and what the company described as £29 million loans had then been repaid. At the end of 1983 NVT paid out over £284,000 on top up payment of creditors of NVT Manufacturing Ltd (the Small Heath operation) and of Norton Triumph International, which meant that all creditors of those companies had finally been paid in full. But after that came a downturn; NVT lost over £1 million for the year ended 31 July 1984. Until late 1984 the Department of Industry had retained their £2.37 million stake in NVT from the original share subscription agreement which limited applications of the Wankel engine and prevented the company acquiring new investment for it.

The Wankel project was in some terms the justification for all the other activities; as Poore put it, 'I would not have begun to plan if I did not think we could make motor cycles.' It was to be located principally in Lynn Lane, Shenstone, Staffs, where in December 1975 NVT had set up shop in a deserted bacon factory, at first working on moped assembly but soon concentrating on other projects. Initially these included the prototype of the last of the 'real' British bikes, the 900 cc Trident, but manufacturing costs were found to be prohibitive. The project was offered to Meriden, but in the absence of appropriate government funding, nothing came of it.

The link with Yamaha, evidenced by the supply of DT engines for the Ramblers, found its most bizarre expression in 1977 as the last of the Norton Interpols were being built. This was a Yamaha SX 750 shaft-driven triple in Police guise, with British accessories—including the Norton name on the tank. NVT management apparently failed to see anything undignified about this bit of total expediency; but only around forty of these hybrids were disposed of, apparently in part due to the resistance by local authorities to buying Japanese. Other fruit of the Yamaha connection from Shenstone was a run of Bengt Aberg Yamaha HL 500 motocross replicas in 1978, as well as some 250 cc Sigma-Yam grasstrack bikes.

Mike Jackson's sales organization from Andover also came to be based at Shenstone, where the bike-building side took the title Norton Motors (1978) Ltd (the NVT name was retained simply as the overall umbrella for the various operations). For the machine which management hoped would represent a genuine revival of the Norton name was an all-British development if not

Saviour or undertaker? A strained Dennis Poore during 1976.

White hope III. NVT's experimental Wankel engine, inherited from BSA.

56

design. This was the Wankel project, which had begun at Meriden and then passed to David Garside at BSA's R&D centre, Umberslade Hall, in 1969. On the face of it the P41, as it was known, was an unlikely machine for Norton to be concentrating on. Previous applications of versions of Dr Felix Wankel's revolutionary rotary engine to motor cycles, the DKW Hercules 2000 and the Suzuki RE5, had been resounding commercial failures. Service problems for dealers, and sales resistance from the ever-conservative motor cycling public, were to be expected. However, the project was already apparently well-advanced, with test rides on Triumph-badged 1974 and 1975 prototypes bringing extremely enthusiastic reactions ('the world's most desirable motor cycle': *Motor Cycle World*, April 1975).

The engine, with twin rotors displacing either 600 or 1200 cc according to your system of measurement, still had to overcome many technical problems after the decision to go ahead in 1976. NVT has come up with many patented solutions to them. Garside and BSA veteran Fred Swift continued on the project, with Bob Trigg in charge. When he left in 1979, ex-Matchless man

NVT Wankel prototypes were road tested as early as 1974.

Tony Denniss took over. Later the dozen-strong development team was joined by Doug Hele, the technical director's job next going to Dr Gordon K. Blair, before he, too, left at the beginning of 1984. NRDC grants have been received, and it is said that the pace of progress has been dictated fairly exactly by the amounts of money from this source.

Designing an air-cooling system for the rotors was a major technical breakthrough over the previous oil-cooled arrangements. Progress was slowed during 1978 by difficulties in reaching agreement with the German NSU company, for German patent holders to the rotary design demanded high copyright fees. By the end of 1979 25 Mk I production prototypes had been produced, but a year after that Poore was blowing cold again, stressing that the Department of Industry's stake gave it a veto on further investment of his company's limited capital in a project that 'remained highly speculative by normal commercial standards'. By the beginning of 1981, in the absence of government objections, a second build of Mk II test bikes began, but Poore was emphasizing that £1 million investment would be needed, and his speculations as to the likely retail price of a road version began at £4,500, a very high price indeed for those days.

From then on many, many launch dates were either provisionally announced or guessed at, and though NVT has avoided a 'fiasco' (Poore's word) like that of the chairman's personal friend Lord Hesketh, the project has become the butt of much magazine humour, as again and again it failed to reach civilian production. However, the Mk II's specifications as they emerged were not unimpressive; 450 lb kerbside (the engine weighed just 100 lb), over 80 bhp, and at least 130 mph top speed, with the rotary motor's characteristic uncanny smoothness, 'vivid' acceleration (the twin rotors develop, after all, the same number of power pulses as a six-cylinder conventional engine), and steering and handling to match ('better than a Featherbed': NOC Chairman Phil Cox) from the pressed steel monocoque frame (perhaps an echo of that earlier ill-fated Issigonis Wulf prototype?).

These facts gradually came to light during 1981 and '82 while the machine was being tested in an unorthodox but effective way, going out on loan to Police forces, who could then exercise an option to buy. On the whole, the Police were impressed, though inevitably some problems emerged. Initially the rotor seals blew, and though this has been cured, as late as mid-1984 Inspector Williams of the West Midlands Police described

57

the air-cooled Mk II as 'very fast but very noisy, and there are problems with the tickover. It doesn't run slowly'—an important consideration for Police traffic work which is mostly slow cruising. Consumption of around 35 mpg was also not too impressive, but very long intervals between major services were encouraging. The tickover problem is now said to have been cured by changes to the electronic ignition and to carburation on the Mk II's SU-type devices, resulting in smooth tickover as low as 600 rpm.

Also, since 1977, alongside the finned air-cooled engine, a water-cooled version has been developed. It is actually lighter than its predecessor, produces over 90 bhp and a probable 140 mph, and is the basis of upcoming Mk IIIs. A prototype was unofficially tested in the German magazine *Motorrad* during 1984, and they were impressed with everything but the styling, which was after all that of a development hack only. For production versions styling had been in the hands of car-designer Bill Thomas, and has latterly been altered on practical grounds.

From February 1983, as well as seventeen machines supplied to the RAF and Navy, over 140

Interpol 2s have gone to some 30 UK Police forces, and the Shenstone workforce has expanded to around sixty to meet orders. While this is encouraging, it is, as Poore recognizes, 'far from profitable', and so far the Wankel has lost money for NVT. Even the civilian version has never been envisaged for mass production; one hold-up in 1981 came with the imposition of 10 per cent 'car tax' on new motor cycles, and Poore campaigned for exemption for manufacturers of less than 500 machines a year, presumably his intended ceiling. But late in 1984 the project took another step forward when Poore, the man who had once invoked government aid to the tune of £40 million, succeeded in buying with MBH funds the Department of Industry's nominal £2.37 million controlling interest in NVT for £375,000, and disentangled himself from the politicians. Buying out, he said, left the company free to find very necessary new investment; under the previous arrangement, no dividends could be paid, and thus no extra investment cash attracted.

It also lifted a limitation which had only permitted Shenstone to make motor cycles and leisure vehicles. This had already allowed the sale of a manufacturing licence to the aircraft products division of the US company Teledyne Industries Inc, with the Wankel powerplant, either as a twin or single chamber unit, to be used as a revival

Norton Wankel Mk II's pressed steel monocoque frame.

58

Left *May 1984, and the Wankel-engined Interpol 2 was in service with several British forces.*

Below left *Possible hope for an uncertain future—Wankel-engined Interpol 2.*

Right *Always was, always will be. A flat track twin at Ascot Park, California in 1972 storms in to win.*

engine for microlight aircraft. Now Norton are free to seek other and profitable applications for the engine's technology, such as military contracts. This does, however, raise the question, which has been worrying some of the Police authorities, of the degree of management commitment to the less profitable motor cycle production. As one letter in the Norton Owners' Club journal put it sourly, 'there is a hint of a suggestion that the rotary engine will end up with an aeroplane company somewhere, or be sold off to British Leyland, perhaps after a certain person has got his knighthood for developing a revolutionary new British engine.'

So there the story stood in 1985, with the Norton name on the tank of an exciting new motor cycle, and almost total uncertainty as to the future. The Wankel-engined machine (still nameless) has not been released for sale to the public. Norton Motors (1978) Ltd recently acquired a new MD, ex-Lotus man Dennis Austin. Questioned on the possibility of a civilian motor cycle launch date, he stressed that the number one priority was a profitable business, and that nothing could be expected in the showrooms before 1986. But given the consistency of NVT's pronouncements on the subject, after a statement like that, the bike could well have been launched before the original edition of this book! In fact it would be in 1987.

If you share the author's feelings, the preceding

pages will have made distressing reading. So let us remember that despite the obstacles of unsuitable premises, lack of finance, political conflict, and plain bad management, nevertheless during our period machines of character, some of them really outstanding road-going motor cycles, were designed, developed and built under the Norton name.

It should be remembered that the scene was further complicated by external events such as the oil crisis and attendant inflation, and by government inconsistency. But for fruitful achievement in the future, it seems to me there is needed not only the unstinted and imaginative application of the most up-to-date technology. There must also be a rekindling of what was to be found, from management down to lowliest worker, in the men of the pioneer and golden days, and in many dedicated individuals since, engineers and riders, whether at Bracebridge Street, Woolwich, Andover or Wolverhampton: a style of management which can lead to a reawakening at all levels of the most intense commitment, even of love.

Norton: The 16H/Big 4 singles

Like a history of Norton incarnate, the side-valve

500 16H and 600 Big 4 emerged from the mists of the Edwardian era, and came through the maelstrom of World War II like rhinoceros through a brush fire, substantially unchanged.

Over 100,000 of the slow, heavy but unstoppable chuffers, both solo and sidecar, had been produced for the military during the conflict, the Big 4 outfits often featuring a driven sidecar wheel. The WD contracts had been in some terms the fruit of Gilbert Smith's pre-war cultivation of Army officers, with invitations for them to the TT, the ISDT and the Scottish, where Norton's unapproachability could be graphically demonstrated. Smith reportedly even had a company technical man draft the officers' reports for them!

'One in every four was a Norton', as the slogan had it about the wartime bikes and memories of the side-valve sloggers are vivid for the servicemen who rode them. The good bit was that, as Titch Allen pointed out in *MCS*, 'nothing that broke or fell off [on the 16H] could bring it to a halt.' The magneto platform, for instance, could work loose, but a bit of wood jammed between it and the cylinder barrel would keep the drive chain in tension. The traditional ruggedness of Pa Norton's design served the troops well.

The downside could be summed up in one word. Ex-Triumph publicity man Ivor Davies,

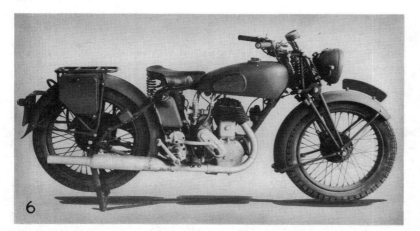

Left *Wartime WD 16H 500 cc side-valve. The word was—vibration!*

Below right *Classic slogger's powerplant—16H side-valve motor dissected.*

recalling DR days in 1939, exclaimed: 'VIBRATION! . . . it was quite impossible to keep even controls tight on the bars. . . One day one of the lads . . . felt his false teeth fly out . . . Don't talk to me about vibration in this day and age!' Another letter to *Classic Bike* stated bluntly, 'The Norton should have been the better bike but in most respects it was a pig compared with a good BSA M20' (the Small Heath 500 side-valve which was 'no slower than the Norton and handled better, particularly on the loose stuff.')

Since the Norton singles had not been particularly remarked for vibration pre-war, the culprit seems to have been the WD specification of a seventeen-tooth engine sprocket for the Big 4, and eighteen-tooth for the 16H, rather than the trusty pre-war nineteen-tooth variety. This was to lower the gearing so that the machine could be ridden at marching pace. In combination with the absence of a headsteady—one was fitted for the side-valves for 1951, but no ohv Norton roadster single boasted this piece of equipment until the Featherbed singles of 1959 on—this seems to have raised the vibration level to the denture-ejecting variety. The seventeen-tooth sprocket stayed on the civilian Big 4 but reverted to nineteen-tooth for the 16H. There is some evidence that Norton were aware of the vibration problem, but during the war and in the boom demand that followed it, there was no time to do anything but produce what was to hand. By then the vibration, and the engine clatter and barking exhaust note, had got itself noticed. Bert Hopwood, while he was designing the Dominator twin engine, recalled how one dealer begged him not to do it, as he feared that a Norton twin would be twice as noisy as the Norton singles!

The heart of these side-valve machines had been laid down by J. L. Norton himself. In 1908

his first production single had been the Big 4, which was honoured thereafter with the Model number 1; and in 1911 he had selected the classic long-stroke 490 cc (79 × 100 mm) dimensions for a 500 side-valve, which dimensions were later to be shared by the ohv Model 18 and ES2, the trials 500T as well as the ohc International, the pre-1936 works racers, and (slightly bored out) the Manx production racers until 1954. The 'H' in the side-valve 16H, incidentally, had originally been for 'Home', to distinguish it from the 'C' suffix of the 'Colonial' models with their higher frames suited to export markets' more primitive road conditions.

By the post-war period the simple design of the powerplant was still essentially as it had been since the last major update by Edgar Franks in 1931. The 16H and the Big 4 were virtually identical to each other, and shared together with much else a substantially similar bottom end (though there were minor differences in the machining of the right crankcase half) with their ohv equivalents the Model 18/ES2 and the 19. For 1931 they had shifted their magnetos to a less vulnerable position behind the cylinder and acquired dry sump lubrication with the trusty Norton double gear oil pump being driven by worm from the right hand side of the crankshaft.

The post-war versions of the 16H engine had its valve-springs enclosed from the first. Then for 1948 these hardy perennials had the benefit of some updating by Bert Hopwood, who had arrived at Bracebridge Street the previous year. Diehards shuddered as the Big 4's stroke was reduced from 120 to 113, the same as the pre-war ohv 600 cc Model 19. This gave both a capacity of 596 cc and despite the stroke being shortened, it was still the longest in the post-war British world. The timing chest, still with internal webs from the bearing-housings to the walls, was smaller than previously but still of generous proportions. This gave plenty of clearance to the substantial grey iron flywheels, which were now smaller in diameter but thicker in width than the previous 8 in diameter, 1 in thick, 55 lb items. The shorter flywheels permitted the use of a longer piston skirt. Norton balanced the flywheels' rotating weight and 50 per cent of their reciprocating weight.

The built-up crankshaft had its mainshafts of case-hardened nickel-steel pressed into the flywheels. It was carried on the drive side by a ball bearing on the outside, then a spacing ring, then a caged roller bearing; an identical roller was used on the timing side. An immense crankpin with a $1^7/_{16}$ in diameter roller track carried the H-section connecting rod on a double-row crowded roller race; the little end was an equally capacious $^7/_8$ in diameter phosphor-bronze bush, the latter material being used for all significant plain bearings. There was a hole beneath the drive side bearing housing, which registered with a corresponding hole in the crankshaft when the piston was descending and thus formed a timed

breather. Compression ratios were low, eminently suited to the low-octane pool fuel; 4.9:1 for the 16H, 4.5:1 for the Big 4. Their power outputs, about which Norton Motors tended to be cagey, were equally lowly, 12.5 bhp and 14 bhp respectively for 1951.

Another main feature of the redesign for 1948 was the valve gear. Previously the valve spring enclosure box had been cast with the cylinder, though with an air space between the box and the iron cylinder walls. A pair of tappets ran in guides screwed into the top of the crankcase, transferring the cam lift directly to the valves. With adjusters built into their top ends, they were returned by single springs. There was a simple valve-lifter, and this valve gear was shielded by a steel cover retained by a single screw and embossed with the Norton name. Drive for this timing gear was taken, unusually, from the crankshaft to the exhaust cam, and thence to the inlet cam. For 1948 came a new detachable aluminium valve-spring housing, strangely H-shaped like a twin chimney pot. It was clamped between the crankcase and barrels with insulating washers, and so was better insulated from the heat of the cylinder walls. On the cylinder finning there was now a vertical division between the inlet

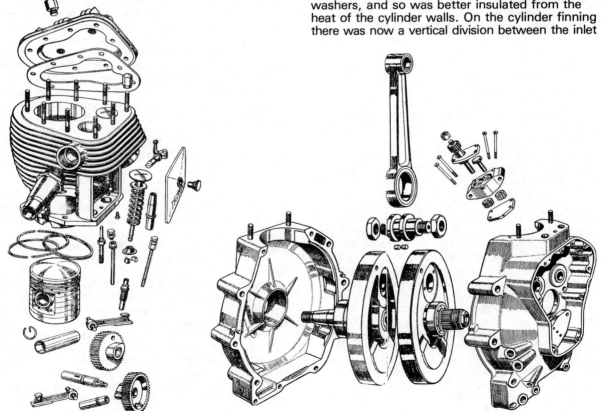

1950 16H, good-looking, old-fashioned but ultra-reliable.

and exhaust port finning. The cover for the valve gear lost its 'Norton'.

Above the barrels came the other big innovation for 1948, a light alloy cylinder head with copper and asbestos head gasket, in place of the previous iron head. The alloy head had its bronze plug seating cast into the aluminium, the plug size now being 14 mm. Both head and barrels were masterpieces of the foundryman's art. Seen from the drive side, the barrel fins' virile yet graceful swelling up from the timing chest is very characteristic, and as Peter Watson pointed out in *Classic Bike*, unlike the head-finning on the equivalent Ariel and BSA, which merely halts when it meets a head stud and then continues after interruption, the Norton's head fins curve sinuously on. But as Watson also points out, this excellence helped push the price up; at £180 for 1948, the Big 4 Norton was £20 dearer than the Ariel VB, and £30 more than BSA's M21, which was not however to follow the Norton lead with an alloy head until 1951 (it was 1952 for the Ariel).

The object of the revamp, for both side-valves and ohv singles, was to try and bring them in line with modern conditions a little more by building in the ability to travel for longer distances at higher speeds, and to improve their ability to rev beyond the 0–2,500 range. Strong pulling in the latter was the fundamental requirement of the sidecar work for which many of them were destined, but it limited solo top speeds to around the 65 mark. This redesign worked better for the 16H than for the intransigently long-stroke Big 4, the 500 returning a top speed of 73 mph in a 1949 test, though with vibration unabated from 55 mph upwards. Possibly this was nature's, or the Norton's, way of telling you to ease off, as traditionally if revved for too long, the cast-iron flywheels could work loose on their mainshafts and disintegrate. (A cure discovered by the early

racers was to dip the shafts in sal ammoniac, which resulted in an absolutely immovable chemical bond of rust!)

Cycle parts for both the side-valves were based on the simple, but strong, single downtube full-cradle type rigid frame. This had featured on the pre-war ES2—the wartime 16Hs had been a different version of the old Colonial frame that used the engine as a stressed member. Electrics were by separate Lucas magneto and dynamo. The machines were handsomely finished in the traditional Norton fashion, with black cycle parts save for a chromed 2¾ gallon petrol tank with silver panels lined in black and red, and a silver wrap-around 4-pint oil tank on the timing side similarly decorated. For 1947 in common with the rest of the range, the side-valves had adopted Norton Roadholder telescopic forks, of the 'long', pre-Featherbed variety. These were not interchangeable with their 'short' successors since the steering column assembly was completely different. In the 'long' forks the springs surrounded the main tubes, and damping was soft, controlled by a double-taper plug. These and the cradle frame gave good handling for the engine's limited output. (Around 1950 there appear to have been a few plunger-framed 16H and Big 4s produced, though these were never catalogued).

The ammeter and light switch were carried in a small panel to the rear of the headlamp shell, while the speedometer was mounted in the fork top. A saddle was standard equipment. Both wheels and tyres were interchangeable 3.25 × 19 in, and both brakes the Norton 7 in single-sided jobs with 1¼ in wide alloy shoes each on their own pivot, which for 1949 were at last linked by a brakeshoe pivot tie plate. The qd rear wheel was of the kind common to the range, the hub having equal size flanges held against the combined sprocket and brake drum by the three long sleeve nuts working on conical rebates within the hub. If very thoroughly neglected these could work loose and either fall out or seize up.

The next (and last) major change came in 1950 and concerned the Norton four-speed footchange gearbox, manufactured for them by Burman since 1935, and housed in an upright rectangular casing. A full description of it will be found in the next section, but for 1950 in a rationalizing move, the singles were given the benefit of the redesign that had been necessary to suit the box to the Dominator twin. It was now 'laid down' rather than standing vertically as previously. Before, too, for tensioning the primary chain the box had pivoted about the lower of its two substantial mounting lugs; this lower lug was housed between two frame members with no problem. However, the top lug was split into two and fitted either side of a frame member, with a single clamping bolt. If this bolt was allowed to work loose, the frame chewed into the gearbox forked lug, and when it was eventually tightened one of the alloy ears of the upper gearbox lug would snap. With the new arrangement the top mounting was altered to suit extended engine plates, and the gearbox pivoted on simple lugs both top and bottom (though the bolt on the top one was inaccessible). Now, too, the positive stop mechanism was at the front of the mainshaft instead of above it. A further useful feature was the kickstart return spring, now like the positive stop mechanism no longer external but housed under a small pressed steel cover on the shaft, and quick and easy to replace if broken. Otherwise the internals were as previously; the cam plate was

still at the front of the box, but its detente spring was now on the underside, and turned by an internal quadrant which linked directly to the change mechanism. The 'laid-down' horizontal box was tucked well in and presented a neater appearance than before, was more reliable, and the pedal movement for changing was shorter. Sidecar gear ratios were usually standard for the Big 4 and 16H.

So the side-valves entered the '50s. A *Motorcycle* road test of a Big 4 and Swallow chair in 1950, while admitting the low-ish cruising speed of just over 50 mph, with top speed of just 55, emphasized the positive; the day-in, day-out reliability, the acceleration which while 'brisk' rather than 'sparkling', varied little whether the chair was full or empty, the ground level or hilly. This was, after all, essentially the same engine that had stormed Porlock Hill twenty consecutive times to take the 1924 Maudes Trophy. They liked the absence of overheating (unusual in a side-valve), the exceptional low-speed torque with the ability to pull from 12 mph in top gear (this with a chair attached), and the smoothness of the gearbox, but were less impressed by the brakes, especially the front one in the wet. At a steady 50 mph the outfit's 596 cc engine returned 35 mpg, the figure improving to 48 mpg at 40 mph; all about normal for a side-valve. Fleet orders from the RAC showed that there was still some market for side-valve dependability and stamina. One of the engine's few weak points was the tendency to burn out exhaust valves if thrashed while pulling a chair. A recent *Classic Bike* test mentioned that, with the tappet set while cold at the recommended gap, the owner of the Big 4 in

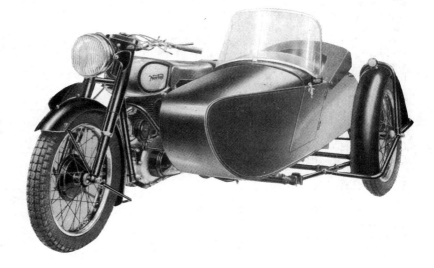

The bike is an OHV, but this Norton own-brand model G sidecar was more often hitched to a side-valve.

1954, last year for the 600 cc Big 4.

question had found the motor losing its exhaust valve clearance when it became hot. He found that setting the clearance with valve hot caused a little more engine clack when cold, but cured the problem.

The 16H and Big 4 benefited from some detail improvements for the range over the next four years, fitting among other things a larger 3½ gallon petrol tank and improved brakes for 1951, a dual-seat for 1953 and an 8 in front brake for 1954. Then, with the AMC takeover established, time ran out for the sloggers. The 596 cc ohv Model 19 was reintroduced to take over the sidecar work, and for 1955 the side-valves were gone. But 43 years hadn't been a bad innings!

Today, attached to a suitable chair, they make a pleasing link with the past, and are probably the most desirable post-war examples of the sv engine type. Spares are reasonably available, though it must be remembered that many of them are for the WD 16H and Big 4s, on which the frames, girder forks, and gearbox (the 1937-type 16H box had the linkage of its foot change mechanism exposed), as well as cycle parts including toolbox, oil tank, headlamp stays and silencer, all differed from the post-war civilian model.

Norton: The 16H and Big 4 singles—dates and specifications
Production dates
Civilian 16H—1946–54
Civilian Big 4—1947–54

Specificiations
16H
Capacity, bore and stroke—490 cc (79 × 100 mm)
Type—sv single
Ignition—Magneto
Weight—(1951) 389 lb

Big 4
Capacity, bore and stroke (from 1947)—596 cc (82 × 113 mm
Type—sv single
Ignition—Magneto
Weight—(1951) 413 lb

Norton: Roadster side-valve singles—annual development and modifications
1950
For 16H, Big 4:
1 Gearbox altered to 'laid-down' type (for details see text).
2 Oil feed and return pipes now terminate in a common junction box fixed to the crankcase, as on the Dominator twins.
3 Voltage control unit was located in toolbox.
4 Dynamo output increased from 35 to 60 watts.

1951
For 16H, Big 4:
1 Prop-stand fitted as standard.
2 New front brake shoe-plate, a rigid alloy die-casting.
3 New fuel tank with capacity enlarged from 2¾ to 3½ gallons, and no recess for the nose of the saddle.
4 New shape for 4-pint oil tank replaces wrap-around type.
5 Steady struts fitted between front down tube and cylinder head.

1953
For 16H, Big 4:
1 Dual-seat fitted as standard.
2 Pillion footrests fitted as standard.
3 Lucas Diacon stop-and-tail lamp now fitted.
4 Rear wheel sprocket changed from 42 to 43 teeth.

1954

For 16H, Big 4:

1 8-in diameter front brake fitted, with die-cast light alloy shoe-plate, 25 per cent increase in brake lining area, and additional brake adjustment available by removing operating arm and turning it over before replacing it on cam spindle.

Norton: The Model 18/ES2/19/Model 50 singles

Like the side-valves, the ohv Norton singles represented the far end of a long tradition. In their case, the heritage went back to Pa Norton's first ohv design of 1922, the Model 18, in the same classic 490 cc (79 × 100 mm) dimensions and with much the same bottom end as his previous side-valve 500. As in the beginning, so after the Second World War, the Model 18 was the first ohv Norton to be offered, in 1946, with the same cycle parts and substantially the same bottom end as the 16H and Big 4; for details of these components see the preceding section.

For 1947 Roadholder forks were grafted on to the Model 18's rigid frame with its malleable iron casting cradle, bestowing on it a rather front-heavy, slightly awkward appearance. This did not apply so much to the sister model that reappeared that year, the 490 cc ES2. There is some controversy as to just what 'ES2' originally stood for when the model was introduced as a sports roadster for 1928, but concensus of opinion seems to favour it signifying 'Enclosed Springs' for this No 2 model in the '18' line. In keeping with the sports bike image, for 1947 it came equipped as standard with rear plunger springing, though in the opinion of *Classic Bike*'s Peter Watson, 'the plunger models are best avoided despite their

good looks, as the rigid chassis offers a better and safer ride.' On the plus side there was marginally more rider comfort from the few inches of movement the plunger's spring-boxes provided, and somehow the system was catalogued as only adding 5 lb extra weight to the ES2 or the Model 18's 374 lb dry. By 1950 the story had changed, with catalogued weight, still only separated by 4 lb, more accurately announced at 409 and 413 lb respectively.

The powerplants of both were similar, beautifully swelling barrels, slashed with the splayed chrome steel of long pushrod tubes, thrusting up tall from tapered yet substantial timing chests. With the 100 mm stroke, these were genuinely long-stroke 500s, even compared with the 93 mm of their AJS/Matchless plonker equivalents.

Bottom end, with the slight exception of the machining on the right-hand crankcase, and bearings, were as for the side-valves, and like the latter the last major redesign for the ohv had come from Edgar Franks in 1931 with the adoption of dry sump lubrication via the double-gear oil pump. This bolted to a face in the timing chest beneath the crankshaft rather than more conventionally (and awkwardly) fitting into a close tolerance hole. It had two gear pairs, and was driven from the right hand end of the crankshaft by a threaded worm wheel, which also secured the timing pinion. Its famous fault was the likelihood, when the machine was left to stand for some days, of oil draining past the gears and into the crankcase, whence it had to be drained off and the system topped up. Some riders provided for themselves what the system lacked to prevent this happening, a ball-valve in the oil feed line from the tank, but this is a potentially dangerous solution. John Hudson believes that the trouble arose because nobody ever thought of servicing the pump itself, but just let it run on forever.

Predecessor. 1936 ES2. Motor changed little to the end.

66

The immediately post-war ohv engines featured flat cam followers, acting directly onto pushrods which had adjusters at their upper ends behind an access plate fastened by two screws. The splayed pushrod tubes, angled in at their upper end, were attached to the crankcase with unions and nuts, and ran outside the iron cylinder barrels right up to the rocker-box in the iron head. There the pushrods worked on three-piece rocker arms, oscillating in grease-lubricated bushes in the rocker box. Screw adjusters allowed for clearance on the rather small valves.

But for 1948, as part of the effort by Bert Hopwood and others to both pep up and quieten the engines, the flywheels were reduced in diameter and increased in width, permitting a longer-skirted piston to be fitted. At the same time the size of the timing case was reduced and the old cam followers were discarded. In their place came tappets with flat feet and a flat on one side of the foot to prevent rotation. The tops of the pushrods were rounded off to create shorter,

stubbier, lighter tubular pushrods, which for 1949 became alloy. The tubes were still clamped between the crankcase and the rocker box but now had a seal at each end, and the rocker box was redesigned in one piece. Inside it the rockers were stiffer and shorter, and worked on fixed spindles. They were now lubricated by a feed taken from the main oil return pipe just before it reached the tank. This fed a banjo union on the left side of the box, and from there internal drillways connected to the rockers and the ball ends that rested in the adjustable cups at the top of the pushrods. Drillings in the cylinder provided oil drains from the valve wells in the head back to the crankcase.

All this had its effect, and from then on the ohv singles were mechanically quiet, with only slight valve gear rustle and intake hiss. But exhaust silencing, with a straight through conical silencer, was not yet of this order. Frame apart, the two ohv singles were identical. Compression was kept low, with the aid of an aluminium head gasket, at 6.45:1, though by 1950 this had risen a hair to 6.6:1. Electrics were provided by a chain-driven Lucas Magdyno located behind the cylinder. The transmission, as on the side-valves, was by single-row primary chain, and by the diminutive but perfectly adequate ⅝ × ¼ in final drive chain. It is possible, as author Roy Bacon suggests, that the malleable iron of the rear drum and its integral sprocket was kinder to the chain than the hardened steel used in other designs. This small chain had the same breaking strain as the later ⅝ × ⅜ in one, since the pin diameter was the same on both. The problem of wear on the combined drum and sprocket remained and now that they are rare items the only solution is re-toothing.

There was no engine shaft shock absorber, but a vane-type cush drive with rubber inserts was to be found at the centre of the three-spring clutch. These inserts would eventually perish messily due to the ingress of oil and had to be replaced. The take-up of the heavy duty clutch from low speeds could be noticeably harsh if it was not meticulously adjusted. The gearbox, as on the side-valves, was at first the upright Norton type, a simple and robust design with its mainshaft mounted above the layshaft and concentric with the sleeve gear; the pushrod of the clutch ran through the mainshaft. Each shaft carried four gears, one of which was splined to move sideways under the guidance of its selector to engage with the gears either side of it, with either three or four dogs and functional amounts of backlash. The design was such that with every change, as one gear moved out of engagement

Below left *Maybe not exactly built in the light of racing experience, but a handsome single flagship, the plunger sprung 500 cc E52 for 1950.*

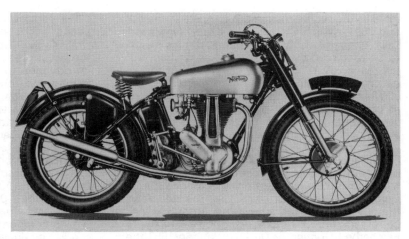

Right *Country cousin, the popular 500T rigid trials iron for 1951.*

the other moved in. Altogether this provided the basis of an outstanding change. For 1950 the singles' gearbox, though altered little internally, underwent the first of two major changes in its life, adopting the 'laid-down' format designed for the previous year's new Dominator twin and described in the side-valve section.

The Norton singles' design may not have been the latest word, but for some riders there was still nothing to compare to the solid reliability of these walloping, workmanlike big bangers. Power outputs of around 21 bhp, with top speeds of just below 80 mph, may not sound overwhelming, but there was also the combination of reliable handling, sure transmission, an unburstable engine and a thoughtfully contrived riding position, with adjustable controls all within easy reach, together with an unusually large, firm and well-sprung saddle. All these things often permitted higher average rates of travel than machines with higher top speeds could achieve in practice. The loping pace of the silver long-strokes had its fans, and the 7 in single-sided brakes, particularly the sensitive and strong rod-operated rear brake, also encouraged the Norton rider to crack on, and justified the additional expense of purchasing a machine bearing the curly 'N'.

The engine's robustness and excellent low-down torque meant that many ohv singles, like the side-valves, were harnessed to sidecars; and indeed Norton, who had begun making sidecars in 1919, still offered their own Model G chair, with 'the body mounted on the Norton double triangulated chassis'. Petrol economy made them attractive too; it might be down on the pre-war 500s' 100 mpg plus, but the Amal 276 carburettor with remote float chamber returned

commendable averages around the 75 mpg mark. These Amals were clip-fixing, and tended to crack along the body nearest to the clip, especially if overtightened. They did however fit a small air filter as standard, as well as a spring-loaded fast idle facility for warming up.

Parallel with the development of the roadsters there ran the separate but equally well-loved 500T and 350T trials singles. Norton began the post-war period offering for trials only the heavy Model 18 with a high-level exhaust, but the first claims to fame in British biking circles of the Featherbed inventors, the McCandless brothers of Belfast, were their swinging-arm conversions for competition work, particularly scrambles, which gave riders an instant edge over rigid machines. Cromie McCandless and the brothers' associate, Artie Bell, though best known now for their road-racing exploits, were all-round riders, and after their association with fellow Ulsterman Joe Craig and the Norton factory had begun, they set about creating a viable trials iron out of available components.

These included the standard Model 18 or ES2 engine, but soon with an alloy head, and later with Wellworthy Alfin alloy barrels, fitted to the much lighter though still rigid WD 16H frame, and topped with a special petrol tank. Most importantly perhaps they went to work on the Roadholder teles. This transformed the big bike's handling and reduced its wheelbase from 56 in to 53 in without adding ground clearance. The forks were good enough for Norton tuner Francis Beart, for whom Cromie rode, to fit them on his racers for 1950, together with smaller (19 in) wheels. The factory adopted this for the Garden Gate-framed racers for 1951, and many privateers followed suit on their Manxes, butchering 500Ts to do so. Late in 1948 the works trials team jumped at the 500T and 350T, which Classic trials expert Don Morley calls 'unquestionably the finest rigid trials machine to be produced by any factory', as well as 'truly unbreakable'. While highly successful at the national level until their withdrawal after 1954, the 500Ts could also perform in other sports, as well as providing daily transport. Today they are much sought after by the pre-'65 mudplugger brigade and by collectors in general.

After the 1950 fitting of the laid-down gearbox (which incidentally the 500T could unfortunately never adopt, due to its restricted wheelbase), there was little significant change for the roadster singles for a couple of years. Like the side-valves, the ohv pair acquired a new and larger 3¾ gallon petrol tank for 1951. 1952 was the year of the first Featherbed Dominator De Luxe, and in 1953 there were suspension changes for the ES2. This adopted a frame in common with the non-Featherbed Dominator, the Model 7. The existing cradle frame, of brazed lug construction with single top and down tubes, had its rear portion redesigned to accommodate a swinging-arm section similar to the one on the Featherbed, with Girling rear units. Wheel movement was increased to 3½ in, while the wheelbase was the same 54½ in as that of the plunger frame. The positioning of the swinging-arm's pivot less that 3 in behind the final drive centre meant minimal chain wear. This frame's handling, while obviously not up to Featherbed standard, was an improvement on the previous plunger chassis, and generally acceptable.

The new 1953 ES2's front fork trail was a compromise at 2¾ in to suit either solo or sidecar work. A new very wide and deeply valanced rear mudguard with a hinged rear piece was fitted, with the same good quickly detachable rear wheel. A new toolbox was fitted in the angle of the rear stay on the left hand side, secured by a one-armed wing-nut, as on the WD 16H. The silencer too was different on this machine. In common with that year's Dominator models, a new bulbous pear-shaped item was fitted, the three internal compartments of which were claimed to absorb less power and to give more efficient silencing; though a year later on the Model 19 600 cc single, a *Motorcycling* test rapped the silencer's note as 'far too robust for comfort, especially when accelerating in traffic'. The ES2's exhaust pipe was now ⅛ in smaller at 1⅝ in and a 43-tooth rear sprocket was substituted for its previous 42-tooth item, as it was on all the singles. Also in common with the whole range was the adoption of a dual-seat and

pillion footrests as standard, along with the new Lucas Diacon stop and tail lamps.

1954, the last year of the side-valves, was also the last for the rigid Model 18, and simply saw the introduction for all of an 8 in front brake; this featured an iron drum riveted to the hub but each shoe still pivoted on a separate pin in the traditional Norton way. For 1955, to fill the gap the flat-tops had left, came the reintroduction of a really big banger, the 600 cc Model 19, last seen in 1939, but now as then featuring the same 113 mm stroke as the post-1947 Big 4 side-valve.

It was available initially in two forms, one being the unsprung 19R, with a strengthened version of the defunct 500 cc Model 18's frame for this last of the rigid Nortons, and a fat 4.00 × 18 in rear tyre to compensate for the absence of a sprung saddle; its dual-seat was of a new type for the whole range (bar the Dominator 88 and the International) with an outlined rear passenger portion. The 19R model was only to last the one year until stocks of the rigid frames had been used up. The other variant was the rear-sprung 19S, with a frame similar to the ES2. While welcoming its comfort, the *Motorcycling* test of a 19S and Swallow Vulcan sidecar late in 1955 noted that the fairly soft springing induced 'a certain looseness of handling'. The very long-stroke Model 19 of the 1920s had been a sidecar TT winner, but now the 19S's top speed of 64 mph with chair attached could scarcely be looked on as pulse-quickening, though it was nearly a 10 mph improvement on a side-valve outfit. The RAC moved from the side-valves and bought 19S models, and later ES2s, for their mobile patrol outfits.

This low performance by the 19S was despite the acquisition of an alloy head for 1955, which the ES2 shared. But the compression ratio stayed nearly the same at 6.8:1 for the 500. The two bikes were almost identical, the giveaway in appearance being the difference in engine height, with the 600's rocker box being almost completely recessed into the fuel tank cutaway. Common to the whole range for 1955 was the adoption of Amal Monobloc 376 carburettors, plus boxed in number plates with a rear reflector, polishing rather than enamelling for the lower ends of the alloy fork sliders, a new shape for the front number plate, and a modified handlebar, with the horn button built into the right hand side (as had previously been the case with the Dominator 88s). With the dual-seats redesigned, petrol tanks were again smaller, reverting to the 2¾ gallon size and sporting thinner knee-grips. The new round three-dimensional plastic tank badge was featured with a big N at the centre of a quartered design reminiscent of the BMW logo. Probably adopted at the behest of AMC, it meant, for the first time since before World War I, a slightly ominous displacing of the unadorned curly Norton name on its own on the tank. Overall these were good-looking versions of the big bangers.

1956 saw more restyling, and indeed the middle '50s are a testing time for those bent on accurate restoration, with a multitude of detail changes. Much of this year's effort reversed the previous year. Petrol tanks were bigger, deeper and more bulbous again at 3¾ gallons, with knee-grips secured by screws, and there was a new flat-top dual-seat. The rear mudguard as valanced to an increased depth, and the new front guard was of deep section. The design of the headlamp was changed, with the previous separate panel holding the light switch and ammeter now made deeper to take the speedometer, which had previously been remotely mounted above it. The headlamp shell no longer carried an underslung pilot light. The fork top area was modified to accommodate the panel, and within the Roadholders the action was modified slightly with different coil springs to provide a softer initial movement. Toolboxes and oil tanks were restyled to matching pannier shapes, and recessed within the frame loops; a pressed steel plate connected the forward ends of oil tank and box, with a hole in it for an air filter, though this fitment was standard only on the twins, becoming an option for the singles for 1957 on.

Alloy full width hubs were now fitted (as on the twins) and no longer incorporated grease nipples for the bearings. The cover plates were polished to match the brake plate. The handlebar was new again, sweeping upward and further rearwards to improve an already good riding position. The prop-stand was shifted further rearwards under the crankcase and was strengthened. At the rear, Armstrong suspension units now embodied the external cam-type two-position adjustment for load. Also the pivoted rear fork for the whole range featured a new forged-steel lug to support the wheel spindle, where formerly the fork ends had been simply trapped and slotted; screw type adjusters were provided for the rear chain. The speedometer drive gearbox was now mounted so that the cable ran from below the level of the wheel spindle.

In the engine department the 500 and 600 were joined for 1956 by a 350, yet another revived machine, the Model 50. This had not been seen since 1939 and was returning with the same 348 cc (71 × 88) dimensions. Compression ratio was 7.3:1, provided by an alloy head and the same

Big brother. The unsprung 600 cc model 19R for 1955 only, to replace the side-valves.

type of wire-wound, flat top alloy pistons as were being introduced for the twins and already used by the other singles. The Model 50 was to be slotted into the same cradle frame with swinging arm as the ES2 and the 19S. Internally, differences were few. The 350 had a slightly smaller Monobloc (1 in, against the ES2's 1¹/₁₆ in), lower gearing (5.59:1 against the ES2's 4.75:1 overall), and rather futilely, six not eight clutch plates, with a deeper alloy pressure plate to compensate. Ex-Model 50 owner Peter Watson advises seeking out an ES2 pressure plate and two more clutch plates, and perhaps using the stronger clutch springs off a 650 SS, particularly if, like him, you raise the 350's gearing, which means some clutch-slipping in traffic. The Model 50 was around 10 mph slower than the 80 mph ES2. The latter's compression ratio rose slightly to 7:1, and a new larger diameter exhaust pipe, now identical to the one on the 19S, had a modified sweep to it. Both these machines also fitted a redesigned exhaust cam and had the area of their cylinder finning increased.

From May 1956 the last variant of the gearbox, the AMC version, was introduced. Less elongated than the first 'laid-down' kind, and lacking the 'Norton' logo on its inspection plate, once again it pivoted on its lower bolt. Elongated holes were provided in the mounting plate for the top bolt so that, as before, the gearbox could be moved backwards and forwards to adjust the primary chain. A drawbolt fitted to the gearbox top bolt had a ³/₁₆ in Whit hexagon nut on either side of a stop riveted to the off-side mounting plate, to pull the gearbox back until the chain was tight.

Within the box, engagement of all gears except bottom was still by dogs, but the positive stop mechanism was improved, with the layshaft bottom gear pinion being provided with holes for engagement by pegs on that side of the layshaft sliding member. The clutch was redesigned, and inserts of Klinger material were now used in the driving friction plates. Although still the three-spring type, its cam-action clutch thrust mechanism now incorporated a ball and roller which required an adjuster for the springs in the clutch pressure plate. While making clutch action less harsh, this was awkward in that it required access to the clutch centre which the pressed-tin chain covers could not provide without removal, and it meant the loss of the large mushroom on the clutch pushrod which had previously ensured it lifting square and free. Also, if the body on which the clutch arm pivoted turned as the locking ring was tightened, the clutch arm did not move vertically and the clutch cable distorted — as the operating arm pivoted, making for a stiff pull. But overall the box continued as the best British design available.

Being an AMC design, the internals were the same for both Norton and AJS/Matchless applications. Yet since in both cases the gearboxes were made to be a direct substitute for their predecessors, the shells had different mounting points and were not interchangeable. An AMC gearbox is identifiable by the prefix letter 'N' if it is a Norton, 'M' if it is a Matchless/AJS.

For 1957 the game changed again with the new 'smooth look'. As on the rest of the range the pear-drop silencers, shapely but by then looking rather quaint, went, in favour of a new, more functional and effective cylindrical design with no tail pipe. The headlamp instrument panel went, everything now being recessed in the headlamp shell. There were new petrol tanks again, this time with their front edges extended further forward, and at the rear the dual-seat blended more closely with the back of the tank. As on the AMC machinery, the tanks were no longer chromed with painted panels, but were painted, with separate chrome-plated side panels retained by four screws, edged with black plastic beading and with a different shape of knee-rubber.

For weight-saving, at the front there was a new cast-aluminium full-width front hub with a cast-in brake liner and there was a new backplate with a forged cam-lever in place of the previous pressing. The shoe assembly was unchanged but the shoe plate was restyled and now fitted inside the open end of the hub. Both end covers of the Lucas Magdyno were reshaped. The rear brake pedal return spring was now concealed, the torque arm discarded and the stop-light switch tidied up. The rear chainguard changed shape, becoming more comprehensive. The footrests were redesigned, changing from the previous built-up type with flat bicycle pedal shape (and what Cyril Ayton calls a capacity for 'spontaneous disassembly' once loosened), to a more conventional kind with round section rubbers, once again no longer with 'Norton' stamped on them; the rests, however, were still adjustable. The handlebar grips changed from rubber to plastic. A modernizing and (with good commonality throughout the range) an economizing hand could be detected in all this, though the results were still handsome enough.

The frame too was changed. The malleable iron casting that previously formed the engine cradle was replaced by a duplex tubular frame, with the

Left *New 'smooth' styling in 1957 for the ES2.*

Above right *Big single in new livery. 600 cc model 19S for 1957.*

rear fork narrowed and tidied; for where the brake torque arm had been dispensed with, the brake backplate now located directly to the fork end. The suspension units were changed this year and from then on to three-position Girlings, like AMC. The upper yoke of the long Roadholders was reshaped, and there was a small increase in front wheel trail, giving more positive steering solo; perhaps this was a reflection of the fact that after the discontinuation of the Model 7 500 cc sidecar twin in 1955, this year's Norton range again saw a twin, the 600 cc Model 77, offered in the old brazed-lug malleable-iron cradle frame and aimed squarely at the sidecar fraternity.

The engines of the three singles also underwent a noticeable change for 1957, the pushrod tubes now disappearing halfway up the barrels into the head, which became a new alloy casting with wider horizontal finning. The vertical finning on the head was modified to improve the airflow and the external lines of the rocker box were smoothed out; but now special care had to be taken when replacing the inspection cover (which once again lost the 'Norton' stamp) to avoid overtightening and subsequent distortion and leaks. Within, the inlet flange was now cast in one with the head, but only the two valve seats, not the complete combustion dome, were cast in. The rocker assembly was modified. The cams gave slightly higher lift, and their quietening ramps were modified to keep mechanical noise down. One result of the redesigned top end was that whereas previously head and barrel had to be removed together, from now on they had to be removed separately. According to Peter Watson, the new shorter pushrod tubes were also, strangely, more difficult to seal at their junctions with the tunnels than their predecessors.

After all that there was no change for 1958, but 1959 saw the last major evolution. The 600 cc 19S went, as the sidecar market shrank forever with the onset of the Mini. The two remaining singles made a strong bid for survival by finally being offered in the current Wideline Featherbed frame like the twins. They also, perhaps less happily, replaced their Magdynos with alternator electrics, and their pressed-steel chaincases were modified to suit this; a simple visual clue to the difference was that the 'Oil-bath Chaincase' badge, previously positioned to the left of the chain inspection cap, was now placed to its right. The adoption of the Featherbed, which gave a claimed weight loss of around 30 lb, led to the 1958-on Model 50 becoming known rather cruelly as 'the safest bike on the road—the best frame and brakes fitted with the slowest engine'. The history

and development of the Featherbed frame will be found in the twins section; here it can be said that for the ohv singles the only difference from the roadster twins' frame lay in the narrower engine plates, the twins' engine mounting lugs being 3 5/16 in wide over the outside of the lugs front and rear, but the singles' front being only 2 1/4 in across. The top speeds of the ohv singles, despite the engine's refinements over the years, remained pretty constant, rising by 1959 to 74 mph for the 350 and 82 mph for the 500. Rider comfort over long distances suffered from the earlier Wideline version's very width, which was one reason why they were changed.

The singles' oil tank capacity was increased by half a pint to 4 1/2 pints. Their petrol tanks, also enlarged to 3 1/2 gallon capacity, abandoned their previous four-bolt fixing and sat on top of the frame rails, held down onto rubber pads taped to the top tubes of the frame by a securing strap running from the steering head to the rear of the tank, where the strap was tensioned by a bolt. Many owners overtightened the bolt and broke the strap. For 1959 the bolt was modified by lengthening it to accommodate a short coil spring under its head, so that the bolt ran out of thread in the steel roller at the front end of the tooltray with which it engaged, before the spring was coil-

Smart 350. Model 50 for 1958.

bound. A new dual-seat, with shaped portions for rider and pillion, was secured by two wing nuts beneath the seat pan. A fully enclosed rear chaincase was now an option. With the Featherbed frame it was no longer possible to remove the gearbox as a separate unit, the engine and gearbox now having to be removed as one from the frame.

Use of the Featherbed meant the adoption of 'short' Roadholder front forks where the springs were housed inside the stanchion tubes. The springs on the 'long' variety had surrounded the main tubes, and the damping had been softer. There were other differences (see the twins section) and these forks are not interchangeable with the previous long ones, since not only is the fork tube length 21.843 in, against the longer components 23.212 in, but the steering column assembly is completely different.

A plus point for remaining sidecar-ists was that the short forks, unlike their predecessors, were offered with alternative solo or sidecar yokes and optional sidecar strength springs. There is room for confusion here, since Long Roadholders also had optional sidecar springs (part no 19481), which were identifiable by red markings on the end, and were a two-rate spring with 22 working coils and a free length of 11 in; solo long springs were part no 18809. Most short Roadholder solo springs, also identifiable by red end markings (green were for the Navigator, blue for the Manx with their shorter external springs) were three-rate (part no 18813/now 06-7723), with 23 working coils; sidecar short springs were coded yellow, part no 15906a/now 06-7660. Heavier springs were also available for the Girling rear units, as well as a steering damper, and an engine sprocket with fewer teeth. For solo riding, incidentally, an

eighteen-tooth engine sprocket was standard for the Model 50 and a twenty-tooth for the ES2. Peter Watson favoured a nineteen-tooth engine sprocket on his Model 50, because it moved the cruising speed of 55–60 mph out of the engine's worst vibration period. However he claims that the nineteen-tooth sprocket for the ES2 and the Model 50 are not interchangeable, while John Hudson says that they are. For sidecar use, a sixteen or a seventeen-tooth engine sprocket could be supplied for the Model 50, and an eighteen-tooth sprocket for the ES2.

The tidying process continued, with pressed steel covers in the AMC style over the engine plates front and rear of the cylinder, and with the 6-volt alternator electrics. These centred round a Lucas RM15, or for 1962, RM19 alternator, mounted conventionally on the left end of the crankshaft. These could provide problems, as they were susceptible to both vibration, with the outer magnet part of the rotor working loose from the central steel sleeve, and to misalignment. (The problem and some possible solutions are discussed in the twins' section.) Another suspect component of the system was the ammeter which was fragile in the extreme, could indicate charging failure where none existed, and could cause a dead short when it failed itself. A third was the infamous Lucas combined lighting and ignition switch, complicated, trouble prone especially in the wet, and now extremely expensive and difficult to replace. Otherwise the rectifier was under the tool tray beneath the seat, the coil under the rear of the tank, and the points, with auto-advance, in the housing where the magneto had been and driven by the same chain, the unit being flange-mounted to the back of the chaincase behind the cylinder. The only additional change within the engine was the adoption of small diameter multi-rate valve springs. Externally the singles marked their new lease of life by being offered in Forest Green with chromed tank panels, as an optional alternative to the traditional silver and black.

For 1960, while the twins moved to the Slimline Featherbed format, the singles stayed with the old Wideline, but now with chromium-plated mudguards as an option. Internally the clutch changed to material bonded onto the driven plates instead of the previous inserts. A steering lock facility allowed the machines to be padlocked with the forks on full right lock, and 'Clayflex' bearings replaced the 'Silentbloc' kind in the swinging arm. The only other change this year was one universal to the range, something that Norton testers including John Hudson had been pushing for since the AMC box was introduced in 1957, but which had been delayed by the parent company, namely altering the gear ratios to close up the gaps between gears. From no 14401 in the singles' case, this meant that all the ratios were raised, with a change in internal ratios from (1., 1.33, 1.77, 2.67) to (1., 1.216, 1.7, 2.55), with a change in the layshaft pinions for third gear from 21 to 20, and the mainshaft pinions for top from 24 to 23. The 23-tooth sleeve gear had its teeth on the same pitch circle as the earlier 24-tooth and so it ran with the same eighteen-tooth on the layshaft. Similarly the twenty-tooth third layshaft had its teeth on the same pitch circle as the previous 21-tooth third gear.

For 1961 the singles followed the twins into Slimline frames (for chassis details, again see the twins section). There were 'Norton straights', available as an eagerly awaited alternative

handlebar, a new dual-seat, flat-top again, in shades of grey, and new two-tone colour finishes in line with the AMC rejuvenation programme. The tank was different again, deeper, narrower and enlarged a fraction at 3.62 gallons, fastened at the front by two rubber-sleeved bolts and at the rear by a rubber band. In the process it lost its chrome side panels and plastic badges in favour of long, chrome-plated zinc-alloy die-cast spiked badges, containing both the Norton name and the narrow knee grips. These separated the tank top dark colour (black for the ES2, green for the Model 50) from what was described as dove-grey but seemed at the time more like cream or off-white, and formed the basis of the author's lifelong dislike of this colour on motor cycles, especially British motor cycles. On the lower tank, mudguards, and upper and lower portions of the rear dampers, it quickly became shabby-looking and was impossible to keep clean. The qd seat, too, was a mixed blessing, with a pair of rubber sockets under the nose engaging with two rearward-pointing pegs on a cross tube at the upper rear of the main frame loops. That was all right, but at the rear the only fastening was a Dzuz screw (which you could untwist with a coin) attaching to an aperture in the rear mudguard. After the Dzuz fastener became loose with wear, the seat wobbled, and I seem to remember losing the screw more than once.

For 1962 there was only a colour streamlining, with both singles now offered in the black and dove-grey finish, and production ended in autumn 1963 shortly after the move south to Plumstead, where AMC had plenty of singles of their own already waiting to be disposed of. To this end, for 1965 and '66 the execrated Model 50 Mk 2 and

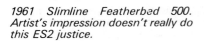

1961 Slimline Featherbed 500. Artist's impression doesn't really do this ES2 justice.

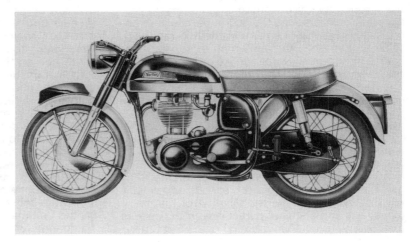

74

Sad end. AMC's 'Model 50 Mk II' for 1966, last year for this disguised Matchless.

ES2 Mk 2 were marketed. These were simply the current Matchless G80/AJS Model 18 500 and G3/Model 16 350, with Norton badges and transfers. At this late stage in the parent company's fortunes they were already sporting Norton Roadholder forks and wheels, and short-stroke scrambles-bred engines (for details see Vol 1, AMC). Export markets, which made up the bulk of AMC sales by then, explain the badge engineering. As a Canadian dealer wrote, recalling 1967, 'Norton was still a big name then, while in the early 1960s the average guy had never heard of a Matchless or an AJS.' Not so true for Britain; they'd heard of them, they just didn't buy them.

It was a whimpering end for the Norton bangers, which in their proper form, through all the variations of frame and cosmetics, always evoked affection from people who rode them, and continue to do so among Classic road-testers today. 'Honest' and 'reliable' are the characteristics ascribed to them. In addition they gave good low speed torque and, surprisingly, excellent acceleration (the 500 in particular is an unusually responsive engine in the mid-range up to 55 or 60 mph). Above 50 mph or so vibration comes in and gets worse, unlike some other singles which smooth out higher up the scale. The name of the game is touring at around the 60 mark, no matter what the passenger and luggage load. They are also physically comfortable machines, the excellent riding position being aided by fully adjustable controls, and mental confidence coming from the handling and the understressed engine's unhurried reliability.

Admittedly at the top end they lope rather than gallop; comparatively low top speeds and solidly weighty cycle parts are the penalty for the robustness and stamina, particularly in the case of the 350s with the 500s' running gear. But both

performance and weight were in line with their contemporaries, like the 500 cc MSS Velocette, which also only just topped 80 mph, or Ariel's VH Red Hunter 500 which turned the scales for 1958 at 375 lb, just 10 lb less than the ES2. It was the nature of the big single species, and the Norton breed were among the finest examples.

The main problem today is locating one, since their solid worth, handsome appearance and associations with the noble marque all make them sought-after items; and dwindling demand coupled with a high price—the late Model 50 was actually dearer than the Navigator 350 twin— meant that comparatively few were built in the '50s. In addition many of the Featherbed-framed variety have been cannibalized to build Tritons or other specials. Their desirability is entirely understandable; the Featherbed really was as good as everybody always says; and in combination with the singles' low power output, as author Roy Bacon puts it, 'you could fall off an ES2 but only after chamfering footrest and silencer until you levered the back wheel off the ground. It was not easy to do.' The brakes too were very good of the type, though with the full width hub on the Featherbed, the rear brake's insubstantial tin backplate was prone to distortion, and once that happened there was nothing to do but substitute, from a specialist like John Tickle, a more rigid alloy backplate, though even these are now no longer available. Nevertheless in combination with the excellent 8 in front brake, 400 lb of 1959 Model 50 on test could be hauled to a hault in 26½ ft from 30 mph. As with the twins, the 'short' Roadholders allow those not bothered by strict authenticity to substitute an even more powerful 2LS front brake off the Commando if desired.

Economy was also always a strong point, with

at least 70 mpg overall being returned for the 350, around the same for earlier 500s and only slightly less on the later spring-framed models. Even better averages could be obtained with a consciously light throttle hand. The long stroke engines probably used less oil than they lost via the oilbath primary chaincase, which distorted easily if, as was inevitable at some stage, its single central fixing bolt was overtightened; modern silicone gasket compound can help with sealing it.

Otherwise problems were few. They were easier to start than most singles. As stated, persistent over-revving can shake the flywheels loose so that they shatter and the power of the thumping powerplant could sometimes knock out big ends and also blow the baffles out of pattern silencers. Vibration, especially if gearing was raised, was easier on the rider than on the later electrics (for which see the twins). The oil draining into the crankcase was a persistent problem, and Loctite on the qd studs and nuts of the rear wheel is a good idea to stop them working loose and wearing irretrievably. Adjusting the primary chain via the gearbox is somewhere between a chore and an art, as it's necessary to check the chain tension in several positions, each after the box has been tightened up again, and of course once that has been done, to then readjust the rear chain.

Like all the over-engineered range of Norton singles, chain wear is slow. With the range's gradual evolution there is reasonable availability and good interchangeability of parts; an exhaust valve from the 1959-on models, for instance, will also fit the 1955-on models, and furthermore can be used as an inlet valve for any 1955-on model too, though they have different parts numbers. Though the Featherbed models must in some ways be the most desirable, any of the ohv singles are well worth considering, and if you are lucky enough to acquire one you will have got a companion for life.

Norton: The ohv singles—production dates and specifications

Production dates (post-war)
Model 18—1946-54
ES2—1947-63
Model 19—1955-58
Model 50—1956-63

Specifications
Model 18/ES2
Capacity, bore and stroke—490 cc (79 × 100 mm)
Type—ohv single

Ignition—(Model 18, and ES2 1947-58) magneto; (ES2 1959-63) Coil
Weight—Model 18 (1951) 409 lb, ES2 (1953) 413 lb, ES2 (1959) 384 lb.

Model 19
Capacity, bore and stroke—597 cc (82 × 113 mm)
Type—ohv single
Ignition—magneto
Weight—19R (1955) 367 lb, 19S (1956) 393 lb

Model 50
Capacity, bore and stroke—384 cc (71 × 88 mm)
Type—ohv single
Ignition—(1956-58) magneto, (1959-63) Coil
Weight—(1956) 382 lb, (1962) 380 lb

Norton: The Model 18/ES2/19/Model 50 singles—annual development and modifications

1950
For Model 18, ES2:
1 'Laid-down' gearbox (for details see text).
2 Oil feed and return pipes now terminate at a common junction box fixed to the crankcase.
3 Prop stands fitted.
4 CVC moved to toolbox.
For ES2:
5 Chainguard extended.

1951
For Model 18, ES2:
1 New 3½ gallon petrol tank, with no recess for nose of saddle.
2 Front brakeshoe plate of greater rigidity in diecast alloy.
3 Different shaped 4 pint oil tank.
4 In mid-1951, due to nickel shortage, petrol tank finish from chrome becomes all silver painted, with panels as previously. Some wheel rims all silver, with red lining.

1953
For Model 18, ES2:
1 Petrol tanks chrome plated.
2 Dual-seat as standard.
3 Pillion footrests as standard.
4 Lucas Diacon stop and tail lamp.
5 43-tooth rear wheel sprocket.
For ES2:
6 New pivoted-fork frame (for details see text).
7 Front fork trail altered to 2¾ in.
8 New wide and deeply valanced mudguard with hinged rear piece.
9 New toolbox.
10 Smaller exhaust pipe.
11 Pear-shaped silencer.

1954
For Model 18, ES2:
1 8 in front brake with 25 per cent increase in lining area.

1955
For ES2, 19R, 19S:
1 Alloy cylinder heads.
2 Amal Monobloc 376 carburettors.
3 Boxed-in number plates with rear reflector.
4 Alloy fork sliders' lower ends polished not enamelled.
5 New shaped front number plate.
6 Handlebar modified with no forward sweep outboard of the clamps, simply up and back; and with horn button built into right hand side.
7 2¾ gallon petrol tanks with three-dimensional plastic badges and thinner knee-grips.
8 Redesigned dual-seat with outlined rear passenger portion.
For 19R:
9 4.00 × 18 in rear tyre.
For ES2:
10 Compression raised to 6.8:1.

1956
For ES2, 19S, Model 50:
1 3¾ gallon petrol tanks with screw-on knee-grips, and new petrol taps and pipes.
2 Pressed-steel pannier-shaped tool, regulator and battery box on the left side, matching 4 pint oil tank on right side, pressed steel plate running transversely across forward end of the two units.
3 New flat-top dual-seat.
4 Rear mudguard valanced to increased depth.
5 Front mudguard of new deep C-section.
6 Softer coil springs for telescopic forks.
7 New headlamp shell with panel on top, no underslung pilot light, ammeter, speedometer and light-switch recessed into panel. Fork top area modified to accommodate.
8 Alloy full width hubs front and rear, with cover plates polished to match brake plate.
9 Combined horn and dip-switch on left bar.
10 Prop stand moved rearwards under crankcase and strengthened.
11 Oil lines altered.
12 Speedometer drive gearbox mounted with cable running from below wheel spindle.
13 Forged end lug for rear fork.
14 Armstrong rear units with three-position setting.
15 Spindle on cam wheel to timing chest now fitted with oil scroll.
16 New handlebar sweeps upward and further rearward.

For ES2 and 19S:
17 New larger diameter exhaust pipe, as 19S, with revised sweep.
18 Redesigned exhaust cam.
For ES2:
19 Compression raised to 7:1.
20 Deeper finning on cylinder.
For ES2, 19S, Model 50:
21 May: AMC gearbox adopted (for details see text).

1957
For ES2, 19S, Model 50:
1 New cylinder head with horizontal fins widened so that casting now incorporates pushrod tunnels and inlet flange, and vertical finning on head modified to improve air flow. Only the two valve seats, not complete combustion dome, cast in. Rocker box external lines smoothed, inspection plate loses 'Norton'. Quietening ramps of the cams modified to keep noise down. Rocker assembly modified: previously steel shim on each side of spring-washer on the pushrod side, now a single steel shim between double spring-washer and aluminium spindle-boss in rocker-box on the pushrod side, with, as before, thicker thrust washer at the valve side. Slightly higher lift cams.
2 New headlamp shell (Lucas MCH 61) with speedometer, ammeter, light switch recessed directly into it.
3 Cylindrical silencers with no tail pipes.
4 New petrol tanks, painted, with screw-on chrome panels holding knee-grips and badges.
5 Cast aluminium full width front hub with cast-in brake liner and new backplate with forged cam-lever. Shoe assembly unchanged but shoe plate restyled and now fitted inside the open end of hub.
6 End covers of Lucas Magdyno reshaped.
7 Frame all tubular, eliminating cradle casting.
8 Rear fork narrower, with brake torque arm eliminated and brake backplate located directly to the fork end.
9 Rear brake pedal spring concealed and stop-light switch tidied.
10 Rear chainguard more comprehensive.
11 Footrests no longer flat built-up type but conventional with unmarked round-section rubbers.
12 Handlebar grips from rubber to plastic.
13 Air filter optional.
14 Rear suspension units now Girlings.
15 Upper yoke of Roadholders reshaped to give small increase in front wheel trail.

1959

For ES2, Model 50:

1 Featherbed 'Wideline' frame and 'short' Roadholder front forks.
2 Lucas RM 15 alternator behind altered chaincase, rectifier under tool tray, coil under tank rear, points in position of previous Magdyno, chain driven, combined light and ignition switch in headlamp.
3 3½ gallon petrol tank with modified fixing.
4 New dual-seat with shaped portion for rider and pillion.
5 4½ pint oil tank.
6 Optional fully enclosed rear chain.
7 Pressed steel covers over engine plates front and rear.
8 Multi-rate valve springs.
9 Rear chains automatically lubricated from crankcase breather or oil tank vent pipe.

1960

For ES2, Model 50:

1 Gearing altered (ES2) from 12.7:1, 8.4:1, 6.55:1, 4.75:1 to 12.16:1, 8.08:1, 5.8:1, 4.75:1. (Model 50) from 14.1:1, 9.3:1, 7.0:1, 5.3:1 to 14.28, 9.5, 6.8, 5.59 (for details see text).
2 Stop-tail lamp changed from Lucas 525 to Lucas 564.
3 Steering locking permitted, by an abutment on the bottom left-hand side of steering head and a hole in the left-hand side of fork crown, permitting padlocking on full right lock.
4 Swinging arm bushes change from Silentbloc to Clayflex.
5 Clutch friction material bonded on to driven plates in place of previous inserts in driving plates and chain wheel.
6 Fibre washer on oil pump nipple between pump and timing cover preventing edge of cover

contacting timing chest changes from $^1/_{32}$ in to $^1/_{64}$ in.
7 Chrome plated mudguards option.

1961

For ES2, Model 50:

1 Featherbed 'Slimline' frame.
2 3.62 gallon petrol tank, narrower, with long chrome-plated zinc-alloy diecast spiked badge containing narrow knee-grip.
3 Grey flat-top dual-seat with qd Dzuz release at rear.
4 'Norton straights' handlebar optional.

1962

For ES2, Model 50:

1 Lucas RM15 alternator changes to RM19.

Norton: The Model 30 and Model 40 Internationals

Everything about the concept of Norton's International single overhead cam engine sportsters is a little complicated.

From their introduction in 1932, the Inters were for a time similar in specification to the works racers of the previous year. At that stage the Model 30 490 cc and the Model 40 which, rather confusingly was the 348 cc, were primarily competition machines; those wanting an ohc roadster opted for the cheaper CS1 (500) and CJ (350) model. The Inter's high price (for the fully equipped racing version, little less than a family saloon car) and uncompromising character meant that they were usually the province of competing sportsmen.

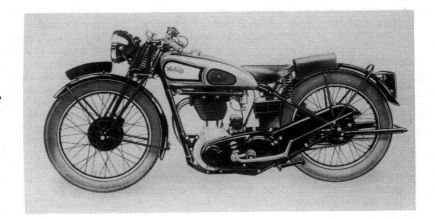

Pre-war, and a hotter number. 1938 Model 30 International 490 cc.

78

Left *Early post-war International for 1947.*

Right *Tower of power. The beautiful Inter powerplant seen here on a 1950 machine used in the Clubman's TT of that year by W. Wilshire.*

But like BSA's post-war Gold Star, they could be had in a variety of options, from fast roadster to out and out road racer. For 1936, following Vic Brittain's clean sheet at the 1935 ISDT in Bavaria, as well as successes by Jack Williams and by director Bill Mansell's son Dennis with Inter-powered outfits, a trials version was offered with high clearance frame, wide ratio box and lower compression. There were also, both before and just after the war, 596 cc works specials aimed at the sporting sidecar-ist.

Post-war, what had been known as 'an International to racing specification' was marketed separately as the 30M and 40M, the full-house Manx production racers (this was the first occasion the 'Manx' title was catalogued). With megaphone exhausts and no lights, they stayed in close touch with the works machinery, in some cases adopting the double ohc engine.

The iron-engined International models did not, because post-war they had in a sense been relegated to the position of the now-defunct CS1. As such, with a complete lack of development, they were left in an awkward limbo, a vestigial nod in the direction of the old Norton policy of providing the public with their own works racers for fast road work. But as sold they were neither satisfactory roadgoing machines nor particularly competitive scratchers.

This was unfortunate, because the potential was there at their heart in the shape of the ohc Carroll engine, as laid out for the works racers in 1929. Its general appearance, big, tapering, and

tall, was similar to the ohv singles on which its predecessor the Moore engine had been based, and which production economy favoured it resembling as much as possible. The cylinder head and barrel were always retained by long through-bolts and at the bottom end were steel flywheels in a pressure-fed, triple row roller-bearing crankpin. Most characteristic of the engine was the square timing box cast into the right-hand side of the crankcase. This contained not only the lower vertical drive bevel, but also the cylindrically housed gear-type oil pump and the casing for the chain drive to the rear-mounted Magdyno.

Above the square timing box was screwed the big chrome tube carrying the vertical drive shaft to the overhead cams. The shaft was jointed top and bottom by Oldham couplings (tongue and groove sliding joints), and ran on a pair of widely separated bearings. At its top end the standard Inter cylinder head, like the barrel, was iron. The cambox was secured by four bolts, and in the style of the Velocette layout which had inspired it, had its rocker adjusters emerging out of slots in the box. These could never be made oiltight. Initially there were felt pads on the rocker bosses intended to stem the flow, but they compressed and wore with use, letting the oil out. The pads were changed shortly before the war to a composite rubber and fabric material, which did just the same thing. Oily inner thighs were part of the price of riding a roadgoing racer, the only consolation being that the real thing, the Manx and works racers, lagged in felt or sorbo rubber, did just the same.

The cambox was split vertically on the longitudinal line, and carried a ball race in each half to support a single shaft. The exhaust cam was keyed to this shaft. On the exhaust cam's left hand side, pinned to it by roller, was the inlet cam. A number of holes in the circumference of the cams to take the roller provided variable adjustment of valve timing. At the right hand side of the shaft, its driving bevel, which meshed with the top bevel of the vertical drive shaft, also had a pin and vernier set up, for the same purpose. Together these enabled timing to be adjusted quickly for open, Brooklands, or road silencers, an extremely valuable facility for last-minute paddock urgencies.

A variety of road silencers were offered over the years before the war, but as Titch Allen points out, it was the Inter's major development lapse that Norton never attempted to produce a 'silencer' cam which would extract better performance from the engine when it had been civilized for the road. As Cyril Ayton says in his *Superprofile* on the Internationals, with this powerplant all silencers, other than the pre-war Brooklands 'can', inhibit the maximum power of a race-developed engine with generous valve-timing overlap. Allen also notes the absence of a cam with quietening ramps to cut down the clack of the engine with its exposed valve springs; Edgar Franks had come up with a design for valve spring enclosure for one of the camshaft engines in 1937 which could have been applied to the Inter, but the factory never used it. 'Mechanical noise, annoying hammering of the valve gear, gear whine, chain whir, piston slap and oiliness' characterized Allen's experience of the Inter, and in an interview with Ayton in the *Superprofile* he rates the Inter road rider as necessarily rugged to the point of masochism.

On the positive side, the engine too was rugged in the Norton tradition, strong and reliable, and maintained its performance even when well worn. Post-war compression for the iron engines (alloy heads and barrels had been an option just before the war) was low, at 7.23:1 for the 500, 7.33:1 for the 50, due to pool fuel.

The ohc engine in any degree of racing tune could test the post-war 'Garden Gate' plunger frame in ways that the ES2's more docile ohv did not. Breakages around the rear chainstays were the most common fault, the rigid frames' triangulation having been lost when rear suspension was added. At the front were the one-way hydraulically damped 'long' Roadholder

telescopic front forks, similar to the Manx's, only made in Reynolds 'A' quality tubing, not the racer's chrome-molybdenum and with different shrouds, since the Manxes had only to support the front racing plate/flyscreen. Inter shrouds, like the ES2s, carried the headlamp with the ammeter and light switch in a small panel in the rear of the lamp's shell with the speedometer mounted in a fork top bridge.

The wheels and tyres however were not the same as the other roadsters, being 3.00 × 21 in front and 3.25 × 20 in rear, the latter's section being increased to 3.50 in for 1951. There was also extra chrome on the primary chaincase, and unlike the other roadsters a headsteady was always a standard fitting though it was not particularly effective against vibration. The post-war emphasis on the machine as a roadster meant some trimming and changes. The big and impressive-looking André racing steering damper was dropped in favour of a normal disc on the steering column.

Most noticeably the beautiful pre-war petrol

tank, though retaining its overall shape including the cutaway on the right for the Amal TT carburettor now came without the crinkled 'piecrust' bottom edge because it was welded up rather than soldered at that joint. It was also only available in the chrome based version with silver panels and black and red lining; pre-war racing versions had had the black lining extending front and rear on a silver base. Mudguards too were a functionally wide kind, not the slimmer pre-war type. The small rubber racing saddle, another prestige fitting, had gone in favour of a more capacious and comfortable fabric-covered Terry's item, but together with higher and wider bars, the same long composite-type footrest hangers and the narrow tank this still gave an excellent riding position. One further go-faster optional extra available later in the '40s was a narrower than standard racing-style petrol tank, bolting through to the frame at four points, with hoops on the tank top for the attachment of a sponge rubber chin pad for when the rider was getting right down to it. For 1950 both the petrol and the similarly decorated wrap-around oil tank had their methods of fixing modified, coming in line with Manx practice in being secured by bolts passing through the tanks, and rubber-mounted.

The International may not have been quite its former self, but sports roadsters were few in the immediate post-war period when most of the new parallel twins were going for export. Norton emphasized the racing heritage when Inters won the first Junior and Senior Clubman's TT in 1947, the first of five victories, including one by Geoff Duke in the 1949 Senior, between then and 1953, as the event steadily became dominated by the BSA Gold Star. But even then the tie with the Inters currently being produced was slender. The 1947 winners, Eric Briggs (Senior) and Denis Parkinson (Junior) were both mounted as the rules permitted them to be, on the more competitive pre-war alloy-engined machines, which were also more suitable for pool fuel. Alloy heads and barrels and central oil feed to the rocker box were being offered as an option again for the Internationals by 1949.

Although the original intention of the races was to provide an initiation for Clubmen new to the island, who were to be restricted to publicly available production machinery, in practice the prestige of the event quickly led to discreet factory involvement. The son of Phil H. Carter, Inter-mounted winner of the 1950 Senior Clubman's, recently wrote in the Norton Owners' Journal, *Roadholder*, that for his father, as a hopeful-looking entrant and 'though it was

supposedly a "production" bike race, Norton had "blueprinted" the motor and also installed Manx cams!' (But it should be noted that according to John Hudson the 350 Model 40 Inter already had the same cams as the Manx (Parts 6466 inlet and 7763 exhaust), and at least by 1953 the Model 30 was fitting 500 Manx cams (Parts 11587 and 11588) as standard).

The Motor Cycle and *Motor Cycling* tested 500 roadster Inters during 1947, with rather different results; the former achieved a top speed of only 86 mph, while the latter saw 97 mph up, with 83 in second, and 91 in third gear! Since both machines could be seen to be equipped with non-standard Brooklands can fishtail silencers, the difference was probably in *Motor Cycling*'s man Charles Markham, who as Titch Allen remarks in his *Superprofile* interview 'could always screw 2–3 mph more out of a bike than any other press man.'

In truth the iron-engined Inters were down on power, the 500 returning 29 bhp at 5,500 rpm and the 350 24 bhp at 6,000. This compared poorly with the contemporary pushrod Triumph Tiger 500 roadster twin which put out 30 bhp at 6,500, or Norton's own Dominator producing 29 bhp at 6,500. The Inter's tall first gear meant clutch slipping in first and then high revving to jump the big gap between bottom and second gear; second, third and top were all very close, and top gear did not favour plonking (though it could be done with an experienced hand on the manual advance-retard lever). All this meant that the beasts had to be ridden with both skill and determination to extract a good performance from them. They were tricky starters, and as mentioned, mechanical noise from the exposed valve gear was cacophonous; tuner Francis Beart, who had negotiated a new 350 Inter as part of his fee from Norton for his successful machine preparation and team management at Daytona in 1949, recalled tersely that 'it was a terrible rattle box—I sold it as soon as possible!'

In the 'Garden Gate' frame, vibration was an ever-present companion at speed, enough to split oil tanks despite the Manx-type rubber-mounting, and sometimes to break the frames. They were also very uncomfortable for the rider at speed over long distances. The frame's handling was better in a straight line than on the swervery, where, according to Phil Heath in the *Superprofile*, they could roll on fast bumpy bends, and although never letting go, once again required a determined hand in control. Inter acceleration through the gears could still be undeniably exhilarating, but it was expensive ecstasy. A final penalty and overriding impression was of weight. The underdeveloped 500 iron motors in 1951 were hauling around 415 lb of roadster cycle parts, with none of the Manx Elektron components to trim this, and the underpowered 350 was in a sense worse off at 409 lb. Halting all that from the high 80s, not with Manx conical hub stoppers, but with the stock roadster 7 in SLS brakes, could be memorable!

Oil consumption was heavy, not least because leaking lubricant was an inevitable companion of the cambox. Internally it could mean an oily combustion chamber and valves; externally, oil emerged from the slots, round the cylinder head, back onto the oil tank and the rider's leg, and ultimately collected in pools under the bike. Adjustment for the oil feed to the rear of the cylinder wall was effected by a screw in the end of the hollow rear crankcase bolt; the correct degree was said to be a half to three-quarters of a turn from the fully open position, or until a faint smoke haze appeared in the exhaust during acceleration. There was also a pressure relief valve in the bevel chamber, which was adjustable at the rear of the crankcase behind the magneto-chain cover; but Phil Heath found this a tricky job ('You need a cooperative, trained snake to help!'), and the manual advised sending it back to the factory. Interestingly, Francis Beart considered that he finally cured the oil leaks on the Manxes by incorporating an AJS breather in the mainshaft and blanking off all other breathing orifices. The pressure relief valve contributed to the familiar Norton trait of oil draining into the crankcase. Some owners went so far as to fit an on-off tap in the oil lines of the Inter to stop this happening— with unfortunate results if they were forgetful

enough to run the motor without switching it on. Petrol consumption too, according to several ex-owners could be high, despite the 1947 tests finding good averages of around 70 mpg: some owners found 40 mpg overall closer to it.

Another interesting thought Titch Allen throws out in the *Superprofile* is that the lack of publicity and prominence, for a model that could have been their own Gold Star, suggests that the factory was really not interested in selling the International at all to the roadgoing public—they were uneconomical to produce, and their temperamental and specialist nature would only have led to disappointment and possibly warranty complications with the bulk of the roadgoing public: in contrast, 'racing men didn't expect guarantees'. Certainly factory publicity emphasized 'the universal *success* attained with this particular type of engine', and Allen reckons most machines were bought by Clubmen racers and run on open pipes.

Low production figures suggest that this is true. What is certainly a fact is the complete absence of factory development from 1947 to 1953. The Inter simply adopted the appropriate changes from other roadsters' running gear. This did not, however, include the 'laid-down' gearbox the other singles acquired for 1950, the Inters retaining the previous upright kind, which had had its clutch mechanism enclosed when the models were reintroduced in 1947. There was the new front-brake shoe plate for 1951, but the six-pint wrap-around oil tank stayed in place while the cooking roadsters altered their smaller versions to a more utilitarian shape that year.

The picture changed quite dramatically for 1953, when the International models adopted both

Offside shot of handsome Featherbed model 30 International for 1953.

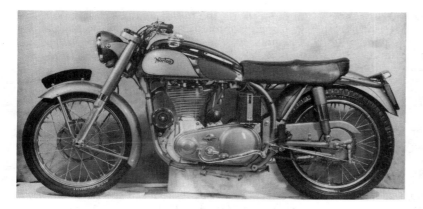

the swinging-arm Featherbed frame with 'short' Roadholder forks, and the alloy head and barrel as standard. The alloy engine yielded a slight increase in power (29.5 bhp at 5,500 for the 500, 25 bhp at 6,000 for the 350), but the package's big advantages were weight loss of over 30 lb, with the 500 now down to 380 lb and the 350 to 366 lb; and the Featherbed's exemplary handling and increased rider comfort.

The Manx Elektron mag-alloy cambox was also now fitted as standard, with pressure fed oiling as on the last sohc racers. Rather than coming through a groove machined in the camshaft sleeve as previously, oil was now fed through a jet screwed into the cambox, giving a better passage to the sides of the cam where it was most required. This countered a tendency of the underlubricated exhaust valve guide to become blocked with carbon. The size of the rubber-mounted oil tank was increased from six to seven pints, and their shape changed to a more conventional one.

The cylinder head was a light alloy casting with iron valve seats, and the barrel an alloy sandcasting with an iron liner. This alloy engine had additional head finning, and so a more tapered shape from there downwards. In 'Moore's Select Few' in *MCS* it is stated that the older engines will not fit the Featherbed frame, and if modified to do so, look wrong. The new engine was now used in conjunction with the 'laid-down' gearbox, and presumably this was the determining factor.

Cycle parts were as for the Featherbed Dominator 88 twin, with that year's pear-shaped silencer (as restrictive as any other to the Inter engine), and a dual-seat in place of the saddle, with a tool tray beneath it, into which went the dynamo control unit. The electrics were still Magdyno, with the switch and ammeter mounted in a panel on top of the fork legs (in front of the

new steering damper, which was now a simple wing-nut), along with the speedometer, like the Dominator. There was also the twins' same 7 in headlamp with the underslung pilot light, and the Diacon stop and tail lamp was fitted. Wheel and tyre sizes were down to 3.00 × 19 in front and 3.25 × 19 in rear, the latter leading to a slight reduction in gearing.

The finish retained the customary broad black outer and narrow red inner pinstriping on the new petrol and oil tank, only no longer over silver and chrome, but now over the Dominator's polychromatic grey. Once again they were good-looking machines. The broad humped tank, wider than the previous one especially at the rear, and at 3¾ gallons slightly larger than the Dominator's, blended with the broad and rather uncomfortable dual-seat. The handling and ride were transformed, with the cycle parts' performance now firmly in excess of the engine's output.

Once again very few were to be produced. The 500 Model 30 at £273 12s for 1955 was nearly £15 dearer than the Dominator 88 twin, which remained a much more tractable and practical answer for fast roadwork. The Inters were now being offered with the optional extras of rearset footrests, gearchange and brake pedal, straight-through exhausts, racing mudguards, Manx handlebars and flyscreen, all indicating firmly the management's continuing notion of their true function. They were still not Manxes, though, lacking the real racers' deeper stiffened crankcase, conical hub brakes and Featherbed frame in superlight Reynolds 531—the Inter's was of 'A' grade tubing.

There were no significant changes from then on, the Inter simply keeping pace with the Dominator 88; for 1954 it adopted the new 8 in front brake and for 1955 it featured the same welded rear sub-frame with larger diameter tubes in place of the previous bolted-up variety, for details of which see the twins section. Full width-hub brakes, similar but not identical to those on the roadster range were also featured for that year. Cosmetically too they kept pace with the range, adopting the round plastic tank badges that year, and for 1957 taking the screw-on chrome tank panels and eliminating the pinstriping on petrol tank or oiltank, together with that year's tubular silencers, new seat and headlamp etc.

By then production had slowed to a real trickle, apparently only about twenty machines a year. If the much larger BSA company were later unable to keep on making Gold Stars on the grounds of disproportionately high production costs, the same went double for Norton who were always on the breadline, and struggling at this point to rationalize production and even up their output. According to a Bob Currie story in *MCW*, it was the enthusiasm for the model of Norton stalwart Bob Collier, then a sales rep for the factory, which prolonged the Inter's lifespan for 1956 and 1957. During the former year it was no longer listed, but in fact continued to be hand-built to special order. Collier was said to have got firm orders from some dealers, which was the only basis on which the factory would continue to supply the model.

In fact by 1957 some Norton dealers were equally keen to see the Inter preserved, so as to have something with which to take on the Gold Stars in Clubman racing. Two such dealers were Reg Dearden in Manchester and Jack Surtees of Forest Hill, South London. The factory prepared two special Featherbed Inters for them, and as was often the case in these final years, Manx components were employed. (Some even featured pukka Manx frames in 531 with extra lugs added and the racing rear fork pivoting not on Silentblocs but on the racers' phosphor bronze bushes.) The Surtees machine is now owned by photographer, author and trials man Don Morley, who finds the Manx engine internals, including cams, hoist the speed above the ton—at the expense of 'a healthy appetite for cam followers'.

The Internationals appeared in a supplement to the Norton model catalogue for 1957, with the 500's compression shown as raised to 8:1 and the 350's to 8.4:1. Production trickled on into 1958, somewhere between five and a dozen models with that year's N11 engine and frame prefix reportedly being made before the end. According to Currie's story this finally came about because the bearing company, Ransome and Marles, had ceased to produce the Inter's big end bearing, and though Alpha Bearings could have supplied an alternative, Norton were feuding with them at the

time and wouldn't go to them. The last Inters were put together using big ends out of factory and dealers' stock.

Like the other singles, any of these 'high-speed batting irons' would be desirable, from the undergunned 350 to the occasional 600 works special. The uncompromising, uncomfortable and even downright rough character of the bike has been dealt with, but this should not obscure the basic Norton strength and simplicity. You could even improve the braking, either as Don Morley does, with Manx hubs which were optional extras towards the end, or on the Featherbed models with the trusty Commando 2LS. But the latter would interfere with a major point of owning one, the look of the thing. Even by the end of its time, many other roadsters could do what the Inter did, and with a lot less fuss, but few could claim as impeccable a pedigree which at the same time kept such a handsomely high profile.

Norton: The Model 30 and Model 40 International—dates and specifications
Production dates
Model 30 and Model 40—1947–58

Specifications
Model 30
Capacity, bore and stroke—490 cc (79 × 100 mm)
Type—ohc single
Ignition—magneto
Weight—(1951) 415 lb, (1955) 380 lb

Model 40
Capacity, bore and stroke—348 cc (71 × 88 mm)
Type—ohc single
Ignition—Magneto
Weight—(1951) 409 lb, (1955) 366 lb

Norton: Model 30 and Model 40 Internationals—annual development and modifications

1950
1 Petrol and oil tank fixing modified, now secured by bolt-through method and rubber-mounted.

1951
1 More rigid prop stand fitted as standard.

1953
1 Cycle parts as on Dominator 88 twin adopted, including Featherbed frame, 'short' Road holder front forks, 'laid-down' gearbox, pear-shaped silencer, 19 in wheels—(for details see text).
2 Alloy head and barrel with deeper finning, and central oil feed to camshaft now adopted as standard (previously optional).
3 Oil tank capacity increased from 6 to 7 pints.

1954
1 8 in front brake adopted.

1955
1 Previous bolted-up rear sub-frame replaced by welded type with larger diameter tubes.
2 Full width brake hubs.
3 Round plastic tank badges.
4 Previously plain knee-grips now with Norton motif.

1957
1 Cycle parts change as Dominator 88, screw on tank panels, plain knee-grips, seat, tubular silencer, plain footrests, headlamp etc (for details see text).
2 Compression catalogued as raised from 7.2:1 to 8:1 (500) and 7.3:1 to 8.4:1 (350).

Norton: The Jubilee/Navigator/ Electra ES400 light twins

Norton's 249 cc Jubilee light twin for 1959 was the last all-new design from the marque to go into civilian production from that day to 1987. A technically interesting engine, laid out by Bert Hopwood and initially produced with the benefit

of Bracebridge Street's expertise and experience, it enjoyed only a poor reputation with enthusiasts and was never a real success. What went wrong?

The story is well known by now that Hopwood's initial design for a 250 featuring a real innovation, the cylinder barrels and heads in one piece, was vetoed by short-sighted AMC management. Though it was Norton managing director Hopwood's name that is always linked with the production Jubilee, and the basic layout was his, it was executed in detail by Doug Hele and by Norton's popular chief designer Bill Pitcher ('a great man to work for', recalls John Hudson). All three men also handled the expansion to the much more impressive 349 cc Navigator. Finally, it was at Woolwich after the Norton move south that in response to prompting from the United States, the twin was developed to its ultimate Electra ES400 form.

One myth that has grown up around the inception of the Jubilee was that the AMC bosses dictated the use of Francis-Barnett cycle parts, and of fairing components from the F-B associated company Clarendon Pressings. But Bert Hopwood confirmed to me recently that the cause for this was not orders from above, but a more familiar Norton situation, simple lack of cash to do anything else.

The Jubilee, so called because its arrival coincided with the 60th anniversary of James Lansdowne Norton's original enterprise, was first displayed at the Earls Court Show at the end of 1958. As the publicity of the day had it, 'the

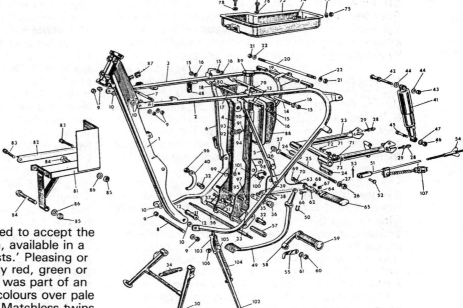

complete styling has been designed to accept the modern alternative two-tone trim, available in a choice of pleasing colour contrasts.' Pleasing or not, the two-colour decor, initially red, green or blue upper and dove grey lower, was part of an AMC masterplan, and with dark colours over pale was also to afflict both the AJS/Matchless twins and the Francis-Barnett/James two-strokes for 1959.

The colours were laid over pressed steel panelling, the fashion for enclosure having been launched with Triumph's own anniversary bike, the 350 Twenty-One twin for 1957, and reinforced by Ariel's Leader the year after that. While far from the worst variation on the enclosure scheme, Norton's squared-off versions could not aspire to the restrained curves of the Triumphs. Characteristically Meriden's was the only marque that got the styling factor right.

To the ever-distrustful public the Jubilee didn't look like a Norton, either cosmetically or even on closer inspection. It was true that this was a parallel twin four-stroke, but there were significant differences from the Dominator twins in the layout of the high camshaft Jubilee engine, the short cylinders of which slanted forward in the frame. As opposed to the long-stroke 500 and 600, the dimensions of the 249 cc unit construction motor were well over-square, with a bore of 60 mm and a stroke of just 44 mm. Also unlike Hopwood's A10 and Dominators, this was a twin cam motor, with the two shafts, gear driven from the right hand end of the crankshaft, mounted fore and aft of the cast iron cylinders. The latter were separate castings, like the AMC twins.

Above them in the alloy head, beneath separate mushroom-shaped rocker box covers the valves

were laid out in a way that was the reverse of the norm, being inboard of the very short pushrods. The rods followed the line of the flat foot tappets, which were angled to give the most favourable rocker geometry. (These 3 in pushrods were so diminutive because in the original composite head and barrel design there had been no pushrods at all—the tappets had reached up to the rocker ends and the valve assembly was to have been inserted into its tunnels upwards from beneath.) Valve adjustment for the production model was conveniently available, after removal of the tank, by eccentric pin rocker spindles, one of several touches aimed at ease of maintenance. The push-fit exhausts were widely splayed, like the big twins, but the included angle between inlet and exhaust valves was just 42 degrees. A single Amal Monobloc 375 carb with 25/32 choke was mounted on a small manifold which bolted to both cylinder heads.

At the bottom end, the cast iron crankshaft, different again from the Dominator in being a one-piece item, ran in reassuringly large bearings, which like the big end bearings were in fact identical in dimensions to the Dominator's (though with a large undercut to accommodate the essential radius where the crank cheek met the journal; so Dominator bearings will not in fact fit the light twins). This robustness meant they were capable of taking any future power increases from the engine, as well as being good unified production practice. The shaft carried a single integral flywheel of 7½ in diameter, which the short stroke caused the pistons to overlap at bottom dead centre, with the sides of the wheel carrying bob-weights matching the shape of the outer weight on each side of the crankpins. Lubrication was by the standard Norton gear oil pump driven by a threaded worm gear on the crankshaft. This was mounted on the outer face of the right crankcase half. One point worthy of note was that there was no timed breather, simply a connection from the crankcase to the oil tank.

The engine was genuinely unit construction, the gearbox internals being those of the AMC 'lightweight' 250 and 350 singles, with the layshaft lying behind the mainshaft, not below it as was normal Norton practice. The clutch was different to AMC however, being the standard Norton three-spring type with the effective vane-type central shock absorber. The gearbox outer cover on the right hand side of the crankcase jointed smoothly with the timing cover, once again giving good accessibility. Primary drive was by duplex chain to a rear-chain even spindlier than normal for Norton at ½ × 5/16 in. Electrics were six-volt and by Wico-Pacy, (who also supplied Francis-Barnett and the AMC 'lightweights'), with a crankshaft-mounted alternator and coils mounted beneath the tank. Each cylinder had its own pair of contacts, driven from the end of the inlet camshaft and mounted on a single backing plate; though as yet the points were awkward in lacking the ability to be adjusted independently for each cylinder.

This engine was mounted in a frame and cycle parts that derived heavily from Francis-Barnett practice, specifically from F-B's 250 cc 1957

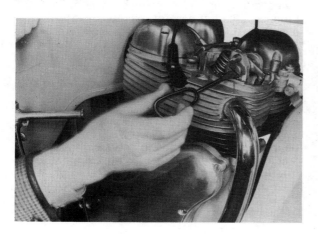

Cruiser 80, which also incidentally shared the same gearbox internals. The frame was a composite structure, with a pressed-steel front frame member and centre post assembly, but the rest a bolted-up tubular assembly. According to the Norton Owners' Club the differences from the Francis-Barnett frame are limited to a different centre post assembly, and to braces in the side members which appear on the Norton frame but not the F-Bs. (These braces were also to differ between the later Standard variants of the light twins and the enclosed De-Luxe versions, as they were to be known when the unfaired versions joined them for 1961.)

For 1959 swathing most of this frame, everything from the cylinders back including the carburettor, was the rear enclosure, which included a full chaincase for the drive chain. The main fairing consisted of two qd side panels, each held by three Dzuz fasteners. The 3½ pint built-in oil tank and the battery sat between them, and a tickler for the carb emerged from a slot in the front of the left hand panel. These two panels were linked at the rear by a fixed tail portion with a lifting handle on the left hand side. This tail piece embraced the rear lamp and the number plate, which was detachable to allow the back wheel to be rolled out easily. The styling was self-consciously 'modern' and therefore dated quickly; but it was far from totally incongruous, and since it had been designed as a whole, was by no means the least graceful of faired models.

At the front a very substantial deeply valanced flowing mudguard with a snub nose and guttered edge lay rather incongruously beneath the diminutive Francis-Barnett 6 in headlamp and a pressing bridging the forks and containing the chromed grille of the very ineffective horn. The front forks were also lightweight Francis-Barnett items, hydraulically damped though not very satisfactorily so, as were the 18 in wheels with their full width pressed-tin hubs and 6 in SLS brakes. It was the front end that probably knocked the model on the head for traditional Norton fanciers, who noted that the distinctly middleweight Jubilee's 325 lb *avoirdupois* was a substantial step up, both to steer and to stop, from the Cruiser 80's 290 lb.

After display at the 1958 Show, production began early in 1959. In road tests and in practice, if the brakes were only adequate, the economy frame was found to give no problems in the handling department except poor ground clearance when cornering hard due to low-mounted footrests. (Later, however, there were to be some instances of the frame cracking beneath the steering head under the stress of the twin motor.) Low, compact, comfortable to ride and tidy, the 250 twin was normally easy to start and reasonably accessible for maintenance. As the short-stroke motor and 8.75:1 compression suggested, it was a buzz-box, needing to be revved through the gears for best results, in a most un-British manner, to an 8,500 rpm maximum. This trait was emphasized by the engine being slightly undergeared; it was also recognized by Norton who provided two sets of valve clearance figures— .002 inlet, .004 exhaust normal, or .004/.006 'if the machine is driven at full throttle for any length of time.' Top speeds may have been modest at around 75 mph, but 65 in third gear and 50 in second sketched the kind of revvy motoring available from the 16 bhp engine. And this was a four-stroke twin, not an old-fashioned plonking single. So once again, what went wrong?

For a start there had been mechanical upsets of the worst kind in the form of broken crankshafts. These came about despite very tough testing of Jubilee prototypes for three weeks late in 1958, in North Wales ISDT country including the dreaded Bwylch-y-groes test hill; John Hudson was there as a pillionist, having sprained his wrist the first day out, and can testify that despite hair-raising riding, nothing broke. But meanwhile, according to journalist Peter Howdle, someone in the Bracebridge Street drawing office had sent out the wrong specification, and 2,000 cranks were made of the incorrect Mehanite type of cast iron; this was rapidly changed to the proper spheroidal graphite nodular iron variety, but not before the damage had been done. Ironically the same thing, only more publicized, was shortly to occur for AMC with their 650 parallel twins.

The next worst point were some of the Francis-Barnett components, particularly the electrics. A feeble horn and lights, and poor switchgear, were just the tip of the problem. Tester John Gill exercises a customary exaggeration when he writes, '[The Jubilees] usually caught fire when we started them. . .' There was a kernel of truth in this however, and it resided not so much in a weak component but in one that was just too good, as Yorkshireman John Hudson revealed when explaining the problems with burnt wiring to *Classic Bike*. 'With the Jubilee, they'd changed from a Lucas battery—where if you had a short, I doubt whether it would have even warmed the wires—to the Exide 3EV11. By, there was some life in that! If you shorted that, the wires were red hot in a minute. With plastic-coated harnesses from Wipac, when the wires glowed the insulation ran off like melted wax.' The contact-breaker set-up also resulted in the light twins' timing going off quickly and often. John Gill continues, 'As soon as the brake and clutch cables were used they stretched like a piece of licorice, and we had a big batch [of Jubilees] which juddered badly on the back brake until the brake anchor stud snapped off.'

Possibly as a result of the breathing arrangements, but with the one-piece design which had then had its head sliced off being a contributory factor, Jubilees also became notorious for oil leaks. The rocker cover castings were of thin section and leaked if they were distorted by overtightening of the securing screws; and like most alternator primary chaincases, these tended to leak where the lead passed through the back of the case. There was considerable mechanical noise, and once again trouble-shooter John Hudson was able to put his finger on a cause. 'There was one thing that was rather stupid about the Jubilee. Its cam followers

Left *Quick adjustment for Jubilee valves—but thin meat on rocker covers meant oil leaks.*

Right *1961 Norton Jubilee 250 in full faired glory.*

Left *Better in every way. Unfaired 'standard' 350 Navigator for 1961, with roadholder forks, bigger brakes.*

Below right *Head on view of 1961 Jubilee De-luxe with Francis-Barnett fork, puny horn and brake.*

worked in guides that were much too short. So the followers would rock back and forth and you'd get this dukka, dukka, dukka noise. The guides were grooved at the side for oil passage. Now these grooves had to be transverse, otherwise they were on the thrust face. But dealers used to bash them in any way on. That was where the noise came from on the Jubilee; tappets oscillating in their guides.' Privately Hudson has admitted that, as well as dealers, Norton's own factory personnel too would install the tappet guides with their oil drain holes pointing in any direction. He also points out that with twin camshafts and twin cylinders, there is a reversal of load with the lift of each cam, and a 'dead' no lift period between each lift; whereas with four cams on a single shaft the 'dead' period is eliminated, and despite the continuing reversal of load, noise from gear drive backlash is reduced.

The short-stroke motor was also a cause of vibration at anything above its cruising speeds, a fact alluded to in a roundabout way during a 1961 road test of the Navigator 350 when it was noted that 'handlebar tremor' made the smooth plastic throttle grip slip at speeds above 65 mph; naturally the solution suggested was to change the grips! Despite the presence of the big twins' bearings, engine wear proved to be rapid if the motor was revved as its characteristics encouraged. With a top limit 1,500 rpm above the Dominator's maximum, the bearings skidded and wore out. In addition to these problems, the bike was perceived as fundamentally underpowered, 'all rev and no guts.'

Probably this image could have been changed; there could, for a start, have been sports styling. Norton man Bob Collier's feat in successfully hauling a Jubilee and Bambi sidecar round the SSDT course in 1960 was impressive if freakish,

but the exploits of Bedford dealer Bob King who took eighth place on a 250 in a Thruxton long distance race, and with a larger carb and other mods pushed the top speed over 100 mph, suggests that the potential may have been there for a sporty quarter litre to rival the Ariel Arrow and Royal Enfield Continental GT. But the light twins remained tourers, the point being emphasized by the offer for 1961 of factory accessories, windscreen, legshields and a bulbous pair of panniers, in colours to match the machines. There was no development, and the Jubilee was left as a mess of contradictions— American-oriented colour schemes that seemed to nod at the two-tone '59 Cadillacs were laid over a pressed-steel frame and enclosures which the Americans had no time for; and a rather sedately-equipped low output tourer, which nevertheless lacked reliability and had an engine with the high-revving characteristics of a junior Café racer. It is little wonder that the two-wheeled fraternity took against the Jubilee from the start, and in 1961, when I was graduating to big wheels for the first time, I well remember being gently but quite firmly steered by our college Norton expert away from the 250 to its successor, the 350 Navigator, a choice of first motorcycle for which I remain in his debt.

The Navigator was launched at the Jubilee London Show late in 1960, on which occasion Norton MD Bert Hopwood, possibly recalling his BSA Docker days, had exhibited a 'Golden Jubilee' of his own, a 250 with its bodyware sprayed with gold leaf and the normally chromed parts gold-plated. At the notoriously pilferage-prone Show this was wisely displayed out of reach, high up on a revolving stand. But more significant was its new 349 cc stablemate. This was offered, as the 250 was from that year, either faired, which was dubbed 'De-Luxe', or in an unfaired Standard version. The Navigator engine was both bored and stroked at 63 × 56 mm, and it was better in every way.

The one-piece crankshaft was of forged steel to cope with a 22 bhp power output. This was also necessary because the longer stroke decreased the overlap between the crankpin and the mainshaft and so had lessened the inherent stiffness of the crankshaft. As with the Jubilee, the cylinder block of the stubby engine was spigoted very deeply into the crankcase mouth, and the cylinder axes were still as close together at 3⅜ in from each other. In conjunction with the larger bore size this decreased the amount of metal around the bore. So for this engine, both for stiffness and for better sealing at the crankcase/barrel joint, the barrels were no longer separate but a single casting, providing an instant external identifier between the two similar machines.

There had been considerable attention to the gearbox. The first Jubilee gearbox had had dogs (in fact they were pegs) on the third gear mainshaft which gave the top gear drive. These engaged with holes in the face of the sleeve gear, similar to the first gear drive on the heavyweight boxes. On the Jubilee these had proved unsatisfactory and the box had been improved by putting male dogs, with undercut, on both sleeve gear and third gear mainshaft. The pegs and holes were thus eliminated for the top gear drive, but retained for the first gear drive more or less as in the heavyweight boxes. At the same time the mainshaft was reduced in diameter where the clutch body fitted; it was also undercut at the end of the splines ie, at the change of section from splines to full circular. In preliminary prototype tests the added power of the Navigator broke them off and on the production Navigator the undercut had been eliminated. To the best of John Hudson's recollection, the spline diameter was also increased to that of the shaft itself. The box was adopted for the 250 also, and he thinks that with this gearbox they got it right.

Valve sizes were the same as the Jubilee, which as one tester found meant that you could soar beyond the 350's lower 7,500 rpm limit without valve float setting in, due to the unusually light reciprocating weight of the Navigator's valve gear. Power characteristics were altered by raised gearing with a nineteen-tooth gearbox sprocket, two more teeth than the Jubilee though otherwise their transmissions were now identical; by new cams that spread the torque more, by a larger (⅞ in choke) 375 carburettor, and by a better power to weight ratio, since a dry weight of 335 lb for the De-Luxe was only around 10 lb up on its baby brother. Other differences included the conrods, the Navigator's split skirt pistons, the pushrods, the engine-to-cylinder fixing studs, the headsteady and the exhaust pipes, though the silencers were the same. The engine could still be buzzed, the tester mentioned above achieving 59 mph in second and 75 mph in third, with a top speed hoisted to 85 mph.

The frame was of the same type as the Jubilee, though, no doubt taking note of the latter's breakages, the front down member had been stiffened. There was also a steeper head angle, giving a wheelbase reduced from the Jubilee's 53½ in to 51½ in. The other major change took place at the front end, where the Francis-Barnett fork and wheel with its fairground mudguarding gave way to Norton Roadholder front forks with slightly shortened springs (coded green), a regular mudguard with two stays each side against the faired 250's one stay, and a front number plate not a painted panel. It also fitted a larger (6½ in) Wipac headlamp common to all the AMC 'lightweight' range (this was one change that the Jubilee too adopted), a new and more effective horn was positioned under the tank and an 8 in front brake on a 19 in front wheel as on the rest of

the range. The result was something that looked much more like a Norton, stopped in 26 ft from 30 mph (despite ovality of the drum on the test bike), and handled with the best of the Nortons. It was in another league entirely from its 350 twin competitor, the Triumph 3TA, and a top speed in the mid-80s had increased respectably to bring it in line with most 500 singles of the day. It was a nice bike; and only a shame that the 1960 restriction of learners to 250 cc and under meant that its benefits were not available for that section of the market.

The Standard versions of both 250 and 350 augured the end of the fashion for enclosure (bad luck if, like me, you were left with a faired Norton a few years later. Not many people had wanted them to begin with, and nobody did by then). They sported ordinary mudguards and the frame mid-section was shrouded by pressed panels which surrounded and blended with the shape of the new left-side tool and battery box matching a new oil tank positioned on the right. The carburettor was exposed, something that eliminated one problem on the De-Luxe models, that of fuel starvation due to the petrol pipe being routed upward over the left enclosure from the tap. Petrol tanks were the same on both versions, with a single fastening bolt at the rear, the other end slotting onto a rubber-bushed peg at the front, but the seats were different on the Standard versions, not being the qd type with a Dzuz fastener at the rear, but conventionally bolted down. For all this the Standard styling still lacked flair.

My memories of my own Navigator, a blue and dove grey 1961 De-Luxe bought secondhand, are complicated by the distance in time and the fact that I was very, very ignorant and inept mechanically. I recall no major frights with handling and roadholding, other than self-induced ones, of which it was forgiving, particularly in the wet. There were also no major mechanical catastrophes in over two years, during which time it took me to Scotland and back, and to the Mediterranean. I was far too fearful to 'buzz' it and explore the upper regions of its performance, but it was a good steady tourer, and the combination of the 3 gallon tank and around 70 mpg gave it the range, though a reserve tap would have been welcome.

But it was often immobilized for causes that puzzled me then as much as they do now. I think the electrics and cables loomed large; except on the long runs, it was always going out of tune and running roughly. For 1961 the points for the whole range had changed to a type that could be

adjusted separately for each cylinder, but if there was any improvement I was not aware of it. To idiots, even the sensible approach can sometimes be counterproductive. My bike had the enclosed rear chaincase (which was optional on the Navigator), a totally sound idea for prolonging chain and sprocket life; but on one occasion the chain jumped off the sprocket with a fearful din, because it had got so loose out of sight inside the pressed tin case, where I or my friends could not see it flailing or drooping. Of course I had not thought to remove the rubber bung and check it. The poor paint and chrome-work suffered further from a life parked outside, though until its final shameful deterioration I had cleaned it quite often—perhaps to appease it for neglect in other areas. And I hated Dove Grey! Motorbikes could be black (for preference) or red, blue or green, but pale colours were just not right. Even I knew that. But despite all the above, its good points had impressed me, and I certainly kept on buying Norton twins.

For 1962 there were only cosmetic changes for the light twins, with chromium plated mudguards becoming an option, and chrome-plated embellishing rims being fitted each side of the 250's front hub and on the right of the rear one; the 350 got the rear wheel trim only. Then following the move south to Plumstead, for 1963 came the last addition to the range, the ES400 Electra, with push-button starting and bar-end winkers such as one had only seen previously on those profoundly impressive (black, of course) police BMWs on which *les flics* purred about *sur le Continent*.

Like many of the later AMC models, the Electra had come about as the result of a suggestion from their American importer Joe Berliner. Reportedly he wanted something to go up against Japanese bikes like the Honda Dream Super Sport 250 which since 1961 had begun to make major inroads into the market over there. For the ES400 the Navigator engine was initially bored and stroked by Plumstead to 397 cc (66 × 58 mm), but in production they settled for 384 cc (66 × 56 mm), which allowed the retention of the Navigator's crankshaft. From January 1963 the first 3,000 machines were for export only, but in July 1963 the Electra became available on the home market. It looked every inch a Norton, as it was offered in traditional black and silver like the current 500SS and 650SS Dominator twins, with silver fluted petrol tank, and the silver oil tank and tool box now standing out well against the black pressing (for the Electra was never offered in faired form).

There had been considerable internal changes.

The inner and outer primary chaincase were different from the Navigator's to accept the starter drive. The crankcase was modified to accept both the larger spigots resulting from the increase in bore size, and a revised gearbox. Crankshaft balance was changed, and in the gearbox there was a revised gear train and larger selectors to handle the increase in power. The gears were arranged as previously but changing was now effected by a drum cam with two selectors fitted on it and this was turned by a revised positive stop mechanism. This gearbox took 2¼ pints of oil, half a pint more than the previous light twins. The lower three gear ratios were slightly higher than the Navigator, though top was unchanged. This drum selector gearbox was a distant step back from the Navigator's, the kickstart pawl being puny and the whole being in the opinion of John Hudson 'a poor thing', which broke frequently. It was unfortunately to be adopted by the Jubilee and Navigator almost immediately at eng. no. 106839.

To cope with the starter the electrics had been raised to 12 volt, with two Exide 6 volt 12 amp hr batteries operating in series. A higher output Wipac 85 watt alternator was fitted. The starter motor was a Lucas M3, mounted behind the cylinder block between the carburettor and the gearbox with drive to the crankshaft outboard of the primary drive and the alternator. The Electra maintained a slim front profile, engine width increasing just 1¼ in and width across the footrests being unaltered, but a *Motor Cycle* tester found that despite the customary low footrests, the starter drive case did foul the rider's left leg. The Lucas M3 had already been used on the Velocette Viceroy and the BSA group Tigress/Sunbeam scooters, and would be found again on the 1981 electric start Triumph Bonneville. Its satisfactory performance on the latter machine suggests that on the Electra, it was lack of amps in the rest of the system, not the four brush motor itself, which generally restricted its use to starting a hot rather than a cold engine.

Drive was by epicyclic reduction gearing in two stages, located between the starter and the chaincase, and a ⅜ in pitch single strand chain to a sprocket concentric with the crankshaft. The sprocket rotated on a short ⅝ in diameter spindle fixed to a light alloy carrier, dowelled and clamped to the chaincase inner half, just outboard of the Wipac generator. When the sprocket was turned by the electric motor, three internal pawls engaged with a nine-tooth ratchet on the crankshaft. As soon as the engine started the pawls were overridden and the drive from the

1964 Electra 400, with electric start and eye-catching winkers.

starter thereby disengaged. With its Wipac Tricon ring switch on the left handlebar, as long as the clutch was pulled in, the starter could be used when the machine was in gear.

Electra chassis differences from the Navigator were confined to gusseting around the steering head, which made removal of the exhaust rocker covers a fiddly job. The ES400 also used the stock Norton 7 in rear brake, though still on an 18 in wheel. Surprisingly the Electra's starting tackle had added only around a dozen lb to the unfaired Navigator's weight giving a kerbside weight of 354 lb. Petrol consumption however on *The Motor Cycle*'s test machine was up quite dramatically at around 50 mpg overall, and the test machine's brakes were definitely substandard, returning a poor 38 ft stopping figure from 30 mph. This, plus the location of the trafficator button on the right side of the bar so that you had to release the throttle to operate it, a headlamp dip beam with poor cut-off and a toolbox lid that would not fit flush, suggested that standards of forethought and production at the struggling Plumstead factory were on the slide; and as with the other light twins, there was virtually no development from then on. In performance terms the Electra was very similar to the Navigator, and the excellent handling of the machine with its low centre of gravity seemed unimpaired by the extra weight on the nearside. Rather stingily, at first the

Another view of a 1965 ES400 Electra, with conventional good looks plus electric foot clearly visible.

Last light twin, 1966 Jubilee in all-burgundy finish.

indicators, as well as the chrome plated mudguards, though standard for the export models, cost extra at home. Initial price was a high £291 5s, over £40 more than the Navigator.

The only change to the other two for 1963 was a slight reduction in compression for the Navigator, from 8.75:1 to 8.5:1. For 1964 however, the scene changed as the De-Luxe faired versions of the 250 and 350 were dropped. So did the price of the Electra in the UK, by £40, and winkers and chrome guards were now standard; but none of this did much good for the ES400's home sales. The 350 and 400 both acquired a Yale steering head lock indicating the fractionally wider Roadholder forks adopted from that year on, and flat handlebars, the famous 'Norton straights' were fitted as standard, along with a wider number plate to cope with the second 'B' year of registration suffixes. For 1965 the last ties with the original juke-box styling passed, with the two-tone colour schemes going, though the blue Navigator retained a dove-grey

frame, forks and headlamp, while the Jubilee was the more handsome in flamboyant burgundy and black. The 250's compression ratio was raised to 9.5:1, and it took on the ES400's gearbox internals, with the rear wheel sprocket dropping from 55 to 53 teeth. With the end approaching AMC, the Navigator was dropped in the autumn, the ES400 at the end of the year, and the Jubilee did not survive the crash of '66.

It had been a tale of sadly wasted opportunities. Restyling the 250 and building the Navigator's strength and cycle parts into it could, if the cost had permitted it, have produced a strong seller for the youth and the medium capacity market. None of these twins was intimidatingly large and heavy, and you could live with the Navigator's noisy engine and rather harsh front suspension because of the handling. The 350 or 400 would still make a nice bike today, but the situation is complicated by very poor spares availability. Also with some components such as the main bearings, the genuine Norton items must be fitted or, according to an *MCM* rebuild feature, the cases will not mate properly. Late gearbox internals are also now in very short supply. Russell Motors and the Owners' Club are reportedly two of the only sources for light twin spares. It would be a shame if this succeeds in sidelining all these machines, because as my own experience of the 350 taught me, they may not be big and heavy, but in some other important respects two out of three of these models were real Nortons.

Norton: The Jubilee, Navigator and Electra ES400 Light Twins—dates and specifications
Production dates
Jubilee—1959–66
Navigator—1961–65
Electra ES400—1963–65

Specifications
Jubilee
Capacity, bore and stroke—249 cc (60 × 44 mm)
Type of engine—ohv twin
Ignition—coil
Weight—(1959) 325 lb (Standard, 1961) 320 lb

Navigator
Capacity, bore and stroke—349 cc (63 × 56 mm)
Type of engine—ohv twin
Ignition—coil
Weight—(1961, De-Luxe) 335 lb (1961, Standard) 330 lb

Electra ES400
Capacity, bore and stroke—384 cc (66 × 56 mm)
Type of engine—ohv twin
Ignition—coil
Weight—(1963) 335 lb approx

Norton: The Jubilee, Navigator and Electra ES400 light twins—annual development and modifications
1961
For Jubilee De-Luxe and Standard:
1 Contact breaker assembly design modified so that the two sets of points are adjustable independently.
2 Headlamp diameter increased from 6 to 6½ in and mounted in a restyled fork shroud.

1962
For Jubilee De-Luxe and Standard, Navigator De-Luxe and Standard:
1 Chromium plated embellishing ring on right of rear hub, and (for Jubilees only) on both sides of front hub.
2 Chrome plated mudguards become optional extra.

For Jubilee De-Luxe and Standard:
3 Front section of 18 in tyre reduced from 3.25 to 3.00 in.

1963
For Navigator De-Luxe and Standard:
1 Compression ratio reduced from 8.75 to 8.5:1.

1964
For Jubilee, Navigator, Electra ES400:
1 Flat handlebars fitted as standard.
2 Wider number plate at rear.
For Electra ES400:
3 Bar-end winkers and chromium plated mudguards now standard.
For Navigator, Electra ES400:
4 Yale steering-head locks provided.
For Jubilee and Navigator
5 At eng. no. 106839, gearbox internals of Electra adopted and hence gearbox oil capacity raised from 1.75 to 2.25 pints.

1965
For Jubilee:
1 Gearbox internals of Electra ES400 adopted and hence gearbox oil capacity raised from 1.75 to 2.25 pints.
2 Rear wheel sprocket reduced from 55 to 53 teeth.
3 Compression raised from 8.75 to 9.5:1.

Norton: The Dominator Model 7/88/88 De-Luxe/88SS/77/99/99 De-Luxe/99SS/N15 Nomad/650/650SS/650 De-Luxe/Atlas/N15CS 'N' Atlas Scrambler/P11/P11A/P11A Ranger/Mercury Twins

In 1947, with wartime restrictions on material slowly lifting, it was clear that the commercial shape of the foreseeable future for the British motor cycle industry was to be determined by Edward Turner's Triumph Speed Twin and its derivatives. AMC, Ariel, Royal Enfield and BSA were all to enter the field shortly, and if Norton Motors wanted to survive they had to produce one too.

Employing Bert Hopwood for the job of designing their twin engine was an intelligent move, for though he had not as yet had an original design produced, he had worked since the 1930s at Ariel and then Triumph with the irascible Turner, and been responsible for important development work on the Triumph engines, being one of several engineers who had helped adapt Turner's inventive flair to the constraints of real metal.

Good looking Model 7 500 cc twin for 1949, with purpose-built tank and mudguard.

From 1 April 1947, working in cramped conditions, Hopwood swiftly laid out a parallel twin which embodied his own desiderata and sought to avoid the Triumph's weak points, which he had good cause to know; engine noise, a tendency to overheating and a lack of robustness in some important areas. In addition to these considerations, there were external restraints. First, and for several years, the engine would have to run on 'Pool' fuel of around 72 octane only. Secondly, Norton's financial condition and antiquated production machinery meant that their existing manufacturing techniques and components would have to be used, whether they were ideal or not. Thus Hopwood would have preferred a one-piece crank, diecast cases and an alloy head and barrel, but had to settle for a built-up crankshaft, sand casting and an iron top end. Also, apart from some cosmetic touches, the twin's cycle parts would have to be those of the existing top-of-the-range ohv single, the ES2. This in turn dictated the production of a compact engine.

The desire to avoid Triumph's problems with excessive cylinder head overheating (to be overcome by the use of alloy for them, which was not yet available to Hopwood), led to a determined improvement of air flow conditions, with the exhaust valves splayed and the exhaust ports set noticeably and characteristically wide apart, out in the cooling wind. Behind them the inlet ports were placed close together, slightly

offset to promote induction swirl. On all but the earliest production versions which featured the original design's integral manifold, the inlet ports were joined by a separate light alloy induction manifold for the 1 in Amal type 76 carburettor. Until 1958, when a twin carb head would become an optional extra for the home market, the roadster Norton twins were to be single carburettor motors, with all the flexibility that high gas speed at low engine revs brings with it. Within the head the steeply angled valves meant that the combustion chamber was notably shallow and provided a compression ratio of 6.7:1. The rocker boxes were integral, access to them being by two separate oval inspection caps at the front, but access to the inlet valves was by a single rectangular cover at the rear. Externally the head featured vertical finning around the exhaust ports, encouraging the cooling air to pass between the inlet and exhaust ports as the latter's splayed configuration permitted it to do.

In contrast to the Triumph motor with its two cams positioned fore and aft of the cylinders and driven by gears, the Model 7's pushrods were operated by a single four-lobe cam set at the front of the engine. This camshaft was chain-driven, as was the rear-mounted magneto, again unlike the Triumph, and like all these dispositions the intention was to diminish engine rattle. It was only partially fulfilled, because Dominator engines would always be known for tappet chatter. Cast integrally at the front of the cylinder block were two pushrod tunnels, with further airspaces between the barrels as well as transversely between the bores and the tunnels. This cured the problem of separate pushrod tubes obstructing engine cooling and being difficult to seal against oil leaks. The steel tube pushrods operated through large, hollow tappets. The flat top pistons and the con-rods were of alloy, with plain steel-backed shell big-end bearings. The crankshaft was a three-piece bolted-up item with a single central cast iron flywheel and forged bob-weighted crank cheeks.

This arrangement, a compromise for Hopwood, did resemble the Triumph design, and he was careful to provide it with a distinctively different central dowel which had a positive function in maintaining accurate alignment, and an offset fixing flange, taking out strong patents on both crank and valve gear. A wise decision, as Edward Turner duly disputed them; at which point, Hopwood writes, he pointed out to Turner that neither of their designs was fully original, since Vauxhall Motors had used a very similar principle, including the central flywheel, on their 1922 3-litre racing engines! While it was true that all the parallel twin designs of the era resembled each other to some extent, with the layout further dictated by the use of a magneto, there were two features that Hopwood built into the Dominator from the start. One was a strong bottom end, with massive timing side ball journal and drive side roller main bearings. These were stronger than those of the Triumph and indeed stronger than most other twins except his own BSA A10 (for which he also specified a drive side roller bearing). The other was an engine with dimensions which, though far from oversquare at 66 × 72.6 mm, nevertheless represented a considerable shortening of stroke from the Speed Twin's 80 mm and BSA's A7 at 82 mm, and for fourteen years only the AMC twins' 72.8 mm stroke was to rival it. Hopwood favoured a shorter stroke engine for rigidity and consequent oil tightness.

Transmission was conventional for Norton, with the single-strand primary chain, 3-spring clutch, vane-type shock absorber and puny ⅝ × ¼ in rear chain. The gearbox, previously upright, was modified to the laid-down type with horizontal oval casing, gear positioin indicator and shorter pedal movement which the singles then also adopted. The box's internals were substantially unchanged, and their strong and proven quality constituted another part of the model's appeal. Lubrication was again by the tried and tested double gear oil pump, mounted in the timing chest and crankshaft driven via a pinion, and, as with the singles, very tolerant of the fit of the worm drive. But its presence meant that the twin inherited the Norton black mark of oil draining past the pump into the crankcase when the machine was left to stand for a period. The factory always denied that this happened, and nothing was to be done about it until 28 years later in 1975...

Engine breathing was via a timed breather keyed to the crankshaft and driven by its end. The 6 volt electrics consisted of the rear mounted magneto (Lucas, or in a few early instances BTH) and at the front of the cylinders a Lucas dynamo clamped to the crankcase by a strap. The ammeter and switch for the system were mounted in a small panel in the back of the headlamp shell. An oil pressure gauge was recessed in the front left top side of the petrol tank.

This engine layout, with many of its original features (splayed ports, oil pump, separate gearbox) substantially intact, was to principally sustain the company's fortunes for the next thirty years. If any one design had to do it this wasn't a bad one, strong, compact and tractable. At the beginning it was slotted into ES2 cycle parts, that is a single downtube cradle frame, with rear springing by plungers which had been lightened and tidied on their appearance after the war. At the front were the hydraulically damped 'long' Roadholder forks with, behind covers, external springs which fitted beneath the lower crown and worked against the top of the lower lug. The springs were colour-coded, solo red, sidecar yellow, and the forks required 7 fl oz of oil as opposed to the later 'short' Roadholders 5 fl oz. A friction steering damper was fitted, with a knurled knob above the fork top crown.

The frame was as for the ES2, but the twin's appearance was enhanced by features special to them alone, mudguards and a swelling 3¾ gallon petrol tank sharply waisted at the rear and of exceptionally pleasing appearance, particularly in conjunction with the solo saddle for which it was designed. The rear mudguard sported a flared lip to its tail portion—Hopwood had not spent that much time around Turner without digesting some of the latter's sense of style and of the importance of style. Wheels and tyres, 3.00 × 21 in front and 3.50 × 19 in rear, were standard Norton, as were the 7 in brakes with their shoes pivoting on separate pins. Finish too was traditional Norton black and silver, with thin red inner lining on the chromed petrol tank, which had teardrop shaped painted side panels.

By the time production commenced early in 1949, Hopwood had gone, dismissed as he was on the point of resigning due to office politics with Joe Craig. Nevertheless, the Dominator was an instant success, and though the first bikes were for export, by mid-1949 some were on test and available in the UK. If the mildly tuned 29 bhp Model 7 with its absolute top speed of just over 90 mph, and realistic road top speeds in the mid-80s, failed to satisfy the expectations of some that Bracebridge Street would come up with a twin 'built in the light of racing experience' which would instantly blow the Triumphs into the weeds, in every other department it was judged satisfactory. It was quick, two to three mph quicker than even the ohc Inter, no bigger or heavier at 413 lb dry, and like a good Norton should be, it was durable; you could ride it fast over long distances and on a regular basis. Hopwood's emphasis on cool running and robustness had paid off. One possible engine flaw was the breaking up of the spigot in the barrel to head joint, but in the experience of journalist and long time Norton rider Bruce Main-Smith, curiously this did not seem to matter.

Handling was good, though there was a penalty

in terms of rather harsh suspension, particularly from the Roadholders, at low speed; and in common with every other example of that system, the plunger rear suspension deteriorated with wear, then provoked slow weaving at speed. The brakes were inadequate for high speed work, and an early test mentioned something that would occur several times over the years with different Nortons on test, namely ovality of the front drum. But as an all-rounder rather than a flat-out roadburner the Dominator, as it was shortly known, shone. Easy to start, reliable, tractable, with excellent acceleration and a good riding position, smooth enough at traffic and cruising speeds though not beyond them, with reasonably good petrol economy by the standards of those days (good, by ours) at a little over 50 mpg overall, and mostly oil tight (with the exception of the pressed steel primary chaincase traditional to Norton and again better than most) — these were delightful and practical twins.

They were hampered only by a 1949 price tag of £220 19s 8d, against £198 2s 5d for a sporting Triumph T100. The price differential would always remain, and always be a handicap. One other drawback was that they were quite difficult engines to work on; due to the integral rocker box, cylinder head removal was necessary to work on the valves, and some of the head nuts and bolts were difficult to get at, being recessed into holes cut in the fins of the cylinder block and needing a box spanner to get up through the finning. There was a special long works socket, or a cut box spanner could be adapted. Either way replacement took longer than removal, with only a fraction of a turn available at a time, and correct alignment of all four pushrods was also tricky (as it was for different reasons on Hopwood's A10). Writer and restorer Jeff Clew, who owned a

Model 7 in the early '50s, recalls taking all day over a decoke.

Little development was needed or received over the next few years. There were no changes for 1950, and for 1951 a new front brake, still of 7 in diameter but with a rigid die-cast light alloy backplate was the only alteration. The drum was of cast iron and riveted to the hub, with both the latter and the backplate being lipped for watertightness and there was adjustment for the still separately pivoting shoes by means of a fitting screwed into a lug cast on the backplate. Then for 1952, which saw the rear wheel go from 19 to 20 in and a minor alteration to the shape of the timing cover, the Model 7 became permanently overshadowed by the addition of the Featherbed-framed Dominator 88, though this model would not be available on the home market until the first trickle were released in mid-1953.

The Featherbed frame was so called because Londoner Harold Daniell, Norton's record-breaking performer on the older 'Garden Gate' plunger framed racers, at the Junior TT prize-giving in 1950 when he was third home of the Norton 1-2-3, declared of the McCandless brothers' frame 'It's just like riding on a featherbed.' Geoff Duke cemented the legend, remarking to a BBC commentator when offered a seat after winning that year's Senior, 'No thanks, I've been lying down all morning.' By comparison with its punishing predecessors the new frame was certainly a revelation—so good, in fact, that it actually caused Daniell, who was one of the pre-war generation of aces, to retire. As Titch Allen explained, 'his reflexes, based on years of back wheels that hopped, skipped and jumped and stepped out at the slightest provocation, found it hard to adjust to a rear wheel that was so glued to the road that a new technique—drifting—could be

'For export only'—late 1952 Featherbed frame 'Dominator DeLuxe'.

employed.' The new generation, like Duke and Ray Amm, had no such problems, and the frame prolonged Norton supremacy on the tracks well into the '50s.

The McCandless brothers, Rex and Cromie, with their partner Artie Bell, ran an excavator and heavy plant repair business in Belfast. Cromie and Bell were both to be world-class road racers, while the self-trained Rex, though also a racer and a grass and hill-climb champion, was probably the most inventive of the partners. By the end of the war he had constructed (with, as Bob Currie pointed out, the unwitting co-operation of the Short Aircraft factory where Bell was working at the time), an inclined-engine Triumph-powered prototype with a duplex loop chassis and his own design of swinging arm rear suspension, using modified Citroen car units. Post-war work on improving the tendency of oil-damped units to aerate in use led to the development of the brothers' own system. An associate of theirs, BSA trials star Billy Nicholson, used the system surreptitiously on his works machine. After the rights had been sold in 1947 to Feridax, though problems with blowing seals on their units were to persist until Girling got it right, the McCandless brothers made a name for themselves, marketing and carrying out swinging arm conversions with rear suspension for scrambling and grasstrack.

According to a recent profile in *Classic Bike*, they had already caught the attention of Bracebridge Street for their part in the support team of Ernie Lyons' unofficial victory with the Triumph Grand Prix racer in the 1946 Manx Grand Prix. Artie Bell was recruited by Norton in 1947, with the brothers soon following. They were unimpressed with the factory team's capability as engineers, and so naturally as Rex recalled, 'there was more trouble with personalities than there ever was with the bicycles!' They worked on the racers' carburation, created the 500T, and then set out to tackle the fracture-prone, physically demanding Garden Gate racer frame. According to the *Classic Bike* piece, 'from the start the new frame was intended to house every combination of Norton engine and gearbox.'

A duplex loop construction like Rex's earlier Triumph prototype; the frame abandoned traditional methods of construction, hearth-brazing with cast lugs, in favour of the sif-bronze welding techniques developed in wartime on tubular assemblies for aircraft engine mountings. Unlike brass, which had previously been used in welded frames, sif-bronze could be built up into fillets. The method allowed structures both stronger and much lighter than previously and thus more responsive and resilient. For the Featherbed, the two main loops of tube were welded to the bottom of the headstock, from where they ran outwards before being bent in to go side by side as the tank top rails. They were bent down to run behind the gearbox, and again to carry them forward beneath the gearbox and engine. At this point they were bent upwards to form the downtubes, and finally not bent but sprung into position *inside* the top tube rails, where they were then welded to both the headstock and the top rails. This crossover bracing arrangement of tubing at the headstock formed the particular brilliance of the design, though as we shall see there was a potential problem associated with it.

Four cross tubes were welded in to brace the main tubes, and there were support gussets welded to the tube loops by the swinging arm. Long, unsupported rails were thus eliminated, one key to the minimizing of bending stresses; even the swinging arm was as short as possible. Three of the cross tubes carried mountings of steel plate for engine and gearbox; these plates, particularly the one constituting a headsteady, caused Rex to be be able to confirm that 'the engine was a very important part of the frame.' A rear sub-frame was bolted on to the main loop, to form the top mounting for the suspension legs, whose bottom end joined the tapered tubes, joined by a further ¼ in wall tube, which formed the swinging arm. The rear forks became wheel spindle carriers by means of tubes being inserted into them, hammered flat and then slotted.

This was the essence of the legendary Featherbed. The McCandless brothers themselves completed the package, with the petrol tank resting on the top rails on rubber mountings, fastened by a strap running over the top of the tank from the headstock to the seat nose; the tank thus needed no capacity-reducing tunnel to accommodate top rails. On the later roadsters, this too would cause problems of rider comfort in terms of tank and seat width of 11½ in, but the initial one for the brothers was that of weight distribution with the tank high up. They persuaded Norton, who in turn pressured the tyre makers to produce a 19 in tyre for the front wheel, to improve the way the weight sat and to put the downtubes as near the vertical as possible for optimum geometry; it was one of the first recognitions of the benefit, now fully being realized, of smaller diameter wheels in this respect. Rex was never to be happy with the way the weight sat high, and continued experiments with lowered petrol distribution up to and including the 1953 'kneeler'.

The machine's geometry was aided further by the use of 'short' Roadholder front forks, with cup and cone steering head bearings, shortened stanchions, fork tubes being over 2 in shorter at 21.843 in, internal springs fitted between the top of the damper cylinder and the top plug, and improved two way damping by means of a rod from the top nut carrying a dashpot system, a piston controlled valve being fitted to the rod's lower end. These forks, while harsh in action, gave outstanding steering in conjunction with the Featherbed. For roadgoing versions the same applied, but there were one or two things to watch. Over-tightening the bottom pinch bolt could break the soft alloy leg, requiring a complete replacement. Roadholders when they wore did so not only at their bushes but also on their stanchions and sliders, and the top cap in the damper tube inside the fork leg wore where the damper rod passed through it. But components were and still are available, and replacement restores damping to a good level.

The brothers completed the prototype in just two months during 1949, it got the thumbs up from the works riders, and as it was known that Norton with their hearth-brazing methods could not construct it, plans were made for Birmingham tubing and frame specialists Reynolds Tubes (later T.I. Reynolds Ltd) to do so. However Rex recently revealed that Reynolds too were initially unable to

produce the frame, which explains why the brothers came to take their jigs to Bracebridge Street and build the first half dozen works frames there for the 1950 season, which Duke, Bell, Lockett and Daniell proceeded to ride into racing history. Reynolds were to begin manufacturing production versions of the frame, at first for the Manx and then for the 88, and here the skill of their development engineer Ken Sprayson was to iron out some problems associated with both racing and roadgoing variants. For the racers, both works and Manx, they used Reynolds 531 tubing, a manganeze-molybdenum steel whose three principal constituents stand in a ratio to each other of 5:3:1; exceptionally light and strong, it retained its mechanical properties and higher ductility values after brazing. For the roadsters, however, the more economical Reynolds 'A' and 'B' grade mild steel tubing was used, the 16 gauge 'A' grade for the Internationals, whose frames were distinguishable by a flat on the tank tube to miss the cam box, and the 14 gauge 'B' for the rest. These were arc-welded not bronze-welded, and the presence of bronze-welding can be used to identify a genuine (and superior) racing frame.

The original design provided for a head angle of 64 degrees but when the whole machine was constructed this became 62 degrees. This, a relatively steep head angle for those days, promoted the excellent high-speed handling as did the frame and the smaller wheels aiding forward weight distribution. Rex had intentionally designed the frame as easy to build, cheap and versatile, and it was he who suggested, against initial resistance at Norton, that it should be used for roadsters. However, his own futuristic prototype design, with a cowled front and a pressed-steel monocoque rear, was too rich for the conventional attitudes of Bracebridge Street.

Though Rex says he had good relations with Reynolds personnel, in *Classic Bike* he dismissed as 'stupid' one of Sprayson's modifications to his design. This was the addition of a gusset at the headstock. But it may be noted that according to Sprayson, the Featherbed had been in production three or four years before Norton provided Reynolds with frame blueprints, and the gusseting was simply a practical solution to a practical problem; namely that though well equal to the intense torsional stresses of high racing speeds, the crossover frame bracing provided insufficient reinforcement when a roadster was simply bumped up onto a kerb, and front forks were sometimes pushed back until the gusset was provided.

99

Below left *Featherbed Dominator finds favour with discerning younger members of the public at the 1952 show.*

Right *Poor relation now, but a very nice motor cycle—swinging-arm Model 7 for 1954.*

One of Rex's other criticisms, however, related to this problem and may be more valid. This concerns the production roadster headsteady, where in place of the original bracing direct from the steering head to the engine and then anchored by a plate to a cross-member at two points (which it will be remembered Rex considered an important element in the strength of the frame), the production roadster version had only a vertically-mounted plate bolted in direct line from the cylinder head via the cross-member up to the steering head. Without the original headsteady in place, there may well have been a weakness at the kind of axis or centre line where the upright tubes from below the engine cross the horizontal ones coming from under the fuel tank, and this could allow the headlug to 'wag' fore and aft under severe working conditions. Certainly Rex claims this headsteady offered less strength under hard braking and contributed to the occasional downtube failures that occurred. Other modifications in production included moving the suspension unit's pick-up point on the rear sub-frame forward a little, as the previous geometry had caused some damper spindles to break. Eventually, in 1955, the rear sub-frame changed from a bolted-up to an all-welded construction. One further weak point of the frame was the Silentbloc bushes for the swinging arm, which could be pulled sideways by pressure, and were often replaced on the racers by bronze bushes.

But overall the Featherbed, much imitated both on and off the track (BMW roadsters were a case in point) provided a genuine, race-bred edge in handling over anything commercially available for the next fifteen years. Triumph and BSA might have their 650 twins, but Norton's handling and roadholding were once again a byword. The frame, as Rex had intended, was not over-expensive to make. Norton maintained a good

relationship with Reynolds to the end. Demand was always high for the frames—by the late '50s three-quarters of all Nortons sold were Featherbed-framed twins—and a limiting factor for production seems to have been Reynolds capacity, which topped out at around 250 a week.

The first Featherbed Dominator 88 was called at the time De-Luxe, but this is not to be confused with the partially enclosed De-Luxe models of 1960 on. The very first model in a politic move was presented to Arthur Bourne, editor of *The Motor Cycle*; and as Cyril Ayton amusingly recounts, the lofty Bourne modified it by raising the already tall and wide seat with a contraption of angle-iron and disused valve springs, which presented distinct problems for the much shorter journalist Vic Willoughby when the model came to be passed on to him! Initially the 88's gearbox featured higher ratios but for 1953 it returned to normal Dominator ratios. On a shaped dual-seat with a tool-tray beneath it the 88 rider sat further forward than had been the case with the racer. The tank was new-designed, initially 3½ gallons but by the time it got to England capacity was 3¾ gallons, when it also acquired thin chequered knee-grips with no Norton logo on them; like the racers it was strap-mounted, and of necessity, for its whole length was wider than the top rail.

This could result in an uncomfortable riding position for short riders, which the firm-to-hard suspension and rather firm seat did not help; unfortunately nothing was to be done about this until 1960. Another problem was the rather limited steering lock. The mudguards too were redesigned, with channelled edges and a deeper valance, the front one initially fixed to the sprung part of the fork, though this changed for 1953 to a lighter section type with two stays. The silencers became the pear-shaped type adopted for the whole range of ohv roadsters for 1953. The 88's

1955 Featherbed Dominator.

oil tank shape was different from the Model 7's, and matched on the left side by a toolbox. Instruments, including the speedometer, were mounted in a panel bridging the form tops, while the headlamp became the kind with the unpopular underslung pilot light.

Finished in polychromatic grey, including (apart from the earliest models) the frame, as well as the teardrop panels on its chromed tank, this was one very handsome motor cycle. At 380 lb it was also nearly 40 lb lighter than the Model 7, and hence marginally quicker. Its light weight paid in other ways; as Titch Allen writes, the Featherbed steering 'was experienced at its best with the Norton singles and 500 twins. . . There was a virtuosity about the lighter models . . . which could not be reproduced on a heavier model . . . The mere transference of thought seemed enough for it to bank and swoop with the grace of a bird.'

For 1953 the original Model 7 did not stagnate prior to withering away; a piece of simple surgery produced an unlikely success. As on the ES2 but with more positive results, plunger suspension at the rear gave way to the same swinging arm system as on the 88, and this led to a really

satisfying matching up of handling characteristics and the power from the iron engine. These 1953–56 Model 7s are one of several neglected gems (so often 500 cc twins) from the industry at this time. 'Long' Roadholders were still fitted, but the frame, while still single down tube, had a new malleable lug brazed to the junction of the tank and seat tubes, and a new steel forging joining the main frame and the seat tube lower end. This supported the swinging arm with its Armstrong units and built up the rear subframe. Wheelbase was the same as for the plunger frame, and the qd rear wheel could be employed. A new tool box was fitted in the angle of the rear stay on the left-hand side, as well as the pear-shaped silencers. Like the 88, pillion footrests, the new Lucas Diacon stop-tail light and the dual-seat were all now standard. The latter provided a niggle in that the oil tank's hinged cap could not be fully raised with it in position.

Norton had doubts about the Featherbed's ability to cope with sidecar work, and no sidecar attachment lugs were featured on the 88. The Model 7 fulfilled this function admirably but was also an eminently satisfying solo roadster, very torquey and with the feel of steering on rails.

This admirable pair of twins remained unchanged for 1954 when the 88 became more

1957 Model 99, 600 cc Featherbed twin. Bottom end could be over-stressed.

generally available at home, except for the welcome addition, which applied to the whole range, of a new 8 in front brake. If properly set up it was a distinct improvement, though many seemed to leave the factory in less than perfect tune. The shoe plate was still of light alloy and the cast iron brake drum riveted to the hub, but there was a 25 per cent increase in brake lining and additional brake adjustment became available by removing the operating arm and turning it over before replacing it on the cam spindle.

Since the onset of the Featherbed-framed model, the iron engine had been somewhat out-performed by the classy chassis, and 1955 was the year when the strong motor's obvious tuning potential began to be explored in production. After works models had tried out the innovation for several years at the Daytona races, both twins acquired an alloy cylinder head. There was only a fractional increase in compression at 6.8:1, and it would take further developments the next year to get the full benefit of the new head. There were other changes. Both twins adopted the Amal Monobloc carburettor, as well as the new plastic tank badges, the lower end of the fork sliders were polished not enamelled, there was more chrome plating to the nuts and bolts, a boxed-in rear number plate and a new shape of handlebar was provided with no forward sweep outboard of the clamps, just up and back, giving a shorter reach.

For the 88 there was a long overdue change to the Featherbed running gear. Ken Sprayson had known all along that the bolted-up construction of the rear sub-frame could never be as rigid as a welded one-piece design, and now Norton adopted the latter format for the roadsters as they had for the racers. To increase stiffness, the sub-frame tubes were now of a larger diameter, and welded to the main-frame tubes. Another change for the 88 was the adoption of full-width light alloy wheel hubs front and rear, with integral spoke flanges and cooling ribs. At the front the hub was now in fact an alloy half carrying the bearings, bolted to a silver-painted cast iron half, a heavy arrangement. At the rear a qd arrangement still obtained, with the rear brake in unit with the sprocket and three holes covered by rubber plugs giving access to the wheel-securing nuts on the off-side, though these needed a special box spanner to undo them. This rear brake was never satisfactory, the problem being the thin backplate which when leverage was applied to the brake, could distort irrevocably. Bracing struts were a possible answer, or a more rigid substitute backplate from a specialist. This brake regrettably remained in service right into the Commando days.

But with the Commando the brake had at least reverted to the underslung type of cam expander lever. It had been replaced on later twins for 1962 by an upturned lever, to accommodate an American-market silencer of some 4 in diameter. The upturned lever had to have much more offset because now the brake-rod had to pass the bottom of the rear damper instead of passing low down alongside the rear fork tube. Only a few big silencers were used, but the upturned lever was retained, and so almost all AMC-built 650 and Atlas models were fitted with it. John Hudson reckons that this, rather than the back-plate, was the brake's weak spot. The underslung type (part 067755, as used on the Commando) can be substituted for it. On the Commando also the bush which carries the brake cam in the brake plate has a steel plate riveted to it which along with a narrower distance piece to allow for the thickness of the plate, passes over the wheel spindle between the distance piece and the inside of the rear fork lug. These parts can also be fitted to the Dominator models.

To return to 1955, the 88 was also fitted with the larger rear mudguard with the hinged tail section as found on the Model 7. A circular, thin, pancake-type air cleaner was now standard. For the Model 7 there was now a new dual-seat common to the rest of the range bar the 88 and the International, and the horn button was built into the right of the bar with the wiring concealed, as on the 88. This was Model 7's last full year, as it was dropped quietly in mid-1956, a forgotten hero.

In its place for 1956 came the first step forward in the capacity race stimulated by American demand, and the start of real sports performance for the production roadsters. This was the 31 bhp 600 cc Model 99, a bored and stroked version of the 500 at 68 × 82 mm, but only five pounds heavier than the smaller capacity machine at 395 lb. The 88 and 99 were very similar, the 600 being externally identifiable by one more fin on its barrel than the eight-fin 500 (though the 650 was also to be a nine-fin engine). Gearing was raised by an extra two teeth on the engine sprocket, making 21 not 19, and the Amal 376 was $1^1/_{16}$ in against the 88's 1 in. This was a rather hotter engine with an alloy head and 7.4:1 compression provided by new flat top pistons, wire-wound as on Plumstead machinery, designed to run with finer clearances and cut down noise from a cold engine. Both it and the 88 whose compression ratio, with Pool fuel a thing of the past, jumped to 7.8:1, featured a camshaft known as the Daytona. Named from the US event for which it had been developed from 1953 onwards, in conjunction with the raised compression these increased the twins' performance in quite a noticeable way, well in line with the Featherbed's capabilities. While losing little of their docility at low speeds, when they came on the cam they could be revved with good results; both 88 and 99 now indicated realistic possible top speeds. More was to come, but with the 99 there was already a price; the 1½ in diameter crankpin could react badly to the 10 mm increase in stroke, and more than one crankshaft broke (which had never been the case with the 500).

There was also a further detail change to the Featherbed, and a good deal of cosmetic activity. The pivoted rear fork, on which it will be recalled the fork ends were formerly trapped and slotted, now featured a forged steel lug to support the wheel-spindle. There was a new style of timing cover, with the previous nameplate replaced by a miniature Norton badge quartered like the one on the tank. The oil tank and toolbox were given three horizontal ribs and a smoother shape within the frame loops, with a pressed steel plate running transversely across their forward ends. The fork top instrument panel went, in favour of one attached to a deeper headlamp shell now containing the speedometer and from which the underslung pilot light was discarded. The sweep of the 88's exhaust pipes were altered, and the cover plates on the alloy full-width hub polished to match the brake plate. On a more practical note a breather pipe from the oil tank now lubricated the rear chain. The Lucas dynamo changed from the E3H to the E3L type.

The action of the telescopic forks was lightened slightly to provide a softer initial movement, though a road test of the 88 in 1957 still found that 'insulation from road shocks could be better'

especially riding solo (a feature with most Norton twins). The same test found the pick-up from 30 mph in top gear not quite the same as previously, but the acceleration from there on was outstanding. The added performance meant that though the engine thrived on revs, at the top end heavy vibration came in from 75 mph onwards. So too did mechanical noise, Norton's legendary chattering tappets. The footrests were also found to be a little far forward for high speed work, and the 12 in width of the seat was found not quite ideal. But overall impressions were good, and the brakes on this one worked well. A *Motor Cycling* test of the 600 cc 99 earlier in the same year found it to be fast, just topping the magic ton at 101 mph, but still excellently flexible and also with very good petrol economy (78 mpg overall), and while vibration was mentioned again at speed through the gears, judged that 'the charm of this Norton was its snappiness'. Once again, a good all-rounder. By then both twins, with the rest of the range, in May 1956 had changed over to the excellent oval-shaped AMC gearbox as production of the box switched to Plumstead.

Late 1956 also saw a revival of a twin aimed at the sidecar man, evidently perceived as a market gap in the range. This was the Model 77, with the 99's 600 cc engine in the old Model 7's brazed-lug frame with malleable iron engine cradle and single down-tube. The frame incorporated the necessary lugs and a steering damper as standard, and the finish was the same handsome polychromatic grey as the Dominators, which is said to have become a slightly darker shade on the later years. A 77-powered outfit on test with *The Motor Cycle* was good for around 70 mph, and gave pleasure with its responsive handling.

Internally for 1957 the twins' engines acquired a redesigned cylinder head with more finning

Left *1957 and the smooth look for sidecar horse, the Model 77.*

Above right *1958, and alternator electrics arrive. Engine cutaway is of 600 cc Model 99.*

between the exhaust ports. Pushrods now changed from steel tubing to light alloy with hardened steel ends. 1957 also saw another self-conscious cosmetic job, 'introducing the new "smooth look" Norton range. . . the result of our unceasing search for perfection', or at least streamlined production costs. The pear-drop silencers were replaced by a cigar-shaped tubular type with no tail pipe. The chrome tank with painted panels sadly gave way to the new 3½ gallon type with plastic-backed screw-on chrome panels and black plastic beading round the edge, the panel containing the badge and a new shape of knee grip. It was still good looking, but the more Romanesque curves of the 1953-56 models get my personal vote on aesthetic grounds. The front edge of this tank came further forward, and its rear blended more closely with the front of the seat.

The instrument panel went, the speedometer, ammeter and light switch now being mounted directly in the headlamp shell. The rear brake control and stop-light switch were tidied up, with the brake pedal return spring now concealed. The old style flat composite footrests like bicycle pedals gave way to more conventional circular ones, though these were still adjustable. There was a new shape to the rear chainguard, the lip at the rear of the mudguard was less pronounced, and on the right-hand side of the Featherbed frames, a sheet steel fairing was bolted to the gusset plate to close the gap behind the gearbox. Girling rear units supplanted the previous Armstrongs, though for 1957 examples of both were still found.

The Featherbed models, but not the 77, acquired a new, lighter, cast-aluminium full-width front hub, with a cast-in brake liner and a new backplate with a forged cam-lever in place of the previous pressing. The diameter at 8 in, as well as the shoe assembly, were unchanged, but the shoe plate was restyled and now fitted inside the open end of the hub. Correctly set up, this was judged to be about the best SLS brake in the business, but many made the mistake of continuing to overtighten the nut on the end of the cam spindle. This eventually distorted the spindle where it passed through the boss of the backplate; it should be loose enough to pass through the boss with just finger pressure. The answer was to remove the cam, smoothing down with emery until it fitted in that way, and reassembling it onto the backplate with a smear of grease, and another where the brake shoes bore on the cam.

1958 was another major change year with the adoption of alternator electrics, not a move that

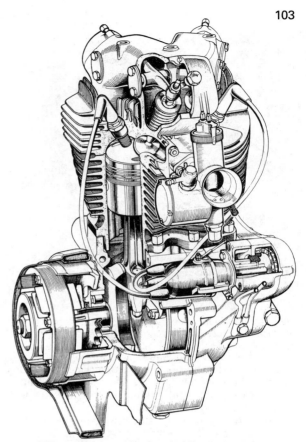

would be welcomed by hard-riding men who correctly equated the magneto with racing speeds, simple wiring and reliability. But as with the other manufacturers, Norton were under economic pressures from Lucas to adopt the cheaper alternator system which was claimed to give easier starting. So the 88 and 99 for that year (but not the 77 which continued as before) fitted a crankshaft mounted Lucas RM15 AC generator, with the stator mounted in a primary chaincase which, for production economy, was still the old pressed steel type. The chaincase had needed only light modification, with its nose radius a little larger, and at its forward end, a circular cut-out of slightly larger diameter than the stator holder; this fitted over a shallow secondary spigot on the crankcase, and the pressing was secured to it by three screws. The previous chain drive to the magneto was also little changed, now being used to drive a Lucas 3812A car-type distributor with points, condenser and auto-advance, mounted behind the cylinders where the magneto had been—making for somewhat inaccessible points.

As part of the reorganization of the timing

1959 and a good idea badly executed. Norton fully-enclosed rear case let dirt in and then kept it there.

cover, the pressure release valve, previously located in a domed housing screwed into the rear edge of the timing case, was now housed within it for neatness, though the filter was still accessible under a blanking plug. Elsewhere in the electrical system, the rectifier was positioned beneath the tool tray, the coil on a bracket on the inside of the right-hand tank rail (for 1960 it would move to a transverse position on the frame cross-tube at the rear of the petrol tank), and lighting and ignition were controlled by the dreaded Lucas combined switch mounted in the headlamp, far from waterproof or shakeproof, with complicated wiring and now rare and expensive to replace.

Both this and the alternator were to mean potential problems for riders. One plus point was that all Norton alternator cranks were to be of the same diameter (though longer than the dynamo cranks) so that more powerful later equipment could be fitted to earlier machinery (though the rotor keyway position was to be altered on the Commando). However, problems arose as the twins' performance began to increase dramatically and vibration (consequently) became a more constant companion. The rotor did not appreciate this and was capable of shaking itself apart, with its outer magnet portion working itself loose from the central steel sleeve; the coils of the stator were also at risk, particularly before they became resin-encapsulated. One solution mentioned in a *Classic Bike* feature was to remove

the rotor and fit special star-shaped spring washers behind and in front of it, as well as turning one of the spacers on the crankshaft to size to suit. Skimming a fraction off the rotor to avoid contact with the stator could also be beneficial, though this will reduce electrical output.

Later in the year the Dominators were presented in alternative colour schemes. In addition to polychromatic grey, you could have a silver petrol tank with the other cycle parts black, or one-colour finishes, still with the chrome tank panels but with everything else, up to and including the chaincase and centre stand, in either metalescent blue or bright Norton red 'with special anti-fade ingredients'. With one more chip knocked off the old image, by the end of the year, though at exactly what point is disputed, wheel rims ceased to be centre-lined in the machine colour with thin red striping and became all chromed.

There were also two optional extras available. One was a full rear chaincase, but this was less than satisfactory. Between its front end and the rear of the primary chaincase there was a gap and road filth would, not unnaturally, insert itself to form a grinding paste with the oil on the chain; some reckoned the case actually diminished chain life. The other option was the offer, from May 1958, of twin carburettors mounted on a suitable splayed manifold. Together with the option of pistons giving higher compression (8.2:1 for the 600, 9:1 for the 500), and of polished combustion chambers and ports, this indicated another step up in the twins' state of tune, and was claimed to provide an 8–10 per cent increase in performance.

These options were intimately connected with an export-only model which had been offered early in 1958. This was the 600 cc N15 Nomad street scrambler, built for American enduro, and the first of a line of production 'desert sleds', as the flamboyantly styled on/off road machines came to be known (the Nomad was red, with a white-topped black seat). At home twin GP carburettors had been offered from 1955–56 for a Clubman's racer 88, and development by Doug Hele and Brian Stimson had proceeded apace, with hot parts being tested over thousands of road miles on selected machines such as Bruce Main-Smith's own 1955 Dominator. The Nomad fitted twin $1^{1}/16$ in Monoblocs, a hotter camshaft and 9:1 compression pistons. But with Joe Berliner's West Coast representative Bob Blair specifying a desert racer's requirements, the quick motor came mounted in the old brazed lug frame, better suited than the Featherbed to the shocks of off-road competition in earnest, and tricked out with twin tubes and bash-plate beneath the engine, a magneto, a wider rear fork and competition wheels and tyres, and alloy mudguards. But the same increase in performance would soon be available in roadster form, again for export only and again at Berliner's instigation, in the shape of the 650 cc Manxman, with a racing cam and flat-based cam followers, two-rate valve springs and barrel-shaped tubular light alloy pushrods. This would eventually influence the form of the ultimate sports Norton twins for the home market.

One casualty later in 1958 was the sidecar 600, the Model 77. Possibly encouraged by Eric Oliver's eighth place at that year's sidecar TT on a standard 88 outfit, both Dominators were offered in an alternative specification suited to service with a chair. There were heavy duty fork springs, stiffer rear units and most importantly a special strengthened fork crown and column, requiring a steering damper with two friction discs which centred on a large-diameter boss on the underside of the crown. (The solo crown steering damper had a single friction disc of different dimensions.) These were coupled with gearing lowered by the use of an engine sprocket with fewer teeth (seventeen for the 500, eighteen for the 600) to create a sporting sidecar mount which led to the demise of the Model 77 by the end of the year. Otherwise 1959 saw both twins acquire a new camshaft with quietening ramps, both inlet and exhaust valves becoming Stellite-tipped. Larger diameter inlet valves became a further option at this point.

For 1960 the major development was the introduction at last of what was offered as a more user-friendly shape for the roadster's Featherbed frame. Those at the factory, however, knew that the main reason the frames were changed was that they wanted to use the enclosed rear tail of the 1959 Jubilee models on the Dominators; hence the 'tea-cup handle' loops and cantilever brackets on the slimline's rear sub-frame, which in the view of John Hudson were inferior to the straight-tubed triangulation of the wideline. Some mythology has grown up around the 'slimline' frames as they came to be known, so it should be noted that both John Hudson and Ken Sprayson of Reynolds have confirmed to me that, like all other Featherbeds outside the very first 1950 racers, every slimline was built at Reynolds' Tyseley works. Differences from the previous wideline were not great; on the same jigs as previously, just above the rear gusset the tubes were bent differently, kinking the back of the main loop inwards, with the tubes at the front

bent a little more to match up. The effect for the rider was to bring the frame loops closer together under the saddle nose, permitting a narrower-nosed seat and slimmer tank, and thus more comfort. The head angle was altered from 26 to 24 degrees, and the extended centres of the rear dampers shortened from 12¾ in to 11⅞ in, with 3 in range compared with 3¼ in previously. To the new rear sub-frame tubular loops were welded steel pressings to form the upper mountings for the suspension units and to provide attachments for the silencers and pillion footrests. There was a new seat mounting system, with a cross-tube at the narrowed rear of the frame main loops carrying two rearward pointing pegs to engage with rubber-lined sockets under the dual-seat nose, and at the rear, spring clips on the base snapped over short transverse tubes welded to the loops.

Over the years there has been some criticism of the slimline frame for causing a slight reduction in Featherbed standards of handling. In *Classic Racer* recently, racer/tester Alan Cathcart referred to it as inferior, and when a reader who raced a Commando-engined slimline Atlas-framed machine wrote in to defend it, Cathcart replied that from personal experience he felt that the narrower spread between the top rails resulted in a lesser resistance to torsional forces when the bike was cornered hard, and that he had never met anyone who thought it the wideline's equal. Conversely, I would add that at anything less than racing speeds, I have never, then or now, heard any criticism of the 'slimline' for fast road use.

Sid Lawton, famous preparer of twin cylinder production racers in the '60s, thinks the fault was one of weight distribution 'which applied to all modern British bikes—Norton, BSA, Triumph, the lot. It was probably caused by a combination of the alternator being slung on the end of the crank and the much bigger clutches fitted to the engines as they were progressively increased in capacity and performance.' On Lawton's racing Nortons he cured it largely by rebuilding both wheels with their rims pulled fractionally to the left. It seems likely that these factors rather than the slimline frame were responsible for any minimal deterioration in handling during this era as power-outputs rose. A final point was cost; in the *Classic Bike* interview with Rex McCandless the latter was very unimpressed with the slimline and guessed 'it must have cost twice as much to make as the earlier type'. But Bert Hopwood has confirmed to me that this was not the case and that Reynolds' costs remained reasonable for both types.

Some slimlines had further brackets attached to the frame and the sub-frame to provide mounting points for the rear enclosure. 1960 was the year when the 'De-Luxe' tag was resurrected, only this time to describe versions of the twins, both 500 and 600, faired in at the rear in the manner of the 250 cc Jubilee which Norton had launched for the previous year. Presumably the theory was that if you couldn't make a Jubilee look like a Dominator, you could at least do it the other way round. As a sales ploy it was to be a flop. The arrangements were identical with the Jubilee's with the twin detachable panels, each with three Dzuz screws fitting close together at the front end, meaning that the twin carb option was not on for these touring models. The whole set-up, with faired in tail lamp and central oil tank was virtually irreversible, as I know to my cost since, too impatient to seek out one of the ever-scarce unfaired twins, I got myself lumbered with a secondhand two-tone dove grey and red 88 De-Luxe, which proved unsaleable for three years. There was the dependable handling and the fact that, when running, it was a handy bike in town; but the engine on mine was a dog, my lack of expertise was as implacable as ever, and the whole experience (seizure, blown head gaskets, snapped head studs, etc) was an unhappy one.

This year all mudguards were of deeper section and the standard models acquired a new one-piece rear mudguard with no detachable tail portion. Finishes for the whole range went two-tone, either black or light blue above and dove grey below. This applied to a new petrol tank, deeper, narrower and slightly larger at 3.62 gallons, and secured no longer by a steel strap on top, but from below by two inverted bolts with rubber

bushes, and held down at the rear by a rubber band. As on the Jubilee, the tank's upper and lower portions were separated by a new chrome-plated zinc alloy die-cast spiked badge containing the Norton name at the front and a narrow kneegrip at the rear. This was the smooth look with a vengeance.

The 1960 engines fitted larger inlet valves as standard, with redesigned porting in the cylinder head and thus a new inlet manifold for the single carburettor with stud centres widened from 1½ in to 1⅝ in. Previously fitted to a few special engines only, this head was identified by a milled-off cast cross on the side of the rocker box between the rocker spindle retaining plates; though it should be noted that the same mark can be seen on the downdraught heads from 1962 on also. For both capacities too there was a new camshaft with quicker lift cams. Compression again rose slightly for the stock engined machines, 8.1:1 for the 500, 7.6:1 for the 600, with the 99's power output now increased to 34 bhp at 6,500 rpm. The latter acquired additional finning on its cast iron cylinder block. Another welcome and long overdue change came to the gearing of both, with the 99's engine sprocket lowered from 21 to 20 teeth and the 88's from 20 to 19. Since the first Norton 20,000 mile test of the prototype AMC box during 1955, factory people like John Hudson had complained to AMC about the ratios, and as he says, 'it took them until 1960 to do this, which was a big improvement'. The principal effect of the change was to narrow the gap between third and top.

On the cycle side there was a new pattern absorption silencer, more completely cylindrical than its predecessor, on which the bottom had

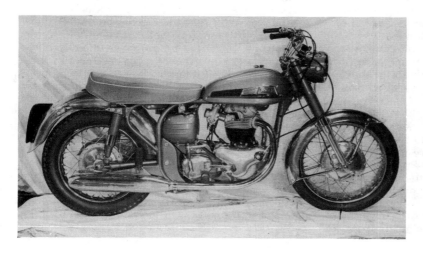

Left *The first 650—strictly for export: 1961 Manxman.*

Above right *Close-up of 650 Manxman engine.*

followed a near straight line from the exhaust pipe through to the rear, while the silencer top took a step up after the junction with the exhaust; the latter shape would appear again on the twins from the following year on. 1960 also saw the introduction from the factory of a short, flat handlebar bent just slightly rearward, the famous 'Norton straights'. These had apparently finally been offered after a factory representative addressing the Owners' Club was challenged to explain why they persisted in supplying the previous swept-back bars. When he suggested that they were what the customer wanted, he was led out to the bike park where every Bracebridge Street twin without exception sported Vincent straights. To the factory's credit the 'straights' were catalogued as an option the following year and were soon to be standard on some machines.

1961 saw the performance war break new barriers, but the most significant, the 650 Manxman, was for export only. For the home models however there was another compression rise, the 500 going to 8.5:1, the 600 to 8.25:1. There was a minor change in the fixing arrangement at the rear of the dual-seat which was now by a standard Dzuz fastener to the rear mudguard or fairing, as on the light twins. Then in April 1961 the various developments and options came together for the 500 and 600 which were offered in a third guise, the SS (Sports Special). These machines had twin carburettors as standard, with ports opened out to suit and polished, as were the combustion chambers. Compression remained the same at 8.25:1 for the 600, 8.5 for the 500, but there was selective assembly of the pistons to make sure this was achieved. From the 600 Manxman came the camshaft and flat-based cam followers, plus two-rate valve springs and hollow barrel-shaped light alloy pushrods with a diameter of ⅜ in in the middle and ⁹⁄₃₂ in at the end. The wishes of the sporting riders were acceded to and for 1962 a Lucas K2FC magneto was fitted for ignition purposes to the 500 cc version. A lower output alternator was retained for the auxiliary functions; about 200 of the very first 88SS 500 cc models also came with a handlebar ignition lever for advance/retard. A final major boost to performance came with the option of a siamezed exhaust system, with the specially developed silencer running along the right-hand side. Vic Willoughby, testing a 600 cc 99SS, confirmed that this made an appreciable difference to power. Other special parts included the flat bars and ball-ended control levers as standard, extra strong clutch springs, and as an extra for the 600, a 21-

tooth engine sprocket against the standard 20-tooth, and for the 500 higher 9:1 cr pistons.

Willoughby was highly impressed with the example he tested for *The Motor Cycle* — a 108 mph top speed and 14.4 second standing quarter from the 44 bhp at 6,750 rpm motor, lightning throttle response compared with the standard machine and realistic 90 mph cruising were all there. He was objective enough to note that there was a price, since at revs below 4,500 the new engines had slightly less punch than the standard versions, a bit more appreciable vibration at top revs in the gears, as well as a slightly heavy thirst for oil and petrol (55 mpg at 60, suggesting an overall figure in the mid-40s). For long journeys he also didn't like the flat bar in conjunction with normal footrest and pedal positions. Rear-sets were available as an optional extra, as was a rev-counter; and for machines having a boss on the timing cover for a rev-counter gearbox, a larger oil pressure relief valve with a fine mesh gauze filter on its inner end was fitted, being accessible via a cap nut from the rear of the engine cover. Willoughby correctly predicted that 'the Sports Specials cannot help but make their mark in production machine racing.' Success was already happening for Norton twins; not only was 1961 the year of Tom Philis' feat in coming third at over 100 mph at the Senior TT on the 500 cc Domiracer, but since 1958, nineteen-year-old Paul Dunstall had been racing a modified 600 cc twin with some success. From 1960 he turned to the sponsoring and preparation of the big twins, also offering a full range of goodies for road riders including his famous swept back exhausts. Syd Lawton's achievements will be mentioned later.

Motor Cycling tested a 500 cc 88SS whose claimed output had risen to 36 bhp at 7,000 rpm, and were not disappointed in a best one-way speed of 111 mph with a following wind, suggesting a still air top speed around 104 mph, about 7 mph up on the standard model now. Given a change of plug from hard KLG FE100 to a soft FE 75 for around town, the hot 500 was tractable enough, though once again high speed acceleration, even from 85 mph on, was more marked than low down torque, and the motor could definitely be revved to the limit. The vibration situation was a little smoother on the 500 than the 600. The tester liked the good ground clearance the siamezed system provided, and the excellent braking (Willoughby's front brake drum had been oval), but noted that at high speeds the oil tank vent pipe coated the left wall of the back tyre, and that lubricant also got past the oil filler cap. Excessive oil from the breather could in fact mean a sticking valve on the pressure-release assembly. Lights and horn could have been stronger, but overall impressions of punch and roadholding were very favourable. The word 'stretchable' was applied to the engine, and certainly the tuners were to find the engine's basic robustness served them well. Exhaust valve clearances had a tendency to close up, but the only major weak point was fragility of the barrels in the 600 and later the 650, particularly if they were fitted with high compression pistons and overbored, which left dangerously thin spigots at the top. This could cause splitting of the barrels, or the breaking off of the base flange, most

particularly on the late 750s.

1962 saw what was, in many ways, the apotheosis of the Norton twin tradition, the Dominator 650SS, released in the UK, along with single carb Standard and De-Luxe faired variants of the larger machine. The 650 engine, while still retaining good commonality of parts with the other twins, had been redesigned with a significant diference. There was no boring out and the bore of 68 mm was that of the 600. So the extra capacity of the 646 cc engine was achieved with a crankshaft redesigned to give a crank-throw of 89 mm, putting this twin into the longer stroke category. In practical terms this meant an excellently flexible motor. Crankcases were redesigned to suit, and a 600 cc could never be converted to 650 capacity without major engineering work. In the new crankcases the breather became the rotary timed type, with surplus oil vapour from the breather now assisting lubrication to the rear chain. This arrangement was fitted for 1962 on 88 and 99 models also, and was a direct substitute for the previous item.

The new crank ran on larger big-end journals of 1¾ in diameter to avoid the crankshaft problems experienced on some 600s, and featured a wider flywheel. An external clue was the absence of the small Norton badge on the timing side of the crankcase. Solid skirt pistons were used, giving a standard compresion ratio of 8.9:1, and featuring a Twiflex oil-control ring, an unusual type of scraper ring comprising two thin rings, called rails, located on each side of the stepped portion of the expander ring. Some early 600 cc models fitted with Automotive wire-wound pistons had suffered from piston failure around the oil ring, so this was possibly an attempt to combat the problem. Syd Lawton also found that piston-to-barrel clearance

Getting there—the definitive 650 for some, the Norton 650SS in 1962.

on the early 650s was very tight, two and a half to three thou, which could, and did, cause seizure; he honed out the barrels on his production racer to five thou, and was able to use the same barrels for three successive and successful racing years.

The 650 also featured an item developed specifically from the Domiracer by Doug Hele, who as Lawton observed 'regarded production racing as a means of improving the breed'. This was the downdraught cylinder head which now was also offered on the 88SS twin, though not the 99. Twin $1^1/_{16}$ in 389 Monoblocs were fitted, with a balance pipe between the induction tracts to aid smooth running at low engine speeds. The inlet passages had originally been of 1⅛ in bore, but these had been sleeved down by the makers to the lower figure to aid mid-range power and Syd Lawton for one found that competitors who tried to run with the sleeves removed and marginally larger 1⅛ in carbs fitted were not as fast as his bike with the standard head.

The new downdraught arrangement could cause a few complications. They were prone to flooding and needed little or no tickling unless you wanted to find yourself push-starting the bike to clear it. Similarly if the petrol tap was left on for long periods when the bike was stationary, the petrol drained past the inlet valve and piston rings into the crankcase, making for thin oil and subsequent trouble; this applied to all SS and Commando models, and always switching off the petrol and the avoidance of long periods on the sidestand are recommended. Finally on SS models the chopped-float twin carbs could sometimes suffer from fuel starvation; one cure was the removal of the standard valve and needle and replacement with Amal dope valve gear, or today, substitution of Concentrics as on the Commando, 28 mm appearing to be the correct size. Standard and De-Luxe 650s fitted a bifurcated inlet manifold and a single 389 1⅛ choke carburettor.

On all the 650s multi-rate valve springs, the barrel-shaped pushrods, sports cam and an additional (fifth) clutch plate was to be found. The 650SS was in line with the 500 sports models in using magneto and alternator electrics, the alternator for all changing that year to the Lucas RM19. Also in common with the other SS models it fitted an Avon Grand Prix rear tyre which had been developed in conjunction with Nortons. 18 in rear wheels had been fitted to the export 650s and these were available as an option at home, but riders found they got better roadholding from the 19 in variety. One respect in which the 650SS did differ from the others was the recommendation for a conventional twin exhaust system to be

fitted, for although the siamezed system was offered as an optional extra, it had been found on the 650 to impede acceleration slightly though it did not affect top speed. The 650SS gave a claimed 49 bhp at 6,800 rpm.

A final point was finish. Happily the 650SS from the start had no truck with the other twins' greens or blues over the pale dove grey, and appeared at home from the start with a tank of traditional Norton silver, and everything else black or chrome. Little heavier than the smaller capacity twins at a shade under 400 lb dry, quite long with its 56 in wheelbase but compact, low and almost unassuming, the arrow-like straight, functional lines of the silver and black 650SS nevertheless breathed power and purpose to the informed eye. The addition of the chrome-plated full mudguards, optional from that year, completed the package. Other options included a folding kickstart, the rev-counter and the fully enclosed rear chainguard. Finally for 1962, the last Bracebridge Street year, even more beef was promised in the shape of the 750 Atlas, but once again this was for export only.

Norton had finally hit the sports 650 market at the height of the rocker era, with a machine whose frame and forks, identical to the smaller models, handled as well as ever they did, and a good deal better than the contemporary Triumph/BSA/Enfield opposition. The speedometer was a 150 Smiths job, and the engine was to prove itself capable of a shade under 120 mph top speeds, meaning 112 mph on a regular basis; the justification for dropping the previous guvnor, the T120 Bonneville engine, into Norton cycle parts could no longer be found in terms of speed.

Syd Lawton pushed the point home that year where it showed most, in production endurance racing at the Thruxton 500 miler and the BMCRC 1,000. His riders Phil Read and Brian Setchell won both events within months of the machine's appearance, though the Bemsee event at Silverstone had at first been led by another Norton ridden by Bruce Main-Smith and Ron Langston until a con-rod let go. Lawton's bike won again at Thruxton the following year, but only took a third in the Bemsee event. In 1964 the 'Lawton Norton', as legendary in its day as the Trident Slippery Sam would be a decade later, won at Thruxton for the third time with Setchell and Derek Woodman up. Lawton confirmed in *Classic Bike* that, except for the addition of a home-brewed Manx-derived close ratio gearbox, 'we didn't tune for extra power or performance.' The 650SS was voted *MCN* Machine of the Year for 1962 and 1963. Road tests endorsed the high

performance, and the more practical points for the road rider such as excellent handling in both dry and wet, a comparatively modest thirst at around 50 mpg overall, reasonable vibration and also at road speeds, good braking by the standards of the day (28½ ft from 30 mph). Excellent ground clearance was praised and above all, as BMS put it in *Motor Cycling*, a 'sporting top end without the bad manners associated with such urge at low speeds.'

The last bikes built at Bracebridge Street were a batch of 650SS Police machines destined for escort duty in Australia. The 650 engine even in SS tune really was as tractable as that fact suggests, as I can testify personally. I was lucky enough to own one, a 1966 example, again bought secondhand. True to form, I never really did explore that power-step which existed above 75 mph/4,300 rpm; in the whole two years that I ran it the engine never really gave of its best at speed, something I put down to a combination of the carburettor problems and lack of intestinal fortitude on the part of the throttle hand. Both are failings I now regret, as in most other ways the bike seemed well up to it, and proved to be an excellent tourer; as well as a regular London to Norfolk run, journeys to Southern Ireland, France, Spain and Morocco and back were completed. Nothing broke, and the only negative aspect was comfort; the ride was hard, the seat not thick. The trip to Morocco is the only time I've seen a pillion

passenger in tears after a 300 mile day, and he was no sissy either.

But if the 650 Norton was that good, why didn't everyone ride them? Brand loyalty, particularly to Triumph with its long history and extensive tuning lore explained some of it, and from then on through the '60s with Doug Hele at Meriden, Triumph were to get better and better, while Norton development was only spasmodic. Nortons were comparatively highly priced and lack of availability (due to low production levels) kept secondhand prices up. In 1963, the year of the move south, altogether only 2,500 Nortons appear to have been built at Plumstead, and the figure seems little better for the subsequent years up to and including 1968 when the Commando came on stream, averaging out at around just 4,000 machines a year, including the light twins; Triumph were building nearly ten times as many.

Like any new machine, the 650 was not without its problems initially. That the barrels sometimes let go under stress has been mentioned (though John Hudson disputes this, saying the problem was confined to the 750 engine), and early SS alloy con rods were prone to breakage until changed to a stronger type after engine no 11920. Vibration at high revs could loosen bolts and fracture the oil tank mountings; regular checks were advisable. The early type copper oil feed pipes to the rockers could fracture unless replaced with the later type of special rubber, and feed to

with the AMC alloy primary chaincase and Matchless/AJS gearbox shell and slotted into the AMC 650 frame with Norton forks, brakes and wheels. The Scrambler's fork stanchions, however, at 25 in were 2 in longer than those on the Norton Atlas roadster, and their rear wheel spacers were longer. With a rev-counter, detachable lights, trail tyres and topped with a scrambles tank (but without the silencers shown in the publicity material), the Atlas Scrambler was the first of a line of Atlas-engined hybrids. They came about only after the AMC twin motor had been unsuccessfully expanded to 739 cc; it had not been halted, as stated incorrectly in Volume 1, at prototype stage, but was produced as the Matchless G15/G45 in very small numbers (less than 200) from 1961 to 1963, until replaced with the Atlas engine. The hybrids, until now, were for export but they hit Britain for 1965 in the form of the Atlas-engined Matchless G15 and G15 CSR/ AJS Model 33 and Model 33 CSR, the first of several variants, details of which can be found in the AMC section of Volume 1. In 1967 in a further complication to the tortuous tale of the hybrids, after the AMC crash of the previous year, the G15 CSR while ceasing for the home market was converted to street scrambler spec for export. However, a few found their way onto the home market due to cancelled export orders.

Police versions of the 745 cc Norton Atlas were offered in Britain from September 1963 and from February 1964 the big bike was released to the public for the home market, the first batches being snapped up quickly; once again the Atlas (and Atlas spares) would always be in short supply, the majority going abroad. The export engine had originally been developed by Doug Hele to meet American requirements. The high performance 500 and 600 cc SS models were found too fussy across the water; what they wanted was a machine so torquey that it could accelerate in top gear from 20 to 100 mph. On the first Atlas machines there had been a problem with the Featherbed frame; some early ones were returned to Ken Sprayson at Reynolds with the twin downtubes broken just above the motor's front mountings, by the engine's sheer grunt. Sprayson had recommended inverting the welded-on lugs so that their tails were uppermost, and this had cured the problem.

Early Atlas engines had been known to throw their con-rods, but soon gained in reliability. Clanking pistons seemed to be a problem area for Norton at this time and the Atlas clutch too could sometimes prove inadequate. Like the AMC 750 engine, the Atlas also had the problem of

the rockers could be improved by substituting a Jubilee restrictor piece for the bigger engine's item, giving a greater feed. In addition to the discomfort, the 650SS was a mechanically rattlesome motor, with valvegear noise heightened by the generous settings recommended for high speed work.

For 1963 the 600 cc engined machines were deleted, which explained why Norton had not bothered to strengthen their crankshafts and adopt magneto ignition as they had for the 500SS the previous year; the 600 was eclipsed by the 650. Not before time, the faired De-Luxe 500 and 650 models were also axed. The foreign market orientation of AMC as they struggled for survival was to lead to some hairy hybrid beasts in the tradition of the Nomad, kicking off in August 1963 with the Atlas Scrambler. This was export only again, and to distinguish them from the previous N15 600 cc Nomad, the 1964 versions were suffixed N15CS 'N' (or G15 CS 'M' when they were marketed as Matchlesses—Joe Berliner of Hasbrouck Heights, New Jersey, was now handling both marques, and would happily swap badges and transfers when necessary—he once sold a batch of the Matchless G15 CSR model as the 'Norton SS 750'). For 1967 the Atlas Scrambler was restyled and became known as the N15CS.

In 1963 the early machines consisted of an Atlas engine with twin carbs and a sports cam, modified inadequate meat for a cylinder base gasket once the 650's bore had been enlarged to 73 mm, and one of the external distinguishing marks between the 650 and 750 Featherbed Nortons was the latter's taller cylinder base holding down nuts (though they had a smaller hexagon— ¼ Whitworth against 5/16 in on the other twins). The crankcase breather pipe was positioned at the front on the left, not the timing side as with the 650. When the crankcase mouths had been enlarged to accept the larger diameter spigot of the barrels, the breather outlet on the 650 had had to be blanked off. Other changes for the 750 included concave pistons and a different shaped combustion chamber, giving lower compression. It should be noted that Doug Hele had been emphatic that the compression ratio on this stretched design should on no account be raised above the 7.5:1 cr he originally specified. The raise to 9:1 shortly after the move to Plumstead, and the subsequent Combat Commando follies, were all in direct contravention of this distinguished developer's recommendation.

The Atlas fitted matching speedometer and rev counter heads, and its rear wheel differed from the 650 in being 4.00 × 18 in as standard. But like the 650SS it featured magneto ignition and in common with all the other twins for 1964, fitted 12 volt electrics, with two Lucas MKZ 9E-2 ultra-lightweight batteries in series. For all the twins the forks were also widened to accept a larger tyre for the US market, the visual clue being a steering head lock in the top crown if the wider crowns are fitted. The standard 500 cc 88 and 650 models were no longer available this year.

The initial power output of the Atlas was identical to the 650SS, 49 bhp, at 6,800 rpm. It was an extremely flexible engine with plenty of power from right down low for relaxed top gear

cruising, and incidentally ideal for sidecar work. Testers noticed a marked increase in vibration at anything above 4,500 rpm, though paradoxically in a 1967 'Rider's Report' on the Atlas, some found that the shakes actually smoothed out above 70 mph. But with high gearing and by the standards of the day (which included the BSA A65 and the Matchless G12), it was not considered excessive by some. Paul Morin of Hy-Cam, the information exchange for the Norton-Matchless hybrids, and at the time a young rocker, bought a new Atlas in 1964. After initial problems dealt with under warranty involving a disintegrating main bearing cage, Paul enjoyed 16,000 trouble-free miles and concluded that the handling, the speed (117 mph at 6,800 rpm) and the reliability of the low compression 7.6:1 Atlas 'sold me on the motor for life.'

This was after Plumstead had done some considerable development work on the 750 engine. Wally Wyatt was a development engineer principally involved. Though allowances must be made for Norton v Matchless factory rivalry, Wyatt in a *Classic Bike* interview recalled how unimpressed he had been with the engines as they had arrived at Woolwich early in 1963, after a year in production for export. Wyatt reckoned that the cylinder head porting was so bad that he couldn't get his finger down it; Wyatt says that he shortly improved on the Bracebridge Street power output 'with a bit of file work', getting 59 bhp from the engine, and by 1967, on versions intended for racing, a claimed 66 bhp. John Hudson maintains that, as with the compression ratio, Wyatt 'should never have done it [boost the power]' if he had known anything of the designer's intentions.' It was these good results with the Atlas that were partly responsible in 1967 for the demise of an alternative twin project, the dohc

Norton 650SS for 1963.

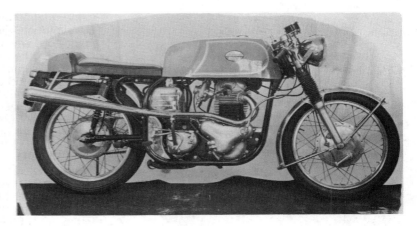

A Dunstall racing variation on the 650SS theme.

800 cc P10. In the 1967 Production TT the Wyatt racers dropped out in practice with disc brake, oiling and ignition problems and it was Ray Pickrell the following year who proved the strength of the engine by winning the race; but that was on a Commando.

Wyatt also had a hand, as part of a team with ex-Velo designer Charles Udall in charge and Tony Denniss as chief draughtsman, on a major modification to the Atlas and 650SS oiling system. On Wyatt's own account, while testing the 750 engine he fixed gauges to the bike and found that at 6,000 rpm the oil pressure dropped to zero, while the temperature increased greatly. Quarter inch oil pipes, with ⅛ in holes in the unions, were reckoned to be at fault.

John Hudson, however, says that there were no oilways anywhere as small as the ⅛ in that Wyatt mentions—$^3/_{16}$ in was the minimum, which is very much larger in terms of flow capacity. He reckons that the oil pressure may well have been zero in the pressure line where you can measure it; but the 44 mm long column of oil 'flying' up the web of the crank would 'suck' oil up to put pressure on the bearing itself at 6,000 rpm. When they had tested the first 650s at Birmingham they ran them flat out on the recently opened M1, and with a gauge fitted, Brian Stimson found a zero or near-zero pressure reading at 6,000 rpm—'but we never had any big end failure.'

At any rate the Woolwich team opened up the drillways from the crankcases to the oil pump, fitted larger unions and a ⅜ in pipe and claimed 350 lb oil pressure at 6,000 rpm. But once again John Hudson from Bracebridge Street, whose profound knowledge of Norton twins was initially rather ignored by some at Plumstead, maintains that Udall 'left out the most important [oilway]— the one from crankcase up to

the return entry into the pump', so the new system was not as satisfactory as it might have been. He also states that 'they could not get anything like 350 lb PSI—the relief valves were all set to blow off at 70 lb PSI!'

From engine no 116372 which appears to have been made during 1966, the speed of the already large oil pump was doubled by the use of a six-start worm-drive. Bleed holes in the con-rods were also provided. Since they were now fed from the delivery pipe to the engine not the return side, there was pressure oil feed to the rockers, with the rocker spindles having previously been made plain and reduced ¼ in in width to resist the added pressure and prevent flooding of the head with oil; and a change to Wellworthy 'Duaflex' 5-piece piston rings to control the extra oil now emerging from the crankshaft. Fitting the new pump to an existing engine was not recommended unless the larger feed pipe and enlarged internal oilways were also provided, though Hudson believes they can be safely fitted anyway. Finally a tendency to blow cylinder gaskets was claimed to have been overcome by eliminating the spigots on top of the

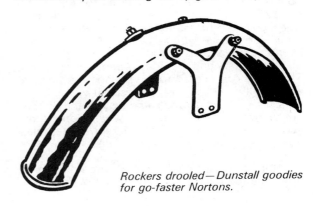

Rockers drooled—Dunstall goodies for go-faster Nortons.

block and their matching recesses in the cylinder head, giving greater efficiency in the production of gas-tight faces; a metallized asbestos head gasket replaced the previous copper-asbestos one. Once again John Hudson points out that spigotless heads and barrels had been tried in Birmingham but the previous arrangement retained as better engineering; at Woolwich, he says, the spigots were planed off simply on the score of cost.

1965 saw only one useful change announced for all three capacities of twin—a heavier ⅝ in × ⅜ in rear chain was finally adopted for a longer life. The Atlas, which in the UK had initially been offered in the 650SS silver and black trim, with an optional red or black tank, sported for this year a cherry red tank. The following year it would be Burgundy, but for some the styling lacked flair compared to the hybrids, or the AMC twins, or even the Atlas' own export styling with peanut tank, high bars and a chromed primary chaincase. The home Atlas called forth words like 'attractive' and 'neatly finished' in road tests. It was handsome in exactly the same way as the 650SS, but didn't flex its muscle; that would come three years later. As a rocker-in-the-street at the time, Paul Morin's comments on his Atlas are interesting.

After his initial troubles there were no major problems for 16,000 miles, no oil leaks despite

being ridden hard, good compression and low oil consumption. Once he had cut off the centre stand foot which had grounded and which he considered dangerous, both handling (especially on rough sufaces and in the wet) and braking were very good up to a limit. This limit was further than others, but to Paul Morin it indicated that the Featherbed was probably at the edge of its efficiency with the Atlas and 650SS output; both Dunstall, with his own frames, and later the JPN team, reached the same conclusions. The problem was a hint of whip on fast bends and when decelerating hard. But the major area of dissatisfaction was more personal; the machine's styling lacked the necessary aggression for Paul, and this meant that his next bike was a Matchless-framed G15 CSR, very quick and with the Atlas engine reliability intact but handling was considerably hairier, especially in the wet.

1966 was the year of the crunch for AMC and an intant casualty was the 500 cc 88SS. Just the Atlas and the 650SS continued in production with the modifications already mentioned. For 1967 the 650 was equipped with the same paired speedometer and rev-meter as the Atlas, these being mounted in a chromed bracket across the fork top yoke.

Meanwhile in 1966, after an unsuccessful bid to bail out the company, Joe Berliner came up with a further mix-and-match hybrid suggestion to help dispose of Plumstead's remaining stock. His West Coast representative Bob Blair of 2DS Motors was heavily involved in the 200 mile races held in the Mojave desert. For a while the last Matchless competition 500 cc single, the G85CS with superlight cycle parts, had been competitive but it was now down on power against Triumph-engined Metisse machinery. The Atlas-engined scramblers had been good but heavy at 410 lb (against the 350 lb Bonneville in TT spec). Why not, mused Berliner, combine the two, the Norton twin engine in the Matchless single's cycle parts? He got on the phone to Bob Blair, who promptly shoe-horned two of the modified Atlas engines into G85CS frames of Reynolds 531. These had malleable iron headstocks and Matchless front forks; some models had scrambler springs with no buffers. These machines are dangerous if the factory's recommendation is ignored and they are ridden on the road without the buffer springs. One machine was tested the hard way by racing in the desert, the other was brought to Plumstead for evaluation prior to production.

This P11, as it was to be known (or sometimes Cheetah 45 in America where 750 cc = 45 cubes) was an export machine, though a few found their way onto the home market; but they had some interesting effects on current and future Nortons. All the series had coil ignition and twin Concentric carburettors. They inherited the Matchless aggressive styling, with beautiful minimal G85 competition 2.2 gallon alloy petrol tanks topping minimal cycle parts, high level or upswept exhausts, chopped off mudguards, abbreviated side panel and oil tank, short seats and chainguard and fat tyres. All this may have been impractical for Britain but it was to have a direct effect on the Commando concept and styling, the similarities being particularly apparent between the last and most road-oriented of these models, the 1969 P11A Ranger, and the 750SS and Roadster versions of the Commando.

With the P11 the initial emphasis was on specialist competition, and the big twins ruled in desert racing for two years or more, taking the 'No 1' plate in the Mojave. Initially the former

Atlas scrambler, the N15CS, took over as the dual-purpose road machine, adopting Norton silencers and extended Roadholder forks for 1967. The factory didn't much like the P11s, which were extremely difficult to marry up. There were many separate engine mounting spacers, resulting in the danger of parts loosening if not really firmly tightened up. If the spacers were not positioned correctly, chain alignments would not be true, and this could damage chaincases etc. If incorrectly positioned the propstand lug could damage the thin-walled 531 frame. Criticism of the bikes that came into press hands over here tended to be inappropriate, centering on weaving at speed on the road, vibration, and 'handling not to Featherbed standards'. With their light weight at 381 lb they were capable of 110 mph on the road, but their intended arena was the rough—where the ground clearance of a Featherbed Atlas was inadequate and the looped frame could bend

Left *Hunky—1965 Norton 750 Atlas.*

Another shot of the US-only 1964 Atlas scrambler.

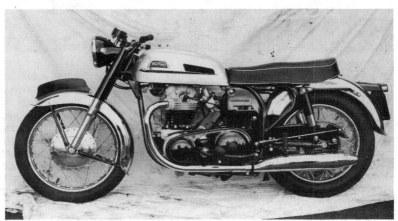

Classic lines of this 1967 Norton Atlas talk speed.

Hybrid. Norton N15CS, taking-over the street scrambler slot for 1967 with modified Atlas engine in Matchless cycle parts.

Peter Pykett, now ace singles restorer, looks distinctly dubious about shoe-horning Atlas engine into G85's 531 frame to make a P11.

Right *When is a Matchless not a Norton? Marketing the N15CS and P11 could get complicated.*

under the pounding. They were so handsome with their candy apple red tanks and panels, and in America and Canada, as one dealer wrote, 'most guys used the scramblers as road bikes, and enjoyed blasting along the highways with them. They vibrated like hell and didn't last long—but many preferred the leaner styling of these Norton-Matchless scramblers.' Even if the vibration shook their lighting systems off and split their seats and oil tanks, they did look the business. The series ended in 1969.

Back in Blighty in mid-1967 the 650SS and the Atlas were modified in mid-season to accept Concentric carburettors and coil ignition. A back-up capacitor system, developed by Lucas for the ISDT, enabled machines to be run, including their lights, without a battery. Then in September 1967 the Commando was unveiled and the writing was on the wall for the traditional twins; unified production of the one model was to be the direction for Norton-Villiers, and the survival of the other remaining models would be pretty much tied to the life of Plumstead, now running down under a compulsory purchase order.

Atlas production ceased in January 1968 though the model was catalogued for that year, as was the 650SS, both now with seat humps at the rear. In September 1968 the remaining Featherbed model became the 47 bhp Mercury with a single Amal Concentric carburettor mounted on a steeply angled manifold which reduced a 20 degree downdraught angle at the head flange to 15 degrees at the carburettor itself. No rev-counter was fitted and the light switch was placed alongside the speedometer. The seat was the humped one, there were side reflectors front and rear in line with US legislation, and the handlebar, lowish and pulled back but quite wide, was a compromise between the Ranger's and the straights. Though stainless steel ones were optional, mudguards were painted Atlantic blue, as was the chaincase, oil tank and battery covers, with the tank silver. Billed as a cost-cutting exercise, this may have been true for the company but not for the customer, as the Mercury was £10 dearer than the preceding 650SS with its higher level of equipment. From 1970 they were offered with as-standard chromed guards and a rev counter to match the speedometer, and this pleasant roadster was the final Featherbed

model, the last one being made in February 1970.

The respective merits of the Commando against the Dominators and Atlas would be hotly disputed. What cannot be denied is that in certain important areas of the motor cycle experience, steering, roadholding and performance married to flexibility, Norton had set a standard in the Featherbed roadsters that could fairly claim to be the ultimate for roadsters of its day. Today the good commonality of parts, extending to the improvement of braking with a Commando TLS front brake for any Featherbed model, is attractive, though there are some tricky areas currently—pistons, Atlas crankcases and 'laid-down' gearbox spares are all hard to come by. But given their obvious qualities, it is strange that today, while sought after, they do not always command the prices of some other less suitable but more flamboyant and assertive machines. Perhaps that is the key; with their minimal styling, the twins were in the Norton tradition of unassuming, solid worth; unlike a Rocket Gold Star, say, or the Bonnevilles of the '60s, the slimline machines in particular didn't *look* that special. But they were.

Norton: The Dominator and Atlas Twins—production dates and specifications

Production dates
Model 7—1949–56
88—1951–63
88 De-Luxe (faired)—1960–62
88SS—1961–66
77—1956–58
99—1956–62
99 De-Luxe—1960–62
99SS—1961–62
N15 Nomad 600—1958
650 (UK)—1962–63
650 De-Luxe—1962
650SS—1962–68
Atlas (UK)—1964–68
N15CS 'N' Atlas scrambler—1963–66
N15CS Street scrambler—1967–68
P11—1967
P11A—1968
P11A Ranger—1969
Mercury—1968–70

Specifications
Model 7/88/88 De-Luxe/88SS
Capacity, bore and stroke—497 cc (66 × 72.6 mm)
Type—ohv twin
Ignition—(Model 7, 88SS, 1962–66; 88 1951–57)
magneto, (88, 1958–63; 88SS 1961; 88 De-Luxe
[faired]) coil
Weight—Model 7 (1951) 413 lb, 88 (1952) 380 lb,
88 De-Luxe (1960) 395 lb, 88SS (1961) 390 lb

77/99/N15 Nomad/99 De-Luxe/99SS
Capacity, bore and stroke—596 cc (68 × 82 mm)
Type—ohv twin
Ignition—(77, Nomad, 99 1956–57) Magneto, (99,
1958–62; 99 De-Luxe, 99SS) Coil
Weight—77 (1957) 400 lb, 99 (1956) 395 lb, 99
De-Luxe (1960) 400 lb, 99SS (1961) 400 lb approx

650/650 De-Luxe/650SS/Mercury
Capacity, bore and stroke—646 cc (68 × 89 mm)
Type—ohv twin
Ignition—(650, 650 De-Luxe, 650SS mid-1967–68,
Mercury) coil, (650SS 1962-mid-1967) magneto
Weight—650 (1962) 398 lb, 650 De-Luxe (1962)
405 lb, 650SS (1962) 400 lb, Mercury (1979) 398 lb

Atlas/N15CS'N'/N15CS/P11/P11A/P11A Ranger
Capacity, bore and stroke—745 cc (73 × 89 mm)
Type—ohv twin
Ignition—(Atlas 1964-mid 1967, N15CS'N')
Magneto, (Atlas mid-1967–68, N15CS, P11,
P11A, Ranger) Coil
Weight—(Atlas 1966) 410 lb

Norton: The Model 7/88/99/77/650/Atlas—annual development and modifications

1951
For Model 7:
1 New front brake shoe plate, still 7 in but an alloy die-casting of greater rigidity.
2 In mid-1951 due to a nickel shortage, petrol tank finish from chrome becomes all silver painted, with panels as previously. Some wheel rims all silver, with red lining.

1952
For Model 7:
1 Timing cover acquires small oval Norton badge as on export-only 88.

1953
For Model 7, 88:
1 Improved rocker-box lubrication. Spring-loaded ball valve arranged in the oil return line to ensure adequate supply of oil to rocker gear.
2 Pear-shaped silencers adopted.
3 Lucas Diacon stop-and-tail lamp fitted.
For 88:
4 Front mudguard no longer fitted to sprung part of fork.
5 Thin chequered knee-grips (with no Norton logo) for petrol tank. Tank capacity increases from 3.5 to 3.75 gallons.
6 Handlebars rubber mounted.
7 3.25 × 19 in front tyre becomes 3.00 × 19 in.
8 Gear ratios now as Model 7.
For Model 7:
9 Pillion footrests as standard.
10 Dual-seat as standard.
11 3.00 × 21 in front wheel becomes 3.25 × 19 in, 3.50 × 20 in rear wheel becomes 3.50 × 19 in.
12 Petrol tanks chrome plated. All wheels chromed and painted.
13 New pivoted fork rear frame (for details see text).
14 New wide and deeply valanced rear mudguard with hinged rear piece.
15 New shape toolbox.
16 Headlamp with underslung pilot light.
17 Smaller oil tank, capacity reduced from 6 to 4 pints.
18 Oil pressure gauge in tank top left no longer fitted.

1954
For Model 7, 88:
1 8 in front brake with 25 per cent increase in lining area.
2 Oil tank capacity reduced from 7 to 4.5 pints.

3 Petrol tank capacity 3.5 gallons.

1955
For Model 7, 88:
1 Alloy cylinder head; compression ratio increases from 6.7:1 to 6.8:1.
2 Amal Monobloc 376 carburettors fitted.
3 Boxed-in number plate with rear reflectors.
4 Alloy fork sliders' lower end polished not enamelled.
5 Rear suspension units of the two models become similar, and with three-position adjustment.
6 New screw-on plastic tank badges, red 'Norton' insignia on a silver letter 'N' backed with quadrant design, black and lined clear.
For Model 7:
8 Handlebar with no forward sweep outboard of the clamp, just up and back, as 88.
9 Horn-button built into right hand of bar, as 88.
10 New front number plate shape.
11 New dual-seat with passenger portion outlined obliquely.
12 Knee-grips modified to 88 type but (as 88 this year) with 'Norton' name.
For 88:
13 Circular, thin pancake type air cleaner now standard.
14 Rear sub-frame altered from bolted-up type to larger diameter tubes now welded to main-frame tubes.
15 Model 7's larger rear mudguard now fitted.
16 Full-width light alloy hubs with integral spoke flanges and cooling ribs featured front and rear. Rear wheel still qd, with three holes covered by rubber plugs giving access to wheel-securing nuts.
17 Engine cut-out button shifted from handlebar to toolbox as on Model 7.
18 Knee-grips now with 'Norton' name.

1956
For 88, and new 99:
1 Restyled oil tank and matching tool/battery box both with three horizontal ribs, with pressed steel plate running transversely across their forward ends.
For 88, new 99 and new 77:
2 Breather pipe from oil tank lubricates rear chain.
3 Cover plate on alloy full width hubs polished to match brake-plate.
4 Softer coil springs for telescopic forks.
5 New headlamp shell with panel on top, no underslung pilot light. Ammeter, speedometer and light-switch recessed into panel. Fork top area modified to accommodate.

6 Rear pivoted-fork ends, formerly trapped and slotted, now a forged steel lug.
7 Speedometer drive gearbox mounted with cable running from below wheel spindle.
8 Armstrong rear units with knurled lower spring cover.
9 Daytona camshaft fitted.
10 New style timing cover with miniature Norton badge replacing previous name plate.
11 Lucas dynamo changes from E3H (with lubricator) to E3L (requiring no lubrication).
For 88:
12 Sweep of exhaust pipe altered.
For all:
13 May: Change to AMC gearbox (for details see text). Klinger Ferodo friction material used in clutch.

1957
For 88, 99, 77:
1 Redesigned cylinder head with more finning between the exhaust ports.
2 Pushrods changed from steel tubing to light alloy with hardened steel ends.
3 Cigar-shaped cylindrical silencers with no tail pipes.
4 Petrol tanks (88, 99 are 3½ gallon, 77 is 3 gallon) painted not chromed, with screw-on chrome panels, plastic-backed, edged with black plastic beading, containing tank badge and smaller knee-grips with no 'Norton' name. Front edge of tank comes further forward, rear blended more closely with seat.
5 New headlamp shell (Lucas MCH61) with speedometer, ammeter, light switch recessed directly into it.
6 Rear brake control and stop-light switch tidied up, with brake pedal return spring now concealed.
7 Footrests no longer flat built-up type but conventional with unmarked round-section rubbers.
8 Handlebar grips changed from rubber to plastic.
9 Air filter optional.
10 Rear suspension units now Girlings.
11 Lip at rear of mudguard less pronounced, rear reflectors no longer fitted.
12 Lucas dynamo with more shapely end cover.
13 Copper rocker feed pipes now feature a short length of plastic non-reinforced pipe interposed in its length.
For 88, 99:
14 New lighter cast-aluminium full-width front hub, with cast-in brake liner and new backplate with forged cam lever in place of previous pressing, and shoeplate restyled and now fitting inside open end of hub.

15 New shape rear chainguard.
16 On lower right side of frame, sheet steel fairing bolted to the gusset plate to close the gap behind the gearbox.

1958
For 88, 99:
1 Lucas RM15 alternator fitted behind altered chaincase, rectifier under tool tray, coil under tank rear, Lucas 18D-2 distributor with points, auto-advance and condenser mounted behind cylinder in position of old magneto and chain driven in the same way. Combined light and ignition switch in headlamp. Cut-out button moves to handlebar.
2 During year, wheel rims become all chrome-plated.
3 Full rear chaincase optional.
4 From May: Twin carburettors and splayed manifolds became optional.

1959
For 88, 99:
1 New camshaft with quietening ramps.
2 Inlet and exhaust valves become stellite-tipped.
3 Larger diameter inlet valves become optional, as do polished ports.
4 Higher compression pistons (9:1 for 88, 8.2:1 for 99) optional.
5 Bolt at rear of petrol tank for tensioning tank retaining strap modified to accommodate a short coil spring under its lead so that the bolt ran out of thread before it was overtightened.
6 Sidecar options become available in mid-1959; heavy duty form springs, stiffer rear units plus special strengthened fork crown requiring steering damper with two friction discs which centred on a large diameter boss on the underside of the crown. Lowered gearing offered via seventeen-tooth engine sprocket for 88, eighteen-tooth for 99.

1960
For 88, 99:
1 Slimline frame, 3.62 gallon petrol tank with two bolt and rubber band fixing from beneath, new design dual-seat located by pegs at front/spring clips at rear (for frame details see text). Rear sub-frame changed from triangular to tubular loops.
2 99 engine sprocket teeth reduced from 21 to 20, 88 from 20 to 19. Top and third gear brought closer together.
3 Roadholders slightly redesigned, intervals between draining oil increased from 5,000 to 10,000 miles.
4 New one-section rear mudguard with no detachable rear portion. Both mudguards are of deeper section.
5 Larger inlet valve as standard, with redesigned porting in the cylinder head and a new inlet manifold for the single carburettor, with stud centres widened from 1½ in to 1⅝ in, head identified by a milled-off cast cross on the side of the rocker box between the rocker spindle retaining plates. Head has additional finning.
6 Standard compression raised to 8.1 for 88, 7.6:1 for 99.
7 New shorter and flatter handlebars optional.
8 New pattern more cylindrical absorption silencers.
9 Chrome-plated zinc-alloy diecast spiked badge containing narrow knee-grip.
10 Coil mounting moves from tank rail to transverse position on the frame cross-tube at rear of petrol tank.
For 88 De-Luxe, 99 De-Luxe:
11 Rear fairing (for details see text). Central oil tank of 4.5 pint capacity.

1961
For 88, 99:
1 Standard compression raised to 8.5:1 for 88, 8.25:1 for 99.
2 Rear fixing for dual-seat now by Dzuz fastener.
3 Chromed mudguards an optional extra.
4 Silencers revert to cigar shape with raised upper portion.
5 In April, 88SS and 99SS versions: twin carburettors, ports opened out, polished ports and combustion chambers, selective assembly of pistons, Manxman-type SS camshaft and flat-based cam followers, two-rate valve springs, hollow barrel-shaped light alloy pushrods. Siamezed exhaust system optional at no extra charge. Flat bars and ball-ended levers, extra strong clutch springs, for 99 optional alternative 21-tooth engine sprocket and for 88, 9.1 pistons; for both, optional rear-sets and rev-counter; if latter was fitted, larger oil pressure relief valve with fine mesh filter on inner end (this was a reversion to the earlier valve).

1962
For 88, 99, 88 De-Luxe, 99 De-Luxe, 88SS, 99SS:
1 From engine no 103749, rotary timed breather adopted as on 650, with port position in rotary valve altered in relation to driving dogs from previous engines. Surplus oil vapour from breather now assisting lubrication of rear chain. Direct substitute for previous type.
For 88SS:
2 Ignition by K2FC magneto as on 650SS, in conjunction with lower output alternator.

Rolling thunder. A 750 Atlas on the road in 1967.

3 Avon Grand Prix rear tyre as on 650SS.
4 Downdraught head for twin Amal 376 Monoblocs as on 650SS.
5 Strengthened crankshaft, by use of smaller (⅝ in compared to previous ⅞ in approx) bore in the crankpin.
6 Siameze exhaust as standard, twin exhaust optional.
7 Compression raised to 9.45:1.
For all twins:
8 Alternator changes from Lucas RM15 to Lucas RM19.
For 650SS:
9 4.00 × 18 in rear wheel and 3.50 × 19 in front wheel optional plus folding kickstart, chromed mudguards, rev-counter, rear chaincase.

1964
For 88SS, 650SS, Atlas:
1 12 volt electrics with two ultra-lightweight Lucas MKZ 9E-2 batteries in series.
2 Chromed mudguards now standard.
3 Front forks widened with centres increased from 7 in to 7⅜ in to accept larger tyre for USA. Wider crowns feature steering lock in top, and AMC-type steering damper.
4 Larger rear number plate.

1965
For all twins (from engine no 111379):
1 Rear chain altered to heavier ⅝ × ⅜ in dimensions.

2 Adjuster hole in primary chaincase for clutch pushrod.
3 Timing cover modified for rev-counter drive gearbox to permit vertical take-off for drive cable.
4 Welded in cross-tube in frame.
(From engine no 114870):
5 Spigots on top of block and matching recesses in cylinder head removed; copper-asbestos head gasket replaces metallized asbestos one. This permitted more support for outer ends of rocker spindles in cylinder head casting. (To convert earlier wide rockers, ¼ in should be ground off the outside of each boss.)

1966
For 650SS, Atlas:
1 From engine no 116372, six-start worm drive doubled oil pump delivery. Bleed holes in con-rods, larger feed pipe and enlarged internal oilways, pressure feed to rockers, rocker spindles now plain and ¼ in narrower. Wellworthy 'Duaflex' five-piece oil control piston rings. Rocker feed pipes revert to solid metal tubing, but not copper.
(From engine no 116966):
2 Left and right hand Monoblocs fitted, instead of a right-hand one with a chopped-off float chamber.
(From engine no 118752):
3 Nyloc nuts on stator fixing studs.

A last beauty; the 650SS for 1968. One hundred per cent thoroughbred sports motor cycle.

For Atlas:
4 Front tyre changes from 3.25 × 19 in to 3.00 × 19 in.
For 650SS:
(From engine no 111920):
5 Con-rods strengthened.

1967
For 650SS:
1 Paired speedometer and rev-counter mounted on a chromed bracket across the fork top yoke.
For 650SS and Atlas:
2 Force fit studs in stator housing.
For 650SS and Atlas:
(From engine no 121307):
3 Coil ignition incorporating twin contact breakers and Lucas capacitor system adopted.
4 Amal Concentric carburettors fitted.

1968
For 650SS and Atlas:
1 Rear hump to dual-seat.
For 650SS:
2 January, from engine no 125871. Pushrods shortened by 0.1 in and valve stems lengthened by the same amount.

1970
For Mercury
1 Chromed mudguards and rev-counter as standard.

Norton: The Commando 750 Fastback/'R' type/'S' type/Roadster/ Hi-Rider/Interstate and 850 Roadster/Hi-Rider/John Player Norton/Interstate

The joke in *Roadholder*, the magazine of the Norton Owners' Club, went something like this:

First Norton rider: 'But why aren't Commandos *real* Nortons?'
Second Norton rider: 'Because they're faster!'

Since it's now become a cliche that most Commandos had a top speed very little faster than a good 650SS, and some considerably less, the quip needs a little amplifying. Some Commandos, sometimes, did top 120 mph but the point in question is not one-way one-off runs, but high average road speeds over distance. Part of it was the comfort that the Isolastic system afforded, part the larger capacity engines giving more speed less busily. The latter could be said to apply to the Atlas, but Norton specialist dealer and long-time

racer Mick Hemmings in *Classic Bike* recently confirmed that, for the ultimate test of the track, the Commando has the greater potential.

'Just why a Commando goes that much better than an Atlas is hard to say—it just does. It certainly breathes better, has shorter pushrods and is probably more oil-tight and reliable.' (But he did add 'There's not much in it.')

In case this sounds like special pleading, I should say here that I have owned two 750 Commandos and the second one was my main bike for several years. A good friend has also owned two of them. Despite the problems mentioned in the Norton history section and amplified from here on in, neither of us experienced major grief, although my own 750 was progressively and sometimes quite expensively modified to eliminate as many of the troubles as possible when, or preferably before, they arose. So I thought that I would begin this section, which at times will read like nothing but a catalogue of disasters, by reaffirming that within certain limits the Commando can be a reliable and satisfying *roadster*, and that most of the problems do have solutions which the company eventually discovered. The limits in question are principally the handling of the Isolastic frame at speeds over 90 mph, and to a lesser extent the machine's performance in town. If either of those areas are particularly important to you, I should say the Commando is not recommended. But if you look for a good all-rounder in the British tradition, that can be made distinctly practical for today's road conditions, then Norton's last parallel twin deserves practical consideration. I should also from the first acknowledge the debt this section owes to the excellent NOC *Commando Service Notes* and their *Mk III Supplement*, which realistically and in greater detail than this book can, sorts out the pitfalls of Commando ownership. Tim Stevens, Al Osborne and John Hudson did a good job.

In 1967 when the first one was shown, it was a sensation. 'No new model introduced in the past decade,' wrote tester David Dixon, 'has made such a big impact as the Norton Commando.' During the decade British parallel twin vibration had begun to be seen as a disqualifier, and the Commando's revolutionary frame seemed to provide an answer. Getting in before the Honda 750 fours; impressing with its capacity as a 750 version of the parallel twin seen sparsely up to now on the Atlas, rivalled only by the big Royal Enfields and more than five years in advance of Triumph; embodying enough traditional features in terms of the engine and cycle parts to reassure

Right *September 1967 and the all-silver Commando (with orange seat and green blobs) bursts on an unsuspecting world.*

Below right *Early 750 Commando engine—modified and tilted Atlas. Note points behind cylinder, early airbox.*

enthusiasts, yet with the promise of a breakthrough in frame technology as potentially revolutionary as the Mini, and with a style that emphasized all this without going completely over the top—how could the new Norton fail to impress?

The genesis of the model will be found described in the Norton history section, so we will start here with a consideration of the first production versions. Powerplant was a modified Atlas; inclined forward in the frame, the engine had undergone some important changes. The 746 cc dimensions remained constant at 73×89 mm, but compression had been increased from 7.6:1 to 8.7:1 by the use of new pistons. Lubrication for the rockers was by a feed from the rear of the timing cover, from the same point as used on the early Model 7 oil pressure gauge, and at pump feed pressures. The engine breather had been on the Atlas since engine no 103749. It was timed and ported by means of a rotary disc with cutaway segment, driven by the camshaft and backed with a light spring, mating with a similar stationary disc fitted behind the left crankshaft bush in the crankcase. An elbow with flexible pipe from the left crankcase lead to the oil tank, and the oil tank filter was connected with the air filter backplate. Electrics were 12 volt, ignition was by coil, incorporating the Lucas capacitor system in parallel for both running and lights without battery if required, but still with the distributor mounted behind the cylinder. The Commando alternator was a big RM21 job and the ignition switch was down in front of the left-hand side panel, with the zener diode beneath it. The twin carburettors on their downdraught alloy manifold linked by a balance tube were 930 Amal Concentrics.

The Commando carburettors were coupled to a large capacity still air chamber and induction

silencer, equipped with a paper element filter. The gearbox was closer to the crankcase, and on the drive side the triplex primary chain which supplanted the Atlas single strand item lay behind an alloy primary chaincase; this had also been true of the versions of the Atlas engine used to create the Matchless G15 variants and P11 desert sleds.

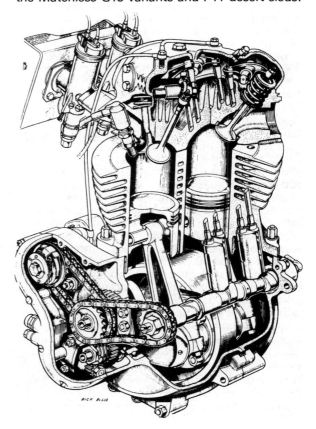

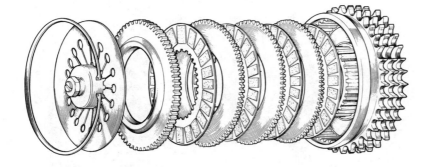

Detail of the diaphragm clutch.

The handsome Commando case was fastened not like the latter by screws around its edge, but by a single central fixing nut. The case, which embodied inspection caps for clutch and primary chain, was sealed around the edges by a sealing band and was generally more oiltight than its single bolt pressed-steel predecessors; unless of course, it was overtightened, or the wrong number of washers were fitted over the central bolt before the inner case was fitted. Care had to be taken not to overfill it with oil, and since the level plug was to prove not strictly accurate, a measured ¼ pint was the best method.

Between the launch at the Show in September 1967, and production beginning in April 1968, there was some development, and this included the conversion by car experts Laycock de Normanville to an up-to-date four-plate diaphragm clutch, so called because pressure was not by the conventional Norton three springs but by a single big diaphragm spring, retained by a circlip around the outside of the extra thick outer plate. A journal ball bearing rather than a row of fifteen caged rollers was used to support the drum, and both plain steel driving plates and Ferodo bonded driven plates had involute splines, rather than simple tongues, to key them for the drum and hub respectively. Clutch withdrawal was by a conventional rod passing through the gearbox mainshaft and bearing on a hardened screw, which was carried in a cup anchored to the middle of the diaphragm. The rod could be a weak point, and the early clutch until 1973 could be rather abrupt in its uptake. The early friction 'postage stamp' inserts were not clever, and were replaced by solid asbestos Ferodo plates in mid-1969, and finally by sintered bronze. The clutch could slip if the early plates became oil-soaked or worn, and all clutches slipped if the chaincase was overfilled. They also sometimes sheared off the two steel pins holding the first drive plate to the drum, and the centre bearings were known to

wear out, indicating this by a low rumbling/grinding noise when the clutch was disengaged. For the rider the clutches could often be distinguished by extreme stiffness at the lever; 1973 mods to its geometry, careful attention to cable run, lubrication and adjustment, and making sure the operating lever in the gearbox was correctly aligned to permit a straight pull, could all help. The clutch's extra strength was very necessary for the Commando engine's initial claimed 56 bhp output, and it usually worked adequately. Other features introduced on the engine between launch and production included provision for timing via a screwed plug on the alternator bulge and timing marks.

But the Commando's big feature was the Isolastic frame. On previous motorcycles individual components had been rubber-mounted, but not since the low-output Sunbeam S7 and Villiers motors had a whole engine/gearbox been cushioned in this way and the Commando went further; not just the engine and transmission but the rear wheel and swinging arm were effectively isolated from the rider above about 2,500 rpm by their rubber anti-vibration mounts. The frame itself consisted of a massive 2¼ in diameter × 16 gauge main spine member braced to the steering head, with a 1 in × 16 gauge duplex cradle looping under the engine and rising to points beneath the seat. Struts from the top tube formed a triangulated structure with the rear members of the cradle loop. All stresses were designed to be taken by the top tube and rear triangulations; the cradle was said to be an engine mounting convenience.

But the genuinely unusual feature was that the rear fork was not pivoted from the frame at all. The pivot was carried by the engine plates; and the engine gearbox and rear fork formed an independent sub-assembly carried at front and rear in outsize rubber mountings with a headsteady and also with insulating rubbers

Right *New frame. Commando spine frame (Mk II—judiciously strengthened at steering head, after early breakages).*

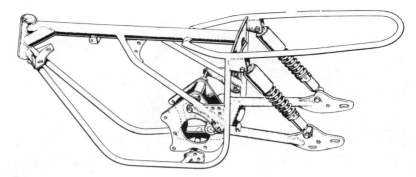

Below right *Early Commandos under construction at Woolwich in May 1968.*

between the sideplates and frame tube thus completing a triangulated mounting set-up and controlling lateral movement of the engine in the frame. The rear mounting, with three Metalastik bonded and two buffer rubbers, was designed to provide maximum support particularly to the swinging arm and rear wheel, while isolating the power unit from the frame; the front mounting, with two bonded and two buffer rubbers, controlled the degree of movement of the engine on the rear mounting, and hence had more flexibility than the latter. These mountings were similar in principle to Silentbloc type rear pivot mountings, but they were considerably larger in diameter and they incorporated plastic thrust washers to permit side play to be kept within strict limits. The degree of side play was controlled by shims. By the time production began, these patented mountings were protected at their ends by plastic gaiters.

These early pre-1970 examples included steel sleeves which were often very difficult to remove. This was important because the Isolastic mountings, as they were known, had to be checked for end play every 3,000 miles and shimmed in about every 5,000 miles, a piece of maintenance that was both tedious and vital; because since the swinging arm was part of the system, handling could be and was adversely affected if the mounts got too loose. While not actually difficult, shimming was quite a time-consuming procedure, and marginally more so after 1970 when the centre stand was bolted directly to the rear engine plate. In retrospect this system is even more irritating since we now know that the vernier system (with threaded adjusters instead of shims) which was finally fitted on the Mk III 850, had been designed by Bernard Hooper during the prototype stage but rejected on grounds of expense. Earlier mountings can now be replaced with the Mk III variety modified to suit, which then makes the maintenance chore a

much shorter one. The bronze-impregnated PTFE thrust washers which eventually replaced the plain yellow polyurethane kind, are also advised as replacements. The Mk III rubber end covers can similarly replace the previous ones which the NOC *Notes* caustically refer to as 'a loose-fitting plastic tube so that the rain and grit which get in cannot get out again.' One of Wolverhampton's lapses was the failure to apply, or recommend applying grease on the shim caps and thrust washers; John Hudson found that when this was done, there was never any sign of perished rubbers.

In addition to the inconvenience in service, the major question-mark over the Isolastic system came in terms of its possible effect on high speed

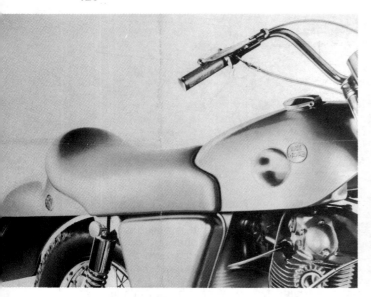

handling. The swinging arm bearing had been made part of the rear engine plate assembly for sound engineering reasons—to avoid the problems of variation in chain tension and chain alignment which would have been particularly prominent in a long-stroke parallel twin if engine and transmission but not swinging arm had been rubber mounted. The tug of the rear chain could also have pulled the engine-gearbox assembly back hard against the mounting bushes and cancelled their effect. But making the swinging arm subject to the variations of the mountings brought its own pitfalls, and this was particularly evident with the earlier type of headsteady as found on the 750, a single piece pressing with an S-bend in the middle which could break straight across; the later box-section 850 headsteady should be substituted, or the Mk III easier-to-adjust spring-loaded type (though I've also had one of those break and John Hudson has no high opinion of them). For the racers Peter Williams substituted a third Isoiastic in place of the headsteady, to help stabilize the engine's lateral location. Commando handling is a rather complicated subject which I shall touch on later, but it's generally accepted that the Isolastic system, while in some ways a breakthrough, and in no way inherently unsafe, did not provide handling of the very highest standard at top speeds.

The spine frame was light at 24 lb, some 10 lb lighter than the Featherbed which the Commando project's team leader, Dr Stefan Bauer, is said to have described as 'bad engineering'. It must

therefore have come as an unpleasant surprise to him when early examples of the Mk I's spine frame broke. Reynolds were to make most of these frames as they had done the Featherbed frame and their development engineer Ken Sprayson had predicted that it would break due to excessive stress concentration from the frame's permanent 'nodding', aggravated by the stiff front forks and an unbalanced front wheel—the break occurring at a welded U-shaped gusset just behind the steering head. Sprayson cured the problem for 1969 by triangulating the bottom of the steering head with a small horizontal bracing tube to a point much further back on the frame spine; from then on the Commando main frames were strong, particularly after 1970 when a transverse strengthening bar was added between the frame loops under the crankcase.

They would fracture at the back, however, if the rear Isolastic mountings were too tight, causing a break where the tube from the seat knobs downwards meet the gussets for the battery carrier—or again if a carrier was fitted at the back without supports to the pillion footrests, causing breaking or bending of the rear-seat loop. Carriers which were overtightened on the top of the rear units could also snap off the damper eye. One other instance of frame trouble, also involving Sprayson, had to do with the examples that were made in Italy. The company established an office in that country and a number of components began to be supplied. According to Sprayson the agent out there obtained a Commando frame and arranged for Verlicchi to

Far left *Flamboyant detailing of the first Commando.*

Left *Action man on an early (now rare) 1968 750 Commando—'The most exciting motorcycle of our age'.*

Right *Early 1969, and the rare 'R' type, plus fastback in the months preceding the 'S' type's arrival.*

produce a replica. The first one was beautiful, and there was a saving of a few pounds on the Reynolds price. Orders were placed around 1973, though Reynolds also continued to produce the frame at the same time. But the tubing of the Italian production version in some instances turned out to be unduly soft, causing the tail end to droop while a passenger and/or heavy luggage was carried. Sprayson says that, ironically, Reynolds made more profit straightening Italian frames than they did making their own!

Back at the beginning, a big part of the Commando's sensational appeal was the styling, with 3.25 fibreglass petrol tank, dual-seat with rear hump, and fibreglass tail fairing (which would lead to the 'Fastback' name), all designed to form a three-piece unit with distinctive, unified horizontal lines, echoed by the silencers. The forward thrust of the inclined engine was repeated, running forward through the angle of the rear suspension, the front edge of the side panels, the downtubes, and the front mudguard stays. The silencers themselves, the alloy mudguard and shrouded Roadholders with a new 8 in TLS front brake were all fairly conventional. But a note of flash was sounded by the elaborate yet solid looking cast-alloy footrest hangers ('the most over-engineered part of the machine'—NOC *Notes*), and the imitation Monza filler cap, chrome headlamp shell, twinned fork top rev-counter and speedometer in chromed cups, and on the 1967 Show model, the Wolf Ohlins-inspired 'N.V.' green blob on the tank (and also on the instrument faces), with a circular 'Norton-Villiers'

badge ahead of it. The finish, silver all over including the frame and engine, topped with an orange seat, was certainly different; and while altered for initial production to a more sober dark green for tail unit and petrol tank (the latter now with Norton disc badge only), with gaitered forks and black frame, barrels and seat, it was still a striking motor cycle.

The early road tests confirmed that it went as well as it looked. Shattering acceleration (0–60 in under five seconds, and 0–100 in 12) was mentioned, and *Motor Cycle*'s Peter Fraser took one to the ISDT in Italy, relishing the beefy power from right low down for storming the passes of the Alps and also the good acceleration from 75 to 100 mph, clocking a top speed of 117 mph. The seat was a little high at 31 in, the centre stand restricted ground clearance a bit and (a perennial problem from now on and not improved by the cable operation necessary because of the frame system), the 7 in rear brake was feeble. Stopping distance was 32 ft from 30 mph. For me in this respect the major irritation is that on its own the back brake won't bring the bike to a halt from *any* speed, which is a nuisance in traffic. But overall impressions were good with the rubber mountings significantly reducing fatigue and the riding position with flat handlebars being reasonable. Though export machines featured a high and wide handlebar, testers in the States were even more enthusiastic and the model was an instant success. Many Commando buffs believe these early 750s to have been smoother to ride than later models, particularly the later Interstates

including the heavy Mk III 850.

Just one version was made in 1968, both production and development centering on Norton-Matchless at Plumstead where standards of finish were still good; some Plumstead-built machines are distinguished by 'P'-suffix and there were not that many of them. Production was troubled from the start; the first eighty bikes off the line were halted when Wally Wyatt successfully appealed to the chairman having realized that they had been fitted by production-hungry staff with the old Bracebridge Street Atlas cylinder head rather than the later item which had had a big hand in boosting bhp from 50 to 59. Total Norton output

for that year appeared to be around 5,000 including some 650SS and P11A models, and most went for export. Aside from the P-suffix, other distinguishing marks were valve covers, footrest supports, gear lever, and kickstart, all sand cast, not polished as later.

The P11A was the inspiration for the next version of the Commando, the S model for 1969 from engine no 131257, with the previous model assuming the Fastback name. As well as styling, there had been some development, with a new type sleeve gear and layshaft pinion tooth form from engine no 128646, late in 1968, and a rear wheel security bolt and, from engine no 129897, the Mk II-type frame, with the headstock bracing tube mentioned above.

But the company's internal divisions and unwillingness to spend money on development were surfacing already. 'Basically, we could do what we liked,' joked Wally Wyatt 'as long as we didn't alter anything.' He said improvements to be made had to be instituted while potential objectors were away from the factory or on holiday; thus were the ignition points transferred from the inaccessible distributor behind the barrels. This meant relocating the rev-counter drive to an integral position at the front of the timing chest (where it was to be the irritating but unimportant source of an oil leak), and reducing the camshaft to drive the points. This work was incorporated on the 1969 Fastback and S models, the Mk II 750s as they were to be known.

Previously, the early 1969 R type was a cross in styling between the P11, the Fastback and the Roadster. 3.00 × 19 in front tyres and narrow

Above left *'S' type exhaust system for 1969.*

Left *The 'S' type. Shiny, Shiny.*

mudguards, gaitered Roadholders and the old style silencers and chainguards were used, and the chrome headlamp shell retained an ammeter as well as the ignition warning light and three-position off-park-main beam toggle light switch. But the 2¼ gallon fibreglass red tank with curly Norton transfer, not badge (though the side panels were still silver), the ribbed ('rolled and pleated' for the US) dual-seat with chromed trim, and the chrome rear mudguard pointed the way forward.

Then from March 1969, at engine no 131257 and engine prefix 20M3S came the Mk II 750 with the points in timing cover behind the polished inspection cap, integral rev-counter drive and sporting styling for the S. However, the Fastback model did not receive the points and rev-counter changes until September 1969 at engine no 133668, presumably when stocks of the old components were used up. The S model had the first unshrouded and polished fork, vulnerable but nice looking and, with chrome wire rim and mountings for the headlamp, high level exhausts sweeping to the left (with the right cylinder pipe higher) and with perforated chrome leg-guards over shallow-angle reverse cone silencers (which with reduced back pressure increased the engine power to 60 bhp) it was a smart looking machine. Compression ratio had by now risen to 9:1 also, but vibration, too, had risen a little, since the silencers were attached to the frame. The ribbed seat acquired a strap, the curly Norton name transfers this time were big and proud on the red, metalflake silver or racing green tank. The name was echoed on the timing cover where it was cast-in, on the horizontal line. These crankcases were also modified at the rear to blank off the previous distributor drive; the primary chaincase was made shallower and the centre stand re-designed to improve cornering ground clearance. The fibreglass side panels were abbreviated and more triangular. They now wore the machine name and capacity transfers, and the left one carried the ignition lock. There was a lot of chrome—for mudguard stays, for the big angled bracket that attached the silencers to a point above the left rear unit, for the extremely abbreviated chainguard with a chopped out portion, and as before around the rim of the front and rear side reflectors which US legislation required. The barrels were silver again, and rocker covers and footrest hangers were polished. Both gear lever and kickstart were chromed. In UK terms, much of this may not have been ultra-practical, but this was the *Easy Rider* era and the S Commando was an absolute magnet to the eye.

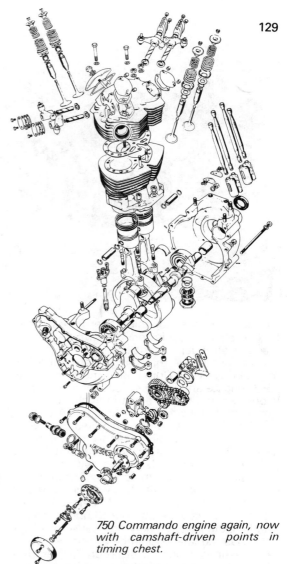

750 Commando engine again, now with camshaft-driven points in timing chest.

High handlebars as always were a limiting factor for speeds over 70, but who cared when you were accelerating into the wind, young, cool, and looking right?

Improvements to the Commando were introduced at will rather than by year, and in May 1969, the 100 lb springs on their rear units were replaced with 126 lb items, although some were to prefer still stronger 150 lb sidecar strength springs. Sidecars, incidentally, were not supposed to be fitted to the Isolastic frame, though I believe this has subsequently been done, for instance by Mundays the Kingston sidecar specialists, though the Isolastics' ability to cope with the side loads a chair would impose, particularly when turning

Right *Bulky British riding gear and skimpy forks, mudguards plus high bars on this 1969 Commando 'S' spell out the contradictions of building for export.*

Far right *1969 Norton Interpol, Neale Shilton's baby, on view to Mods at that year's Brighton show.*

left, is highly questionable. Later fibre clutch friction plates were introduced and the third gear made of stronger material.

This gave a clue that things were not all they might be with the Commando motor as in July 1969, engine and bike production ceased in Woolwich and began again in Wolverhampton in September, (bike assembly being at Andover); the first Wolverhampton engine was 134108. Starting at the top, oil tended to feature strongly; head gaskets could blow and there could be leaks from the rocker spindle covers, with oil running down and back along the cooling fins and looking like a head to barrel leak (this was finally remedied from engine no 203884 in 1972 when copper sealing washers were introduced under the rocker spindle plate bolts). The worst cause of all the leaks was the later incidence of porous cylinder head castings which occurred on 750s around 1971–72, and which there was nothing to do about but either live with or replace.

The engines could smoke from the exhausts due to the familiar Norton problem of the oil draining past the pump into the crankcase. It was always necessary to check the oil level with the engine hot, since if the oil level on a dipstick was taken cold, it looked low; top up, start, and once the oil in the sump circulated, causing smoking from the exhausts, the tank was over-full and the excess oil appeared out of the breather and sometimes over the rear tyre. On the left side the tyre would be spattered from the very over-enthusiastic rear chain oiler, which used a good deal of lubricant and even after a metering device was built into it, produced enough spatter to

decorate a pillion passenger's back. The situation improved with the fitting of a black plastic endpiece to the rear chainguard during 1973, and the option of a rear mudflap shortly afterwards. Blanking off the oiler is the only real answer.

But a smoking exhaust could also be due to worn valve guides to which Commandos were particularly prone, as well as short-life valve seats. One reason for the smoking was that with the inclined engine, oil gathered in little wells around the inlet valve and escaped down the valves in excessive quantities if there was enough clearance for it to do so—which was very often the case due to the worn valve seats. Norton were to get on to this one in early 1972 by changing the pattern of the inlet and the exhaust valve guides and fitting plastic oilseals to the inlet valve, with both exhaust (mid-1972) and inlet valve (early 1973) becoming stellite-tipped. These are identifiable by the fact that they have no number rolled on to them—but some pattern valves of the earlier type don't either! Even after the new guides and seals, it was found that some oil was going down the inside of the guides, while more was trickling down the outside, because they were not a good fit in the head; a partial cure was the use of Loctite when installing them, something Norton was to be advocating at several points throughout the bike. 750 valve guides were thinner than the later 850; boring out to the 850 size and using an 850 guide is recommended by NOC. Exhaust valves hung up and wore out rapidly unless regular tappet checks were observed, especially if the later 'bean can' silencers were fitted. The problem of inlet valve seat wear was to become

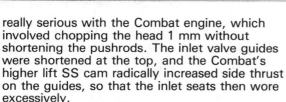

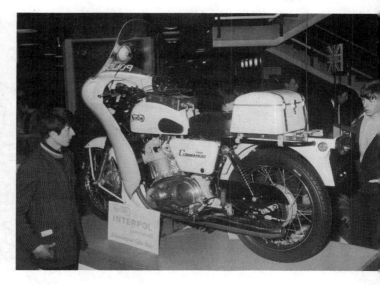

really serious with the Combat engine, which involved chopping the head 1 mm without shortening the pushrods. The inlet valve guides were shortened at the top, and the Combat's higher lift SS cam radically increased side thrust on the guides, so that the inlet seats then wore excessively.

The Commandos also used a lot of oil initially, often 200 miles a pint or less, due to piston ring problems. Since the beginning of 1969, Commandos had fitted a three-piece oil control ring, where the central part was U-shaped in cross section; these were difficult to place in the bore, and not good at oil control. Since the depth of their groove was shallower than that for the oil rings which replaced them, they are not interchangeable with the new type of oil control rings (adopted late in 1971) which are easier to fit and have a circular central cross-section. On my own bike new rings stopped its habit of dumping a pool of oil out on the breather pipe when halted after a long run. It paid to make sure a chrome top rign was fitted, as sometimes two cast rings were supplied.

The pistons themselves could be a problem. All 750 pistons had cast slots adjacent to the gudgeon pin bosses, but earlier ones had a saw-cut which joined these slots through the oil ring groove fore and aft. This weakened the pistons until it was deleted after 1971. According to NOC, the slots themselves were sometimes responsible for the top leaving the piston if the revs were kept up towards 7,000 rpm, the recommended limit. Another notorious Commando production weakness concerned camshafts that had been insufficiently hardened and wore down very

quickly; later camshafts were tuftrided, denoted by an even brownish-grey colour all over the shaft, rather than a bright finish; but inferior shafts have turned up even on the later 850 Mk IIIs. Apparently the problem may have been due to an outside contractor's failure to understand that the shaft's EN32 steel, when Tuftrided, had its original hardness cancelled out by the process and was actually being softened. If replacing, cam followers should also be renewed. The standard Commando 'S' cam was based on the 650SS profile; the one to avoid if possible is the wild 'SS' cam for the Combat specification engine, which caused plenty of problems and required tappet settings of .008 inlet, .010 exhaust. (Incidentally this 'SS' cam is not the same as the Dominator SS item fitted on all Atlas/650SS/88SS and Mercury models; and because of the Commando's cam-driven contact breaker, is not interchangeable with it.)

At the bottom end, with machines that encouraged hard riding with their engine characteristics and image, stress was a factor from the start. Mainbearing life was reportedly not good, 10,000-15,000 miles being not unusual, though no mention of this was made in a 1969 *Riders Report*, and many examples, especially if not thrashed, could and did settle down to amass impressively high mileages. But sometimes the stress had its effect, and if the crank was reground, extreme care had to be taken that the crankpins were accurately radiused, or crankshafts would break; this sometimes happened on new machines also for that reason, though John Hudson never experienced this, and

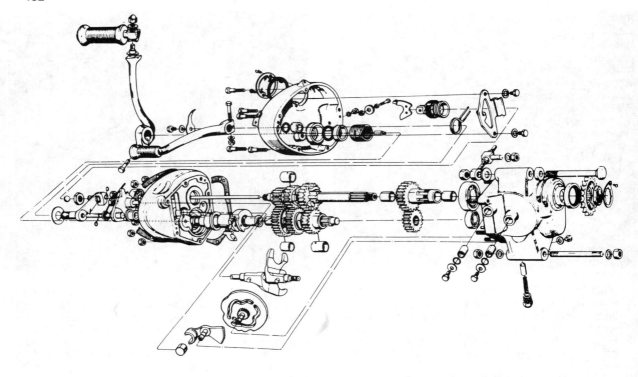

Above *This could be an over-stressed item. AMC gearbox designed for 30 BHP output in a 60 BHP world.*

Left *Next step forward. First Commando Roadster, for 1970.*

believes that the crank itself was a sound design. Later bottom end problems will be dealt with in place.

Clutch problems have been mentioned, and another weak point was the gearbox, which though an excellent design had after all been laid down with 30 bhp outputs in mind. Peter Williams' problems on the JPN production racers highlighted the affliction; the most frequent was teeth stripping off the layshaft pinion that meshed with the sleeve gear. This was the pinion that carried the driving load in all gears except top, and the problem resulted from the flexure of the gearbox mainshaft under full engine torque. On the road bikes the layshaft bearing was usually the first thing to go, especially since Portuguese SKF bearings were employed. Replacement with an RHP 117 bearing or needle roller bearing conversion is the answer here. Around 1974 there was another little quality control lapse and some inadequately hardened clusters got through into production. Sleeve gear bushes could work loose—caught in time, this could be fixed with Loctite. The gearbox/mainshaft oil seals could fail, evidenced by oil weeping at the crankcase to chaincase joint. The kickstart pawls, as ever on the AMC box, broke; after 1971, steel pawls, identified by an 'M' on the side, were fitted and should be used as a replacement. Various sizes of kickstart were used, and fouling the pipes is not unknown; the later 850 kickstarter from engine no 309600 is 1 in longer and helps with the rather healthy kick required to start a Commando.

The Lucas electrical equipment's star weak point was the auto-advance unit on the 6CA points. The advance spring anchorages consisted of a tiny tag secured by a spot-weld, and the whole setup was just not strong enough; the cam-spindle would wear out, the return springs would cut through their posts, the points gap became variable and it would jam on full advance, which was to be particularly disastrous when the high compression Combat engines were introduced. The unit was changed for the stronger 10 CA unit for 1973, but it was still afflicted by the fact that drive was from the camshaft. This was driven as ever by chain, and adjusting it for operation was a complicated servicing process involving removing points and complete timing cover, fitting a slave cover cut away for access, setting the tensioner slipper while holding the camshaft to put the slack in the top run, and then reassembling. If this wasn't done, particularly with the wild SS cams, the thrashing chain pulled the ignition timing about. The answer today is the improved Lucas RITA electronic ignition. Other

Above *1970 Commando production racer, one of an initial batch of fifty.*

Below *Fastback Mk II in late 1970 with roadster pipes.*

electrical trouble spots originally were poor quality HT leads, and a complicated wiring harness since it was in common with the Interpol Police Nortons with their extra equipment.

For 1970 the isolastics changed; previously they had featured steel sleeves which were often very difficult to remove. For this year and from then on, bonded mounting bushes were fitted which were lubricated at the time of assembly. Also the next styling step was taken with the introduction of the Roadster, virtually an S-model with stylish low-level but upswept reverse cone silencers and an optional lower handlebar, a handsome and trendy format with several metalflake colour schemes. It was not until the following year that it would adopt the classic black and gold lining that quite seduced many young riders, me included, who weren't sure about the allusion to (or cribbing from) Velocette/Vincent/Matchless that the finish involved, but loved the classical impression which was in both cahoots with and in contrast to the Roadster's rather brutal styling.

In mid-1970 the Combat engine option was offered for the first time, with better breathing, a 10:1 compression ratio and polished internals. Tuning kits devised in conjunction with Paul Dunstall had been offered from early on, and production racers with larger carbs, hot cam and a cast-iron front disc brake on a Campagnola hub were also available, but this was a road-oriented hot motor which claimed a 68 bhp output. It was later to be big trouble for the company, because it exacerbated all the engine's existing weak spots.

From April 1970 and engine no 139571, the Fastback received the Roadster's upswept silencers and in this form became known as the Fastback Mk II: this rather confusingly muddies the issue of the 'Marks' for the 750 bikes as a whole, which I will continue to record. Already in

February 1970 a 4 gallon tank in steel rather than fibreglass, made by Homers of Birmingham like the Interpol tanks, had become a Fastback option, creating the LR (Long Range) model for '70 and '71 only. As on the other Commandos in 1970, polished hangers and chromed kickstart and gear pedals were fitted, and while it retained fork top covers, these too were chromed. The LR's seat lost its 'ears'.

For 1971 Commando variations of what were, since engine no 141783, the Mk III 750s, proliferated (though that year's Roadster, again confusingly, was known as Mk II). These machines all fitted a revised front fork, redesigned qd rear wheel, a revised Lucas electrical system and handlebar switches, and the centre-stand attached to the engine. The forks were still Roadholders with oval section fork sliders and a fork tube length of 23.161 in. All top tubes were plated and ungaitered, and a larger (4.10 × 19 in) section front tyre was fitted (TT 100s were standard at this time), necessitating a wider mudguard. The fork yokes changed, with a reduction in trail said to be related to racing experience such as the Thruxton 500 win in 1970, so steering head angle was 62 degrees. The steering head bearings altered from adjustable ball journal bearings to the sealed non-adjustable type, and the method of attachment to the frame was now by a steering stem projecting downwards from the upper fork yoke, with a securing nut on the underside of the lower yoke. (Here it can be mentioned that head races were crucial to Commando handling, which up till then had suffered if they were overtightened or pitted.) New chrome-plated shrouds supported the headlamp, and the rear units lost the shrouds on their chromed springs.

The headlamp no longer carried an ammeter,

Left *Variations on the racer theme. A Gus Kuhn racer-ized roadster of 1971.*

Right *The Isolastic system made easy.*

but a two-position toggle switch for park and main beam, the lights themselves being controlled by the ignition switch. There were also three small indicating lights for main-beam indicator, ignition warning light and a winking light for the optional direction indicators (which being Lucas items very often didn't wink, but just stayed on instead). There were more legible figures on the instruments, which still bore the corporate green dot. Facing forward again beneath the left rear of the fuel tank was the rubber covered barrel of what was now a four-position ignition switch; near it there was a luxury touch, a new socket to supply power from the battery for equipment such as an inspection light or shaver. The electrical system was still 12 volt, but the ignition coils were two 6-volt items in circuit with a ballast resistor; this system was designed to maintain consistent voltage through the coils, whatever the state of the battery. The capacitor back-up meant that the machine could be ridden without a battery for cross-country work, and snap connectors under the tank permitted the headlamp to be detached in a few minutes. In a bracket beneath the tank nose were grouped the ignition capacitor, coils, ballast resistor, contact breaker, capacitor pack and ignition light simulator. On my Commando, over the years but not a great mileage, with the exception of the ballast resistor, every one of these Lucas items has malfunctioned and had to be replaced, often more than once. But the capacitor ignition system has got me out of trouble at least once. The handlebar controls were a new Lucas design for that year, with switches which some testers found too short, incorporated in the pivot block. Behind the side panel there was a new battery tray with a quick-action security strap.

The centre-stand now pivoted on the engine mount, not the frame. This improved cornering clearance but that was about the only thing to be said in the stand's favour ('a bad joke'—NOC). It was flimsily mounted, it twisted much too easily, springs had been known to break so it dropped to the road while running, and once misaligned, it bashed the silencers, knocking their internal baffles loose. In addition, with the new arrangement the Isolastics could no longer be checked while the machine was on its stand; bricks, orange boxes, or old oil cans were the order of the day from then on. The quality of the stand itself improved later with the 850 and this could be substituted for the earlier ones. For 1971 the prop stand also tucked in closer, with a wicked curved 4 in extension piece; this long-reach item had originally been fitted on the police models only, but it still lacked the final later refinement of a rubber buffer to stop the clonk when it hit the frame.

The 5-pint oil tank and its rubber mountings had been redesigned; the mountings were always a prime target for fracture from vibration. The tank, behind a fibreglass cover, was redesigned internally. To meet US legislation and to ensure that oil mist from the tank was drawn into the carburettor air filter, the tank had a breather tower with internal baffle plates. Hot oil mist impinged against these and condensed, dropping back into the tank. Seats were restyled with deeper padding, and the chromed chainguards were also new and stronger. At the back end, the qd rear wheel had been redesigned. Previously secured to the brake drum by three studs and nuts, three flat-sided pegs on the brake drum now slid into blind sockets in the hub face, and the assembly merely pulled apart. Clear polyurethane shock

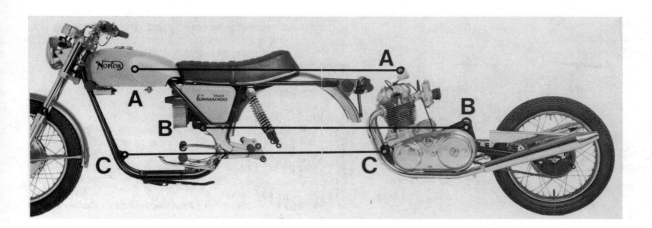

absorbing pads, known for their shape in the trade as 'toffees', were fitted into the hub sockets to promote rear chain life and smoothness, cush-drive at the clutch having gone out with the arrival of the diaphragm. Also, instead of one ball bearing in the hub and another in the brake drum assembly, the hub now ran in two widely-spaced bearings, and the brake drum on a double-row roller bearing. These bearings were tucked away in the centre of the brake drum and often neglected.

Having standardized these features, the stylists let go with five varieties of these Mk III 750s, as well as the Interpol and the Production Racer; it was an economical alternative to building a genuinely varied range of motor cycles. Therer was the Fastback Mk III with either the Roadster handlebar, a 3¼-gallon fibreglass tank and 7 in headlamp, or the Fastback LR with the 4 gallon steel tank and the redesigned seat. There was the Roadster Mk II with its 2¼ gallon fibreglass tank, pull-back bars, and another variation of the seat rising to a hump at the rear. There was the SS model to supplant the S for on/off road duties, with a high front mudguard fixed to the lower fork yoke, a neat 2-gallon petrol tank, a 5 in headlamp, braced moto-cross bar, bash plate and a high-level exhaust pipe curling along each side of the bike, now with the reverse-cone megas and inadequate-looking plain matt black heat shields. Evidently the SS did not work out too well; it was

Side-show. Jawa frame, belt-driven Commando engine, for pacing bicycle track racers.

withdrawn after just five months and dealers were advised that the Roadster exhaust system 'had been found more satisfactory' and were offered a kit to change one to the other. Finally, there was, in deference to *Easy Rider*, a real lemon of a factory custom in the shape of the Hi-Rider, with a tank and headlight as on the SS plus ape-hangers and a Very Silly seat and cissy bar simply stuck on what was otherwise just a 750 Roadster. But they lasted four years, so somebody was impressed.

Commandos were still selling well, and for 1972 the decision was taken to damn the torpedoes, strengthen the bottom end, and raise the power output. In a rather contradictory way, the launch vehicle for this high-power endeavour was the new Interstate, a long-distance tourer. Why they chose to do this is not clear; presumably requests from America. These Mk IV 750s commenced from March 1972 and engine No 200000 — in fact there had been a jump of about 40,000 numbers and from this point on, the system of consecutive engine numbers which had continued since World War II was abandoned, and a new system and numbers were introduced. This and the turmoil at the factory and works for the next 12 months could lead to some confusing results; as one NOC member wrote to another, his Combat 750 was a Roadster, engine no 201695 and 'born in December'. That his friend's Interstate was 205660 and was built in August 'proves how fast a Combat is. Fast enough to go backwards in time!'

The Mk IV '72 750s had a redesigned crankcase. The Fastback, Hi-Rider and Roadster were now known as Mk IVs, the Roadster having skipped the Mark III stage, and the Hi-Rider jumping straight in at Mk IV. The scavenge pick-up for the pump was repositioned in the crankcase base and the case was considerably stiffened by internal webs and by thicker sections and bosses, particularly round the main bearing housing. The mains too were strengthened, the ballbearing on the timing side being replaced by a double roller. The crankcase breathing arrangements were completely revised; the timed flap-valve, never very satisfactory due to its small size, was replaced by a right-angle joint at the bottom rear of the crankcase, venting directly to a full-flow foam oil separator, mounted at the rear of the engine plates, to retain the oil and control the air flow. From there, large diameter braided hoses led to the oil tank. The tank was modified with a higher oil return stack pipe, to prevent oil spilling over into the carburettor air filter and the oiler pipe to the rear chain. More significantly, with one of those production engineering strokes then

current at Wolverhampton, the sump oil filters were eliminated and for some time nothing was installed to replace them. Clean oil and regular oil changes at short (about 1,500 mile) intervals are prerequisites for a healthy Commando, so this inexplicable move was really foolish. One result was that since the 'weak' slotted piston was still fitted, and many on Combat engines broke up, their fragments, in the absence of the sump filter, passed into the oil pump and wrecked the engine. Pace of production was hot, and some 12,000 engines had been built, some of them to Combat specification, before (in March 1972) the Interstate arrived with a small magnetic sump plug which as the NOC *Notes* point out flatly, 'has a chance of catching any bits of metal on the way to the pump—unless the metal is aluminium, brass, or bronze.' Later that year, a replaceable external car-type cartridge oil filter was added to the system, screwing on to the back of the crankcase in the space between the engine plates behind the gearbox. This could be machined quite easily on to Mk IV 750s that don't have it. But for the 850s the sump filter was put back.

Still, with a progressive determined assault on oil problems by the valve guide sealers, rocker spindle copper washers, and new oil control piston rings already described, plus new Hallite gasket material, and with the strengthened crankcase and new roller bearing, this seemed like a serious effort. The Combat engine was identified by the letter 'C' stamped on top of the rocker box, and more obviously by black cylinder barrels as opposed to a new silver finish on the others. With its 10:1 compression, double S cam, 32 mm concentrics replacing 30 mm standard, with cylinder head tracts bored out to suit and gas flowed, it sounded like a hot number. The raised compression had been achieved economically, by using standard pistons and simply skimming down the joint face on the head; 100 octane fuel was a must. On the Interstate, along with the Combat engine as standard went a disc front brake, which was optional for the whole range except the Hi-Rider from the beginning of the year (when both became standard later in the year, Fastback and Roadster could still be supplied with the drum brake and low compression engine for a lower price).

Developed by Lockheed, but with operating gear of Norton design and manufacture, the disc was in cast-iron, chrome plated, and fitted to the right-hand side of the front hub with the calipers behind the right fork leg. Straightaway, that was a snag. For reasons possibly connected to the fact that Commando rear wheels were built ³/₁₆ in

A very silly idea. The 750 Hi-rider for 1971. 'A tasteful chopper'?

offset to the right, to compensate for the engine/gearbox being slightly ofset to the left, according to the NOC *Notes*, the right-hand disc caused machines to pull to the left and made some so bad that you could not steer the machine hands off. Swopping the fork over improved this but was highly dangerous because the wheel bearing lock ring would unscrew if the rotation of the wheel was reversed. The cure was not to come until the 850 Mk IIIs with left-hand disc and caliper in front of the forks. The chrome on the disc peeled fast, turning the surface initially into a grinding wheel which did pad life no good; and very badly worn pads were dangerous, since if worn thin enough they could eject from their housings when applied. After the chrome had gone the discs rusted, which is unsightly, but harmless enough as it goes the first time the brake is applied. All that having been said, the brake itself worked very well, earning high praise from testers accustomed to Japan's best, and bringing the braking of a heavy (Interstate 430 lb dry) British twin into the late 20th century for the first time ever. Feeling may have been a bit wooden, but the brake stopped you. The master cylinder and reservoir were combined in a handlebar unit which incorporated a pressure-operated stop-light switch with the assembly including a bellows seal in the top of the fluid integral reservoir to prevent loss if the bike fell.

The Interstate was initially distinguished by its less triangular side panels and very big 5¼-gallon

Above *1972 and bad news: The fragile Combat-engined 750 Interstate, with disc brake.*

Below *1972 Interstate 750 rolling down the highway. Many did not stay on it for long.*

petrol tank, both in fibreglass, but progressively replaced by steel items, the steel tank being 5½ gallons. They were optional at first, but, as for the whole range, the fibreglass was phased out by 1974 for all but the Hi-Riders, in line with legal requirements. The Interstate's tank was one of the truly big production petrol tanks, a useful touring aid on the wilder shores, and its bulk was subtly played down by the central portion being picked out in gold pinstriping. The bulk was real, though, and it meant that the rider sat with his legs uncomfortably far apart, his knees in the breeze, and his seat further back on the machine. Since those impressively engineered footrest hangers were a very permanent feature, his feet were placed further forward than the vertical axis of the hip, and offered no support to his body, which was stretched forward over the tank to reach the handlebars. If the high and wide pullback bars were used, the body was stretched like a sail and control over the always light front end was minimal; if the flatter European-style bars were fitted, the strain on the wrists was bad, really uncomfortable pains developed across the back and shoulders and the only way to do anything about it was to go faster and let the wind take the pressure off. Over the next three years various tank and bars configurations were tried but they didn't get it anywhere near right until the end. Finally, there were long horizontal silencers, developed for the Interpol to allow panniers to be carried. These were ungainly, and though they lost little power over the reverse cones, were 'noisy by current standards' as a *Bike* tester put it—and that was in 1972.

That test in the early summer of 1972 consisted of a 3,000 mile continental trip and by the end of it, in an almost delicate aside, it was mentioned that the main bearings were on their noisy way out. The Combat engine is by now a well-known disaster; the extra stress of its claimed 65 bhp was catered for by the stiffer crankcases, but no thought had been given to strengthening the crank. This fought the stiff cases, the conflict centering on the bearings; the corners of the new roller timing side bearing dug in and destroyed both itself and the tracks it ran on. Main bearing life of only 4,000 miles was not unusual for a Combat engine. Other aggravating factors for that year's Interstate were the ignition jamming full on (as mentioned) and the fact that the gearing had been lowered which with the flexible engine encouraged forays to the 7,000 rpm blood line and beyond. It just was not that sort of engine, and showed it by self-destructing.

By July the number of bikes returned under

warranty had abundantly established that fact, but the confused way Wolverhampton was operated meant that though in July, from engine no 211891, a cure for the main bearing problem had been found and implemented in the shape of the 'Superblend' bearing, the implications of the Combat had not been properly digested and in October it was announced that all models bar the Hi-Rider were getting the high compression engine (and the disc brake) as standard. The 'Superblend' was still a roller main bearing, running in heavy brass cages, but with slightly spherical, barrel-shaped ends; it was thus self-aligning, which allowed the crankshaft to flex. Types from several bearing companies were used but NOC confirms that the ones to fit are, for the 750, either Ransome and Marles or Fischer AG, with the FAG the only factory recommended one for the 850; the bearing numbers involved are NJ306E (the E being important as NJ 306 is weaker), or 6MRJA30.

A halt was shortly called to the Combat folly. At first they tried to de-tune the 10:1 cr monster with an aluminium alloy gasket, part no 064072 and no less than 2 mm thick. Used together with a cylinder base gasket this reduced cr to 8.8:1. Neale Shilton claimed that the alloy material deteriorated through burning, causing the cylinder head joint to leak, resulting in weak mixture and burnt out valves. John Hudson says that while he does not think he ever saw a burnt alloy gasket, they would certainly compress and 'bulge' out into the pushrod tunnels and foul the pushrod tubes. Shilton describes batches of machines going back and forwards from Wolverhampton to Andover for fitting and then removal of gaskets, and Norton management to their credit had all machines in stock fitted with the new mains, a quieter cam, and lowered gearing. This probably explains the apparently time-travelling Combat machines mentioned earlier, as numbers got out of sequence. The matter of compression ratios is a vexed one, since in addition to the various gaskets and the variable of a cylinder base gasket, or a cylinder base sealed with Loctite instead, there were several different cylinder heads. These included the standard 1968–1972 30 mm carburettor version, the Combat's 32 mm RH3, and then from engine no 211110, the 32 mm standard RH5 giving 8.9:1 cr, and RH6 giving 9.3:1, both without base gaskets. But the possible combinations are multitudinous, and I agree with NOC that a) if you want to find out the compression of your Commando the only sure way is to use a burette, and b) that the factory's eventual solution, part no 063844 available from

Above *1972 750 fastback Mk IV. The last of the line.*

Below *1972's Mk IV 750 roadster. Disc brake and black barrels = Combat = trouble.*

September 1972, is the only answer.

This part is a gasket of composition material, incorporating steel fire-ring 'eyelets' — the 'eyeletted composition' for short. The alloy and the 1 mm copper gasket (part no 064071) will simply not stay oiltight; the latter I know from personal experience. Incidentally, if really low compression is desired, or necessary, John Hudson's solution for a Commando, originally in fact a Combat, which went overland to South Africa and gave no trouble in 26,000 miles, was to use two Hallite gaskets with a solid copper one sandwiched in between.

These measures, a stronger auto-advance unit and higher gearing restored some sanity as Norton prepared to launch one of the reasons why they had strengthened the bottom end in the first place, namely the move up to 829 cc capacity. In February 1973 from engine no 220000, the final 750, the Mk V, was announced. These were in Hi-Rider, Roadster and Interstate form only, with Superblend bearings, full flow oil filter, raised overall gearing and 32 mm carburettors. Benefits from the 850 included the box-section headsteady, a strengthened gearbox, larger and stronger finned ring nuts (but without the collets on the 850), and the latter's strengthened clutch (though without the big bike's extra plate). There was also hard chroming for the fork stanchions and new plastic gaiters to protect the Isolastics. There were changes to the air cleaner assembly and electrics, deeper seat padding, stainless steel mudguards, and French Veglia instruments, now in black cases. The compression was lowered (a nominal 8.5:1 standard for both, with a 9.5:1

option for the Roadster only), ostensibly to cope with West Germany's low octane (lead-free) petrol. With new big square tail light, and optional mirrors, grabrail, Halogen headlamp and winkers, dual-seats with a new cross-hatched top, and with all their good looks intact in black and gold, or cherry red with silver lettering, these were the last and best of the 750s. They were terminated by October 1973, the last known example being engine no 230935. This was a pity as they had now come good, and were faster machines than their successors.

The 850 Mk I came in for March 1973, engine numbers restarting at 300000, and also in Interstate, Roadster and Hi-Rider form. They were identifiable externally by smart double-row pinstriping on tank and panels against the 750's single line; by an exhaust system with a link tube connecting the two pipes; and a cylinder base flange with no visible studs and nuts on right and left of the block. This was because the barrel was clamped to the crankcase by long holding-down bolts. These engines were claimed to have a modest 8.5:1 compression ratio, but as Norton troubleshooter Bob Manns later told *Which Bike?*, 'none that I ever checked did! (This was borne out by others who have checked, usually to find the standard ratio was 7.7:1.)' The 60 bhp at 6,000 rpm figure was also distinctly optimistic—realistic power outputs were down around the 52 mark and magazines checked out later examples at even lower outputs.

To counter front end shake the head angle of the frame was increased by 1 degree to 62 degrees, with the forks brought back to increase

Left *Short-stroke 750, part of a small run for 1973.*

Right *The first 850, a Mk I seen here in Interstate trim early in 1973.*

Far right *1973's Commando production racer.*

trail yet retain the 750's wheelbase. Internally, very little was interchangeable with the 750, though camshafts, cam gear and conrods were the same; later, 850 components were used to make up 750 crankshafts, but the two were balanced differently and the latter identified by 750 stamped on the centre flywheel. Cycle parts were generally interchangeable, and the benefit of having just one base model with many variations was that later improvements could be incorporated easily on earlier bikes.

At the bottom end of the 850 engine the FAG Superblend bearings were fitted, their housings in the crankcase casting being line-bored, and additional metal and reinforcing webs provided around the main bearing housing. The gauze crankcase oil strainer with access via a hexagon-headed nut was back, screwed into the rear underside of the crankcase, as well as a larger version of the magnetic drain plug. The sump itself was deepened and to improve scavenging the crankcase well was repositioned so that it would trap the bulk of oil scraped off the flywheel. The oilways were redesigned, and the full-flow filter cartridge was also in place and connected with steel braided pipes. The crankcase mouth face was increased in area to reduce oil leaks, and the cylinder base gasket made with Loctite Plastic Gasket. The crankcase breathing, always an important factor with oil tightness, was revised for the third time, and this version was really satisfactory, with holes in the timing side chaincase for the crankcase to breathe into the timing chest, from which a short pipe at the back vented into the atmosphere. All this represented a

determined assault on oil leaks, and was largely successful as long as the motor was screwed together properly and not abused. An exception was the copper cylinder head gasket fitted for most of 1973 until the Klingerite-type with metal flame-rings was substituted.

Another element in this was the new clamping methods for cylinder block and head. The two outermost crankcase bolts were now long, their heads located in deep recesses in the cylinder block top face, with helicoil inserts in the crankcase helping to secure all four through-studs. The bolt pattern was rearranged to equalize pressure, as was the spacing of the cylinder head bolts. The pushrod tunnel in the block was smaller, giving more metal between the tunnel and the cylinder bores, and also between the bores and the holding down bolts. The slotted pistons were replaced by the stronger flat top solid-skirt type, though confusingly these were called Combat, being similar to that engine's since its higher cr had been achieved by skimming the heads. For smoother gas flow the inlet ports were redesigned, though the downdraught angle was no steeper than before; and as mentioned when discussing valve problems, the walls of 850 valve guides were thicker, and they were retained by circlips. There was an enlarged drain hole where the cylinder head drained oil away by means of the inlet valve well, the valve seat area was enlarged, and seals fitted to the top of the guides to prevent oil being sucked down the inlet-valve stems. The cam profile reverted to the S, pre-Combat specifications, and the carburettors, while still 32 mm, had different spray tube design, jetting and

needle profile, and also featured a recently introduced shrouded float.

The alternator was the same size but was claimed to have a stronger magnetic field due to different material for the rotor, which increased output at low and medium rpm; a bigger 9 amp hr battery was fitted, and a Quartz Halogen light unit was offered as an option on Interstate and Roadster. With the 10CA contact breakers, the auto-advance mechanism was brazed, not peened, to its baseplate, the contact breaker spring abutments more robust and the attachment of the assembly was improved. The thumb switches on the instruments became longer for easier reach.

The shell of the gearbox was thickened in parts, notably in the higher gear area around the main bearing wall. The clutch was now all metal, with five friction plates with sintered bronze faces, and four plain plates, an increase of one in each. There was new geometry for the clutch lever, reducing the pressure required. The friction rings were faced with sintered bronze, the pressure plate was slimmer, and the backplate was now held in by three rivets, not the previous two pins. Other areas of strengthening included heat-treating for the kickstarter shank, and on the frame, the addition of gussets behind the top mountings for the rear suspension, for extra robustness in the area stressed when panniers were fitted. Wheels were balanced, with straighter pull strokes, and the rear fork was also gusseted; but a basic flaw remained, namely the poor location of the swinging arm spindle in the gearbox cradle. The spindle was held by a single ¼ in screw so, as the NOC *Notes* point out, this one screw effectively held the back wheel in. Tim Stevens, the quality control manager at Wolverhampton, and co-author of the *Notes*, tells how the screw on his machine failed once at speed and the swinging arm spindle came out, with very hairy results. Wear alone here caused poor rear end handling. The oversize spindle was available, and some Interpol-riding Police also had a dodge for improving matters. They shimmed out the swinging fork pivot, using shims from the rear Isolastic, until the fork would just, but only just, remain static under its own weight. They then drilled the pivot cross-tube, brazed on a pair of nuts, inserted a bolt to lock the spindle into place and wired them for security. On the 850 Mk III the spindle was finally to be secured in the engine plate cross-tube with two bicycle crank type cotter pins. Police machines also tended to set the Isolastic clearances tighter than the recommended 10 thou clearance, because it extended service

intervals and although there was a slight loss of smoothness, the Interpols with their heavy equipment were less affected than a lighter machine, and handling was tauter.

In this area shortly afterwards there was another one of Wolverhampton's inexplicable design lapses. On the 750s lubrication for the swinging arm was via a grease nipple fitted to its left hand cover plate. The problem was that it was not intended for grease at all but for heavy EP90 gearbox oil—however it was not marked 'OIL' and an inattentive owner or garage would apply grease. Since the feed for the lubricant was from a centre bore of the spindle via a ¹/₁₆ in hole at each end feeding oil downwards to each bush in the rear fork, and since both spindle and bush were plain, with no scroll, if grease entered those tiny holes they were immediately blocked, and the rear fork was left unlubricated until it seized. But at least the system would work if you knew the form and used a clean Tecalemite grease gun filled with oil. However, from December 1973 on the Mk II and Mk IIA 850s, that is from engine no 307311, the oil nipple was simply left out. Also, as Stevens tells it, hardly any oil was put in at the works, and the feed wicks were very tight in the spindle bore, so that any oil which might be in the centre of the spindle was unlikely to reach the disc wicks; these wicks were located under the core plugs, and were intended to feed oil to the outer edge of each bush. Swinging arm lubrication stayed like that until the end, the only solution being to drill more substantial oilways and inject oil in. Not very satisfactory.

Elsewhere on the 850 the centre stand was strengthened with sturdier stop blocks and improved pivot bushes. There was hard chrome plating for the fork stanchions in place of the previous decorative and short-lived chrome; works standards of chroming were never good, as owners and testers soon realized. To improve the weatherproofing of the Isolastic system, the gaiters at the end of the more vulnerable front mounting were made of softer plastic to prevent cracking in frost; and more importantly, the improved and less vulnerable bronze-impregnated PTFE washers replaced the polyurethane kind, outboard of the shim caps. The internal buffers were also now secured in the tube by rubber circlips. Another perennial problem tackled stemmed from the fact that due to the Isolastic system, the exhaust pipes were unbraced with no pipe-to-frame bracket at any position from the exhaust ports to their attachment point by Silentblocs at a spot down by the pillion footrests. If there was any loosening at the head, it was not unusual for exhaust pipes to strip their threads there and eject, meaning at least an expensive helicoiling job on the exhaust port threads. The problem always remained, but for the Mk I 850 a first step towards a remedy was taken when the flanges of the linked exhaust pipes were fitted with thicker abutments and were sleeved right through into the exhaust tracts. At the same time the less than effective exhaust locking rings were made more robust.

The Interstate's petrol tank capacity had risen to a massive 5¾ gallons, and only the Roadster had the option of a European-style handlebar. Direction indicators were fitted as standard, as was a grabrail, and the seats had deeper padding. The Hi-Rider (and this also went for the 750) had a larger seat, and in 850 form acquired the front disc brake.

The 850 represented a sustained assault on the Commando's problems but the effort was let down by production standards and perhaps by being simply too late—1972 had been the last year that the Commando was *MCN*'s machine of the year, 1973's being the Kawasaki Z1; and 850 or not, the Commando was in another dimension from the big Zed. Even so, there continued to be a market for something reliable, muscular, four-stroke and traditional but the quality lapses kept turning up embarrassingly on road test machines, and testers were no longer loath to mention them. *MCM*'s test bike in June 1973 had enough play in its swinging arm to have failed an MOT test. The bolt holding the inner chaincase to the crankcase came undone due to its tab washer not being properly secured, and by the time this was discovered the bolt had smashed its way through the inner chaincase. It also revealed that the triplex chain had been located on only two runs of the engine and clutch sprocket. *Motor Cyclist Illustrated* had a machine so rough that they returned it, only to find the replacement equally poorly prepared and leak-prone. And these were the test bikes! Poor chrome and paint, especially on the frames which were often rusting in delivery trim, were a constant niggle; stainless steel replacements have done a lively business ever since.

Dave Rawlins performed impressively on the drag strip on an 850 prepared skilfully by John Baker at NV's experimental department, running 142.74 mph with a 24-tooth gear sprocket, and achieving a 12 second standing quarter with a 19-tooth one, which was in any terms an impressive figure for a production roadster. But this was misrepresentative for the 850s which the public were offered were slower than their predecessors—always a difficult pill for bikers to swallow about any machine. Raising the gearing with a 21-tooth sprocket did not seem to affect the acceleration of the Mk V 750, which was also 30 lb lighter. One early 850 was tested by *Motor Cycle* in March 1973 who, despite the low compression, found it 'the quickest yet' at 121/ 122 top speeds, though this rather contradicted previous Norton publicity claiming 125 mph runs for standard 750s. The testers were impressed by the effortless way it managed the high speeds, its oil tightness and the way the new clutch never went out of adjustment despite abuse. Mpg had fallen a bit at 42 against the usual 50-ish overall, but they attributed this to a lot of motorway mileage. They also liked the handling, finding no trace of some earlier 750s' sensitivity to throttle closure on bends—in general, Commando technique, like a lot of other twins, had always favoured keeping the power on and driving through corners.

But by accident or factory design that test seems to have dropped on a particularly well set up machine. *Bike*'s Mark Williams in contrast found the example he tested accelerated surprisingly well for a soft engine to 90 mph, but ran out of breath from there on and took a long time to reach its 111 mph top speeds. He also considered that at least a friction steering damper was a necessity, as the front end lightened even more than previously under hard acceleration, giving rise to 'vicious little wobbles' as the front wheel momentarily left the ground. *MCM* thought that the frame still felt flexible if the throttle was shut off while cornering and also noted the light front end. The vibration period below which the Isolastics stopped damping out the quaking engine had risen to 3,000 rpm in some cases, making for awkward town running.

In September 1973 there appeared Mk IA versions of the 850, aimed at the European market and its progressively stricter noise pollution requirements. There was the large black box of a new low-noise air cleaner, and raised gearing with a 22-tooth gearbox sprocket, which was aimed at slower revs and hence less noise in the speed band at which decibel readings with their 85 db limit were taken. This was also the first appearance of the good-looking upswept annular discharge silencers, the 'black cap' or 'bean cans' as they were known due to the matt black mutes protruding from their rear like the top of a Heinz tin. They were the fruit of an eighteen month collaboration between Dr Roe and Dr Thorpe of Birmingham University, and Bernard Hooper at NV. Unlike the previous detachable mutes fixed to

the end of some Commando silencers by a set-screw, these silencers (which would also appear on the T160 Trident) lowered noise levels appreciably (up to 25 db better) but did not have a restrictive effect on performance; in some circumstances they were claimed to actually improve power output. They allowed exhaust gases to pass down the narrow annular passage between two concentric cylinders, and tuning was achieved by altering the size and layout of the holes, known as Heimholtz cavities, in the central cylinder. It was not the silencer but the new airbox which would strangle the 850.

Late in 1973 a new styling exercise was unveiled in the form of the John Player Norton Commando, a standard 850 frame and engine tricked out very handsomely in café racer trim; it was also offered for more serious scratching with the short stroke (77 × 80.4 mm) 749 cc production racing engine, which was produced in limited quantities for homologation purposes. In 1974 Dave Rawlins used a 69 bhp John Baker variant of one of the short stroke engines to run 11.46 at Santa Pod, a new production class record. The JPN was a publicity exercise in homage to one of the company's major race sponsors as well as the celebration of a successful year on the tracks after Formula 750 and Thruxton 500 wins. Styled on the lines of the 750 racers, it wore a fairing striped with the team's red, white and blue colours and carried twin double-dip headlamps and mirrors. The speedometer and rev-counter were carried in a moulded fascia. A 4 gallon steel tank beneath a

fibreglass tank shroud, clip-ons, rear-sets, matt black exhausts and silencers, a single racing seat and a tail hump bearing the Union Jack, more or less completed the package, but converting a stock Norton to this specification would be a major work, as the parts list supplement for it runs to over one hundred items. Released in June 1974 in a limited edition of 300, it was a fun bike, the chief drawbacks being a cripplingly hard seat, and the fixed footrest position, as well as an awkward 'backward' kickstart; but tester Dave Minton enjoyed sitting in the 'cockpit' and picking off unsuspecting strokers from behind like a booming fighter-bomber, though the matt-black mutes and silencers, and the engine within the fairing, proved quite effectively silenced. He also reckoned it handled better than any other Commando, though on long high-speed curves, when a power change was necessary, the familiar 'Commando creep' set in. He was careful to emphasize that this was not fatal, making the distinction between problems of road-holding (which it wasn't) and handling (which it always was).

For 1974 and engine no 307311 from December '73 the Mk II series of 850s was available, and these included a Mk IIA. The Mk IIs featured more deeply padded seats with a cross-pattern quilting on top, and a neater European bar, called Majorca, an improvement but still too wide. The Interstate tank from engine no 307091 was reduced to 4½ gallons by removing a section from the centre so that it was not so uncomfortably

Far left *1973 850s came in roadster trim too—you just didn't see so many of them.*

Left *Still a silly idea. 1973 850 hi-rider.*

Right *Early 1974, and the restricted Mk II 850 with 'black cap' silencers, plastic airbox (and poor pinstriping already worn away by rider's knee).*

wide at the rear, though still not ideal; the Roadster tank was slightly restyled and increased to 2½ gallons. Cylinder barrels were black again, which at a year's distance no longer carried the Combat stigma.

An effort had been made to improve paint quality, and there was one new and handsome finish for the Roadsters with a broad blue stripe, superimposed low down with a narrow gold one, on white tank and panels. Principally for the USA there were the Mk II versions of the 850, retaining the old silencers and airbox and standard gearing, lowered a little with a twenty-tooth gearbox sprocket, though the 21 and 22-tooth options were available. The Hi-Rider, an ageing hippie now in its last year, remained exclusively in this mode. The Mk IIAs were ostensibly aimed at Europe, though many would sell in the UK too.

For them the black cap silencers and airbox were as previously, and it was the latter, a massive plastic baffle box aimed at suppressing induction roar, and with a larger filter element said to be easier to renew, which really knocked Mk IIA performance on the head. In addition to the previous overall raised gearing with the 22-tooth gearbox sprocket, the second gear ratio had been altered by changing the pinions in the cluster, since it was in that gear that the noise was tested during acceleration. Also in the gearbox a third sleeve gear bush was added. The claimed output of these engines was 52 bhp, and top speed was down on the best Mk Is by 7 or 8 mph at around 114 mph; though mpg was improved at 50 overall,

and that was three star petrol. Mk IIAs had their inlet ports tapered from 32 mm at the carb to 30 mm above the valve; a shape said to have been determined in the light of Dave Rawlins' experience. It was claimed to improve low speed torque, but the marginally slower acceleration figures on production machines did not substantiate this, and the NOC *Notes* advise opening out the ports again. The instruments carried mute testimony to the troubled waters which the company was navigating at Meriden and elsewhere, in the shape of the squiggled NT symbol on their faces. Other detail changes included a flap over the ignition lock, a plastic tool-tray, the lengthened kickstart, the excellent Halogen headlamp as standard, mudflaps and the plastic extension to the rear chainguard from engine no 309600, with fork gaiters becoming an optional extra—this was the sensible backlash. *MCM* found that for once the front suspension seemed too soft on their test model, and had a tendency to wander at low speeds and to wobble, but this was manageable, and once they got used to the handling, the bike's excellent roadholding meant heeling over far enough to ground the prop-stand on left-handers. They appreciated the genuinely low noise levels, although with stiffish controls and 450 lb kerb weight, the 850 remained a tiring bike to ride in traffic. But even with the raised gearing and a top speed down to around 110 mph, the strong point remained the acceleration, and overall they appreciated this version of the biggest parallel twin.

A roadster version of restricted Mk IA 850 for late 1973, with 'bean cans' clearly displayed.

1974 JPN 850, handsome factory custom.

With the company already heading for terminal trouble, 1975 saw the last act, the 850 Mk III with electric starter, left-hand front and right-hand rear disc brakes, left-hand gear shift in line with Japanese practice and hence US legislation, and nearly 140 detailed changes from previous components to strengthen and sanitize the 850 still further. Introduced to the UK in March 1975 at a launch at Ragley Hall, it was offered in Roadster and Interstate forms; a Mk III JPN was illustrated but only a few were produced. The Interstate was distinguished by a new finish to supplement the traditional black and gold or deep metallic cherry red; this was a return to Norton roots in the shape

of 'Manx' silver for tank and side panels, with broad black and narrow red lining, though the allusion was lost on many and the silver always appeared to have a greenish tinge, unlike the great original. One always seemed to see more Interstates than Roadsters among the 850s and this was particularly true of the Mk IIIs. In a two-model range (Commando and T160 Trident), NVT were selling the triple as the road burner and the twin, by now well overweight at 466 lb dry, as the tourer, though Wolverhampton's Norton 76 showed that other directions were possible.

The Mk III had been very extensively redesigned. To deal with the principal points first, in order to eliminate some of the stress on it, the gearbox now stood in fixed relation to the engine and adjustment of the primary chain was done automatically by a hydraulically operated double shoe tensioner, working on the inner faces of both runs of the chain. A new lip-seal was also put behind the clutch on the gearbox mainshaft to stop oil leaks; one tester remarked that for the first time they had a problem with nuts on the prop-stand going rusty because there was no oil leak. Within the box third and fourth gears were altered in pitch and profile to strengthen them. There was only a 4 in spread between the final drive sprocket shaft and the swinging arm pivot, making for minimum chain tension fluctuation. To beat leaks again the single bolt fixing for the primary chaincase had also gone; it was now secured by twelve peripheral Phillips screws and the walls and joint faces had been widened, their material being said to be lighter, more corrosion-resistant alloy.

On the other side of the engine the same applied to the timing cover which was also located by twelve equal length Posidrive screws, as opposed to the previous ten unequal cheese-head variety. Setting the ignition timing was facilitated by an inspection cover on the case. This allowed the cam chain tension to be checked without taking off the whole case and by lining up marks inside, the correct advance could be attained. The oiling system was uprated; the venerable but trusty worm-drive oil pump had always worked

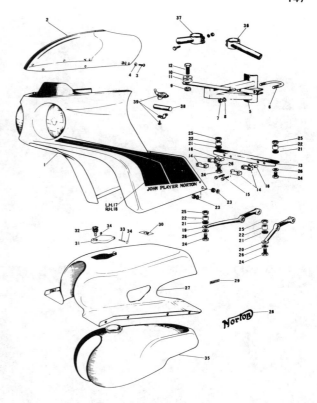

Above right *Part of what it took to make a JPN.*

Right *Another sporting variant—a Gus Kuhn 850 sprinter for 1974.*

The final version. 850 Mk III Electric start for 1975, in 'Manx' silver trim.

850 Mk III powerplant, with 'Prestolite' starter and right foot brake pedal clearly visible.

well, but there had sometimes been air leakage between pump and crankcase due to distortion and wear on the gears. The pump was now held by bolts rather than the earlier nuts and at last, after nearly thirty years, a piston type anti-leak valve was plumbed into the system to prevent oil seeping into the crankcase when the bike was left for long periods. But as a final irony several NOC members with Mk IIIs have reported that though their timing cases carried the small external protuberance signifying the presence of the anti-

leak valve, inside there was no plunger and spring and the cases had not even been machined to take it. Fallen at the last.

The method of bolting up the flywheel and crankshaft assembly had been amended in mid-1974 and now the crankshaft itself was finally strengthened and the con-rods shot-peened. The main bearing widths were extended. The change to left-hand shift meant a by-now-conventional up-for-up pattern—the Commando had been the last to retain the old down-for-up. The left shift was effected by having the old AMC box expensively geared, rather than linked, to a cross-over shaft running to the front of the main gearbox assembly. For some, a bit of the lightness of the old box was lost in the changeover.

The lack of a starter had been perceived as a fault for several years—executive material didn't like to have to kickstart if they stalled at the lights. Sadly, the US Prestolite solenoid-operated starter, placed behind the cylinder in the old magneto position, added weight and little else. Geared to a sprag clutch on the left-hand end of the crankshaft inboard of the primary drive sprocket, it proved only intermittently capable of turning over 829 cc's worth of big Norton, and least of all on cold mornings when the normally easily started Norton might have appreciated it. Luckily the kickstarter was left in place. Another quirk was that in the absence of a safety locknut wired into the lever bracket, you could operate it with the machine in gear and if the clutch was not withdrawn the bike would lurch forward. Sometimes it could be worse; the cross shaft holding the gears and spring mechanism could wear an oval hole in the inner primary case. There was later a Prestolite four-brush conversion which made for efficient operation and eliminated the wear problems; details can be found in the NOC Mk III Supplement to their *Notes*. They also say that a cheap alternative is a Lucas four-brush set (Lucas part no 251108).

The Isolastic system had its rubbers bonded together to prevent their shifting, and finally adopted the original Vernier lockable thread

system, adjustable with a special key, eliminating shimming and reducing job time to fifteen minutes. The covers for the system became close fitting rubber. At the third point, the headsteady, a spring-loaded support, was added to help slow the judder at idle. Both headsteady and Vernier Isolastics can be fitted to previous Commandos.

There was a new wiring harness, and the ignition switch was moved to a console between the speedo and rev-counter along with the warning lights. Switchgear units in flat black were cleaned up and their functions clearly marked in white as was now the pilot/main lightswitch previously mounted on the headlamp—US legislation again. The alternator was uprated to a high-output Lucas RM24, and the battery was (horrors) a Japanese Yuasa (but it was good). The messy rear chain oiler was finally discarded. The problems of the exhaust to head joint were tackled even more thoroughly with a car-type spherical fitting, a convex sealing ring allowing the pipe to pull the new spherical flange of the exhaust pipe up tight without putting too great a stress on the retaining nut and the flange. The seat was reprofiled, softer, hinged and lockable, and an old security problem was settled on the left-hand side panel with its tool space, previously known for detaching itself spontaneously, being removable now only when the seat was lifted. Rear-view mirrors and fork gaiters were standard. New petrol taps with on/off markings were fitted and although the Interstate tank reverted to 5¼ gallons it was the most rider-friendly shape so far. There was even talk of an improved sealing gasket for the perennial oil leak at the rev-counter drive,

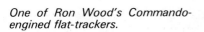

One of Ron Wood's Commando-engined flat-trackers.

but it is not clear whether this ever happened. Today's answer is the BL Mini valve stem oil seal, plus Superglue.

At the rear a disc brake of the same 10.7 in diameter as the front one was installed on the right side, operated by a chromed forged steel pedal on the right, with a master cylinder behind the gearbox. This brake involved a new hub with a different design of shock-absorber between the hub and the sprocket on the right and with the speedometer box on the left.

So that was the final Commando, scarcely changed from then on as production tailed to the last trickle in 1978. It had gained several desirable features, many happily applicable to earlier Commandos. But it had also gained to the extent of a 492 lb kerbside weight, some 70 lb heavier than most 750s. With the breathing and emission restrictions, it had also lost the edge of its performance; compression was now billed openly as 7.8:1, and though the tachometer showed a 7,000 blood line, this was a hangover from the 750, as the Mk III's limit was 6,500 rpm.

Top speed was a little over 105 mph, and mpg down at around 40. The Mk III was fundamentally a pleasant and relatively reliable tourer. You can boost performance by substituting the reverse cone silencers, but only in conjunction with the earlier airbox, and with jetting up from 230 to 260 on the main jet. 10 to 15 mpg can also be gained by going over to a single carb with an inexpensive manifold from Stewart Engineering, obtainable

from Les Emery's Shop and elsewhere. But steady long distance going with plenty of acceleration is really the name of the game. 750 or 850? You trade off some speed for some reliability.

Despite the pitfalls, I would still say the Commando represents one of the few Brits that are a practical ride for today's conditions. With 70 mph at around a lazy 4,000 rpm they can cruise the motorways with plenty in hand, and with disc brake or brakes they stop accordingly. They don't like sustained flat-out blasting but they're friendly to twisty A-roads and to mountains. They also don't like towns; how the Interpols handled it, I don't know. There is a restricted steering lock, plus a tendency to stall at tickover due apparently to the carburettors normally having a high float and to frothing in the bowl caused by low-speed engine shakes, which also bounce the rider about in slow traffic. The controls are on the harsh side and the transmission can quickly become so; the engine runs hot, the weight is not the most easily controllable at low speeds, the harsh suspension clobbers you on rutted city streets and an added irritant is the poor back brake. So town is no picnic.

On the open road, in top gear, which is so flexible that you rarely need to leave it, it's a different story. You feel relaxed, sitting on grumbling rolling thunder, though rarely graceful and in perfect harmony; look at the shots of the bike on the road shown here and you will see how the rider sits on top of the bike rather than at one

Late Interpol, the 1975 Mk III electric start.

A final classically black and gold Mk III at a 1975 show in Holland.

with it, with the weight and 31–33 in seat height making it more awkward for shorter pilots. What seems to me the single greatest aid to a comfortable riding position, for Roadsters but especially Interstates, I deliberately left out of sequence; it's the 850 Mk III handlebar, with which they finally got it right. A low, quite narrow T-shaped configuration that will take the disc brake master cylinder, it puts your hands and wrists just where they should be; but it has to be the real Norton thing. I have had patterns which were close and they were not good enough; I finally found a genuine pair at Gander and Gray.

Without becoming too fanciful, the Commando is also one of those machines that gives of its best if you are in the mood, responding favourably to a confident approach, the handling working well, within its limits, only when driven decisively, the harder but not harsher the better. The handling is a subject in itself; the slow weave at high speed cannot be denied, and has best been described as a tiptoe feeling, nervous and delicate but predictable once learnt, and rarely developing into serious trouble. Many factors are involved — tyres (Avon Roadrunners seem to me to be the ones, though the factory fitted TT100s for a while), condition of the steering head bearings, shocks and swinging arm, whether a hydraulic steering damper is fitted (again personally they seem to make a slight but definite improvement), whether you drive abruptly or progressively, and how the bike is loaded. Commandos are one of those machines that like two up and can carry

reasonable amounts of luggage (the factory set a limit of 40 lb) as long as it's sensibly distributed, low down and not too far back; a medium tank bag is a good idea.

Set up thus you have a machine ready for years of long distance hauling. Plenty were built and the spares situation and interchangeability is good. It will be a love-hate relationship; deal with one niggle and another crops up. Get the NOC *Notes* for constructive solutions to many of them. But to return to the original contention, yes, the Commando seems to me, with its endurance, strength, and power when you need it, to be a real Norton, and the qualities all those sidecar motocross men and production racers, Police, dragsters and flat-track artists discovered in the big twin can work for you, in a properly set up example, over the miles and over the years.

Norton: The 750 and 850 Commando — dates and specifications
Production dates

750	Date	From engine
Mk I		
750 Fastback Mk I	April 1968	(no 126125)
Mk II		
750 Fastback Mk II	March 1969	
750 'S' type		
750 Roadster Mk I		(no 135140)
Mk III		

750 Fastback Mk III
(includes LR)   January 1971   (no 141783)
750 Roadster Mk II   (no 142534)
750 'SS' type
750 Hi-Rider
(January 1972, consecutive numbers abandoned)
Mk IV
750 Fastback Mk IV   March 1972   (no 200000)
750 Roadster Mk IV
750 Interstate
(Combat)   (no 212278)
750 Hi-Rider
Mk V
750 Roadster Mk V   March 1973   (no 220000)
750 Interstate (non-
Combat)
750 Hi-Rider
End of production   October 1973   (no 230935)
850
Mk I
850 Roadster Mk I   February 1973   (no 300000)
850 Interstate Mk I
850 Hi-Rider
850 Roadster Mk IA   October 1973   (no 306591)
850 Interstate Mk IA
Mk II
850 Roadster Mk II   December
1973   (no 307311)
850 Interstate Mk II
850 Roadster Mk IIA
850 Interstate Mk
IIA
850 Hi-Rider
850 John Player
Norton
Mk III
850 Roadster Mk III   February 1975   (no 330000)
850 Interstate Mk III
End of production   1978

Specifications
750 Commando
Capacity, bore and stroke—745 cc (73 × 89 mm)
Type of engine—ohv twin
Ignition—Coil
Weight—(1969 Fastback) 415 lb, (1971 Roadster)
395 lb, (1973 Interstate) 430 lb.
850 Commando
Capacity, bore and stroke—829 cc (77 × 89 mm)
Type of engine—ohv twin
Ignition—Coil
Weight—(1973 Roadster) 418 lb, (1974 Interstate)
430 lb, (1975 Mk III Interstate) 466 lb.

Norton: The Commando 750 and 850—annual development and modifications

Because Norton Villiers/Norton Triumph employed series production with the Commando rather than production by model year, and because many modifications were introduced in mid-year, the following development tables will often be by engine number, and where available by month, though the latter are necessarily approximate datings. Where a month is printed in italics it represents the probable commencement of a change in the factory; where not italicized the month indicates the approximate date that the change was notified in service bulletins. For reasons of space, changes to the different 'Mark' series as they were introduced are described in the text and not duplicated here.

1968
For 750 Commando Mk I:
1 *Sept* No 128646. New type sleeve gear and layshaft pinion tooth form.

1969
For 750 Commando Mk I:
1 *Jan?* No 129897. Rear wheel security bolt and Mk 2 type frame with horizontal bracing tube in place of gusset.
2 *Feb?* No 130979. APEX three-piece oil-control ring replaces previous five-piece type.
3 *Mar* No 131257. 750 Mk II series and first 'S' type, latter with points in timing cover, integral rpm drive, 6 volt coils (for details see text).
4 *May?* 126 lb rear springs replace previous 100 lb.
5 *Mid-year* No 132576. Fibre Ferodo clutch friction plate replaced small friction inserts.
6 *Mid-year* No 133488: third gears in stronger material.
7 *Sept* No 133668. Fastback receives 'S' type mods—points, coils, etc.
8 *Late year* No 134108. First Wolverhampton-built engine, lacking 'P' for Plumstead engine number suffix.
9 *Late year* No 134738. 'Hylomar' Rolls-Royce sealing compound adopted.

1970
For 750 Commando Mk II:
1 Transverse strengthening bar added between the frame loops under the crankcase.
2 *Feb* 4 gallon steel tank becomes optional for Fastback.
3 *Mar* No 135140. First Roadster model with low pipes and upswept reverse cone silencers.
4 *Apr?* No 133618. Blanking plate fitted in old

magneto position recess where experimental starter motor was to have been.
5 *Aug* No 138973. Taper piston rings (compression).
6 *Sept* No 139571. Fastback Mk II receives Roadster exhaust system.
7 *Late year* No 140061. Plastic oil feed pipes to rockers.

1971

1 *Jan* No 141783. Mk III models. New forks and steering head bearings, 4.10 tyres, centre stand on engine, bare stanchions, handlebar switches etc (see text).
2 *May* No 146584. New type 'SE' oil control ring; to No 147176. Then again fitted from no 147259.
3 *July* No 147730. Rear brake drums screwed and riveted.
4 Mid-year Drain holes were incorporated in the brake drum, breaking through the casting between first and second fin from the drive (left) side
5 Sept Three tabwashers and exhaust pipe lock rings with shorter threads.
6 *Aug?* No 147896. Toughened kickstart pawl.
7 *Sept?* No 148895. Modified inlet valve guide (for oil).
8 *Sept?* No 149670. Plastic oil seal fitted to inlet guide.
9 *Sept?* No 150120. Oil pump paper gasket fitted.
10 Oct Revised main bearings for use with crankshaft of latest production size part no 063106 of reduced overall width with letter 'R' stamped on timing side crankshaft cheek adjacent to bearing location.
11 *Nov?* No 151175. Increased chamfer on cam followers to increase drain from head.
12 *Nov?* No 152000. Rear drum strengthening webs.
13 *Nov?* No 152499. Replaceable (screw-in) footrest pegs.
14 *Dec* No 153120. Riveted clutch back plate.
15 Dec No 153362. Chaincase outer incorporating cap 'O' rings, not leather washers.
16 Dec No 153324. Rev-counter housing gasket.
17 Dec Front disc brake conversion kit for existing drum brake models.

1972

For 750 Commando Mk IV:
(consecutive engine numbers abandoned, and a complicated year for engine numbers due to production difficulties—see text).
1 Jan No 200000. Mk IV 750 introduced, stronger crankcases, double roller mains. Also revised 'D'-shape handlebars (Tomaselli). Standard cylinder head with increased inlet guide support

(deleting two NM 23392 heat insulating washers). Rear units chromed springs, lose top shrouds.
2 *Early year* No 200976. First (?standard production) Combat engine, 10:1 cr, black barrels, 'SS' cam. Interim pistons with oil slots.
3 *Early year* No 200708. Cam follower locating plate modified to accommodate 1972 Combat camshaft.
4 *Spring?* No 212278. First Interstate; Combat, disc etc.
5 Jan The Roadster exhaust system 'had been found more satisfactory than the "SS" type.' A kit offered to change one to the other.
6 Feb New type camshaft bushes of smaller outside diameter, with oil groove. The two appropriate types of camshaft and bushes must be used together, though both with grooves is not harmful.
7 Mar No 202116. To improve thief-proofing and to prevent headlamp being turned on in parked position, previous Lucas master switch (39565) redesigned to incorporate a fourth terminal, meaning a new main harness and headlamp harness. 1972 switch is part no 39784.
8 *Mar?* No 202760. Revised front brake lever (disc master cylinder).
9 *Mar?* No 203200. Steel petrol tank and side panels (Roadster) alternative to fibreglass.
10 Mar No 203136. To stiffen up TLS front brake support plate (and as kit no 063410).
11 Mar No 203884. Copper washers, part no 063129, introduced to fit beneath the heads of the rocker spindle retaining plate bolts to prevent oil seepage at that point.
12 Apr No 201778. Clutch friction plate 061339 now incorporated oil dispersal grooves on both sides to help disperse oil causing clutch slip.
13 Apr No 202341. On some early Combat engines (no 200004 to 202340) valves were not opening properly due to valve springs not depressing far enough: this needed new thinner bottom valve spring cup, part no 063396, identified by the marking 'IN' on its inner face.

From engine numbers 202341 to 202665, thinner valve spring bottom cup fitted. From 202666, heat-insulating washers NM 23392 and standard cup washers NMT 2073 were reintroduced, cancelling mod at no 200000.
14 May Design of exhaust valve guide NMT 2011 revised to prevent excessive oil passage between valves and guides. Upper end of guide shortened so taper on valve stem cannot enter neck of guide, which would cause a pumping action. The lower end of the valve guide lengthened by a similar amount. Modified valve guide (part no 063527).

15 May Left and right hand switch clusters reversed, to give right hand operation of direction indicators. Functions of kill button and headlamp flasher, and spare button and horn, are also reversed.

16 May After three different prop stands used on 1971 and 1972 models, the latest, equipped with a rubber bump stop can be used in place of any of them (part no 063389) and use an extra spacer where necessary for the pivot bolt.

17 June Quartz Halogen headlamps now available as a kit for all 7 in headlamp models (ie, not Hi-Rider and SS).

18 June For Combat-engined models, where silencing mutes have been fitted to the silencers, a new mute (part no 063763) is fitted to improve acceleration.

19 Aug No 211891. A change in the roller main bearing to one designated 'Superblend', supplied under part no 063906—manufacturers part no R and M 6/MRJA30 (previously specified bearing was part no 063114, two dot single lip roller bearings). Now fully interchangeable, should be used in pairs, and could be fitted with advantage to 1971 and earlier Commando engines, provided care was taken fitting the inner spool to the right side crankshaft journal (was 1.1807 in to 1.1812 in, is now 1.1812 in to 1.185 in diameter). Also crankshaft fitted end float should be checked, and shimmed where necessary to provide 0.010 in minimum, 0.020 in maximum end float (see also text).

20 Aug Front and rear engine mounting buffers of new type (new front part no 063960, new rear part no 063928) to improve location and seating of engine.

21 Sept No 212173. Revised cylinder head gasket (part no 063844) incorporating steel fire ring 'eyelets' which provide more positive gas seal under arduous conditions; a direct replacement for previous. Alternatively a thicker copper gasket (1 mm thick), part no 064071 also available, or an even thicker alloy (2 mm thick) part no 064072, to reduce compression. With Combat (063327) head and a cylinder base gasket, the eyeletted type gives a 9.8:1 cr, without a cylinder base gasket, 10:1, both as previously. The 1 mm copper gives 9.5:1 cr with cylinder base gasket, 9.8:1 without. The 2 mm alloy gives 8.8:1 with cylinder base gasket, 9:1 without. 'Eyeletted' material gasket preferred providing Premium (minimum 97 octane) fuels are used. Discontinuation of use of alloy gasket later advised.

22 Sept An oversize swinging arm-pivot spindle (part no 064077) available to enable reclamation of rear engine mountings where excessive spindle bore wear has taken place.

23 Sept No 211110. A 32 mm carburettor version with silver painted barrels of the standard Commando unit replaced previous 32 mm Combat specification. This necessitated the introduction of two new cylinder heads, the RH5 (part no 064048) and the RH6 (part no 064097) to replace the Combat's RH3. RH5 gives 8.9:1 compression with a cylinder base gasket, 9.2:1 without; RH6 gives 9.3:1 cr with a cylinder base gasket, 9.6:1 without, and was the 'preferred item for stocking purposes'. Use of copper head gaskets lowered compression further.

24 Oct Interstate/Roadster/Fastback fitted with Combat engine as standard.

25 Nov No 212278. A new type of clutch friction plate introduced, comprising two sintered bronze friction discs bonded to either side of a plain steel plate. Extra clutch capacity was provided by the inclusion of five friction plates in place of the original four fibre material plate. Other changes were the incorporation of an additional plain driving plate, and an identical but hardened clutch centre, together with a new thinner section pressure plate. All were fully interchangeable with previous, except that the new sintered faced driven plates could only be used in conjunction with the new hardened clutch centres (part no 063779, and identifiable by its darker 'Heat Treatment' colouration).

26 Nov Also no 212278. The method of bolting up the flywheel and crankshaft assembly amended from bolts, nuts and lock-tabwashers to studs, nuts and dowel retaining plates.

1973

For 750 Commando Mk V:

1 *March* Engine No 220000. Mk V Commando (for details see text).

2 New centre stand kit, 850 type (kit no 064874) converted any Commando fitted with stand attached to engine plates. Fitted to engines 222145 to 221644, and to engines 230536 to 230685, and from engine number 300000.

3 New-type headsteady (part no 064179) fits all Commandos.

4 Inlet valves 064034 now stellite-tipped, interchangeable with previous (and for Atlas).

5 New engine mounting spacers (part no 063960 front, 063928 rear) used circlips (part no 063927) to locate bump rubbers. For all Commandos.

6 New rubber (part no 063961) oil tank mountings to avoid contact with battery terminals.

7 No 208754 Cartridge oil filter available as kit no 064283 for all Commandos, but needs two holes drilling in gearbox cradle.

8 Sept Recent 750 Commandos fitted with twin horns mounted on coil brackets beneath the front of the petrol tank.
9 *Oct* No 230935. Probable last 750.
For Commando 850:
1 *Mar* No 30000. 850 Mk I, for details see text.
2 New PTFE Isolastic washers (part no 063556) replaced polyurethane type. For 750 also.
3 New type of FAG Superblend main bearing (part no 064118) with higher load capacity replaces previous Superblend, and can be fitted also to 1971 and earlier models. End float in excess of between 0.010 and 0.024 can be eliminated by fitting mainbearing shims NMT 2196A between the inner race and the timing side crankshaft. For 750 also.
4 Improved inlet valve (part no 064034) incorporating a stellite tip similar to exhaust valve, fitted from engine 221317, interchangeable with previous. For 750 also.
5 No 220000. Improved version of original top engine mounting engine steady plate (part no 064179), of stiffer construction and fabricated as a 'box section' member, interchangeable with previous.
6 No 300003, swinging arm stiffened by the incorporation of box section gusset plates.
7 *May* 'Majorca' type lower and reduced width handlebars available, developed to accept existing disc front brake master cylinder and hydraulic equipment.
8 *May* No 301700. New 'quick action' throttle twistgrip (part no 064600) introduced.
9 *May* Monograde (SAE 40, with SAE 30 for winter) engine oils now recommended. For 750 also.
10 *May* Rear mud-flap becomes available as option. For 750 also.
11 *May* Grab-rails for Roadster and Interstate commonized.
12 May No 307091. Rear chainguard with detachable black plastic extension end piece fitted. For 750 also.
13 July No 302000. Adjuster facility to rear chain oiler by means of an additional clamp, applicable to all previous Commandos. For 750 also.
14 July Auto advance unit changes from Lucas 6CA to Lucas 10CA (interchangeable). For 750 also.
15 July Existing front disc brake caliper modified by the addition of two 2.35 mm diameter holes on the rear face, to allow incorporation of a fully-floating, self-aligning disc scraper to prevent dust etc, entering the caliper yoke.
16 *Sept* No 306591. 850 Mk IIA European model. Annular discharge silencers, gearing changed

with a new pair of second gear-pinions, parts no 064639 and 064640, interchangeable with previous but only in pairs, plastic airbox, for details see text.
17 *Oct?* No 307091. Slimmer 4½ gallon Interstate tank.
18 *Dec* No 307311. 850 Mk II, Mk IIA, Mk II for America with old type silencers and airbox. Mk IIA revised second and third gears (for details see text).
19 *Dec* 850 Mk II silencers with integral mutes (previous mutes were an optional fitment via a small self-tap attachment screw) are now standard. The 850's coupled exhaust system with balance pipe required mutes with silencers to be fitted. Main jets for 850 Mk I = 250 (v 260 without mutes), 750 = 220 (v 210 without mutes).
20 Dec No 305427, new rear wheel bearing spacer (part no 062070) to overcome impression from the bearing inner spool and consequent slackening off of rear wheel spindle while in use. Interchangeable with previous.
21 Dec For 850, alternative wire mesh reinforced 'Klingerit' fibre cylinder head gasket incorporating steel fibre ring eyelets, part no 065051 superseded previous copper head gasket, maintained nominal 8.5:1 cr.

1974
For 850 Mk II, Mk IIA:
1 May The latest and subsequent machines have the front disc brake on the left side.
2 Dec No 317312. New design of exhaust pipe introduced on 850 Commandos, with spherical connection flange. New arrangement comprises a convex seating ring inserted into the threaded exhaust port prior to placing the new spherical flanged exhaust pipe into position, which is then located in situ by means of a spherical collet of matching section, held and tightened into position by the current finned lockring. Not directly interchangeable with previous except as complete set, unless the exhaust cross tube is shortened.

(It is regretted that these lists are far from complete, but hoped that even so they will be of some use to Commando owners in need.)

Norton: engine and frame numbers
Post-war Nortons (until 1960) used a letter and number code to indicate (1) model year (the first letter), (2) model (the first number sometimes found together with a suffix letter to denote model variations, (3) a number for the machine itself (which should apply to both engine and frame), and finally, (4) on the engine numbers and

following the machine number, a number giving the engine bore and stroke dimensions.

1 Letters for model years
(generally from September of the previous year):
1950 = E; 1951 = F; 1952 = G; 1953 = H; 1954 = J; 1955 = K; 1956 = L; 1957 = M; 1958 = N; 1959 = P; and 1960 = R. These year letter prefixes were also stamped on gearboxes. After 1960 the system was discontinued, reportedly due to large stocks of machines left unsold at the end of the year. After that, although the model prefix (2) was retained, the frame numbers (see below (3)) alone provide an approximate way of dating a machine.

2 The model number code

	Model	Code
Singles	16H	2
	Big 4	7
	Spring-frame Big 4 or 16H	8
	18	3
	ES2	4
	19R	6
	19S	9
	50	13
	Inter 40	10
	Inter 30	11
Twins	Dominator 7	12
	88	122
	99	14
	77 and Nomad	15
	Nomad	16
	Jubilee	17
	Navigator	19
	Electra	EL
	650	18
	Atlas	20
	Commando (pre cam-shaft driven points)	20M3
	Commando (camshaft driven points)	20M3S

Suffix D = De-Luxe
Suffix SS = Sports Special and Mercury

3 Frame (and hopefully also engine) **numbers,** after 1960

For 1961	From
Singles	
Model 50	n/a
ES2	92270

Twins	
Jubilee	92485
Navigator	94573
88	93235
99	92270

For 1962	
Singles	
Model 50	n/a
ES2	99498
Twins	
Jubilee	99598
Navigator	99110
88	n/a
99, ends August 1962 at—	103929
650	100200

BMC73B

For 1963	
Singles	
Model 50	104029
ES2, ends at—	106837
Twins	
Jubilee	103575
Jubilee De-Luxe	103446
Navigator	103275
Navigator De-Luxe	99172
88	101918
88SS	102911
650	104267
650SS	104123

For 1964	
Twins	
Jubilee	107988
Navigator	n/a
88	n/a
650	n/a
Atlas, from February	10800

For 1965	
Singles	
Model 50 Mk II	n/a
ES2 Mk II	111627
Twins	
Jubilee	111026
Navigator	106980
Ends September at—	114519
88SS	109512
650SS	110375
Atlas	111377

For 1966	
Singles	
Model 50 Mk II, ends July at—	43058
ES2 Mk II, ends July at—	135290
Twins	
88SS, ends July at—	118151

650SS	n/a
Atlas	n/a

For 1967
Twins
650SS, July 1967	123164
Atlas, July 1967	121307
P11	121007
Ends June at—	123012
N15CS, introduced October	123672
Ends November at—	124371

For 1968
Twins
650SS, ends February	126124
Mercury, introduced October	129147
Atlas, ends January	125770
P11A, from September	124372
P11A Ranger, from September	128646
Ends November at—	129145
Commando 750, from February	126125

For 1969
Twins
Commando 750 S Mk II, from March	131257
Commando 750 Mk II Fastback, from March	131180
Commando 750 S, from Sept	133668

For 1970
Commando 750 Roadster, from March	135140
Commando 750 S, ends June	135088
Commando 750 Fastback 'Mk II', from Sept	139571

For 1971
Commando 750 Mk III, from Jan	141783
Ends October at—	150723

For 1972
Commando 750 Mk IV	200001
Commando 750 Interstate	212278

For 1973
Commando 750 Mk V	220000
Ends October at—	230935
Commando 850 Mk I, from Feb/March	300000
Commando 850 Mk IA, from October	306591
Commando 850 Mk II and Mk IIA, from December	307311

For 1974 n/a

For 1975
Commando 850 Mk III	330000

Norton: colour schemes

1950 Singles: All cycle parts black, all wheels with chromed rims, black centres with thin red lines. 16H, Big 4, Model 18, ES2, chrome petrol tank with silver panels outlined with broad black outer and thin red inner lines. Oil tanks black. Internationals, petrol and oil tanks silver, with wide black and thin red inner lining. Twins: Model 7, cycle parts, wheels, as singles. Petrol tank chrome plated with 'teardrop' silver panels outlined in broad black, narrow red inner lines. Oil tank black.

1951 Singles: as 1950, but mid-year, due to nickel shortage, chrome tanks became all silver painted, with panels as previously. Some wheel rims finish silver, with centres and lining as before. Twins: Model 7, as 1950 and as singles.

1952 Singles: as 1950, but with new tank panel shape, with ¼ not ½ in thick black outer lining, same thin red inner lining. Wheel rims chromed, with silver centres lined in red. Twins: Model 7, as 1950, with wheel rims and thinner outer lining for tank panel as singles. 88, polychromatic grey for frame, oil tank, mudguards, chaincase, forks, wheel hubs, headlamp shell and tank panels (tear-drop, but different shape from Model 7) on chromed tank, with panels outlined in outer black and inner red lines. Wheel rims chromed with grey centres lined in red.

1953 Singles: as 1952 but 16H, Big 4 petrol tank silver not chromed; and International as 88 twin for 1952, only wheel rims chrome with silver centres lined in grey. Alternative finish in Manx silver and black. Twins: as 1952, but 88 optional finish as Model 7.

1954 As 1953.

1955 As 1954, but all models fit round plastic tank badges, fork sliders are polished as are some nuts and bolt heads after plating.

1956 As 1955. Twins: 99 and 77 as 88, ie, cycle parts all polychromatic grey.

1957 Singles: as 1956, but petrol tank now painted matt silver with chromed screw-on panels with black plastic beaded edge, except International where tank colour is still polychromatic grey. Twins: as singles, with tank colour polychromatic grey.

1958 As 1957, but wheels now all chromed by year's end.

1959 Singles: Model 50, ES2, cycle parts and tank (bar chrome panels) in Forest Green; with optional black and silver finish as 1957. Twins: Jubilee, two-tone trim, with red, blue or green for upper petrol tank, forks, headlamp shell, upper part and front of enclosure panels, with dove grey frame, mudguard, primary chaincase, optional rear chaincase, oil tank tool tray and lower tank and enclosure. 88 and 99, as 1958, but options of Norton Red or Metalescent Blue overall, or black and silver, available.

1960 Singles: Model 50, ES2, as 1959 but optional chrome-plated mudguards from now on. Twins: Jubilee as 1959. 88, 99, two tone trim, with either black or light blue upper petrol tank, fork shrouds, headlamp shell, and (if De-Luxe) upper part of enclosure panels; and dove grey lower tank, mudguards and (if De-Luxe) lower enclosure, with black upper fitting black frame, oil tank and primary chaincase, and light blue upper fitting those parts in dove grey also. New long spiked tank badge.

1961 Singles: as Twins for 1960, with upper petrol tank, fork shrouds, headlamp, frame, oil tank, side cover, chaincase and chainguard in black for Model 50, Forest Green for ES2, with lower tank and mudguards dove grey for both. New long spiked tank badge. Twins: Jubilee as 1960, Navigator De-Luxe as Jubilee with blue, or black, upper, dove grey remainder. Standard versions two tone also, with petrol tank upper, oil tank, tool box cover red, blue or black, remainder dove grey. Others continue two tone trim but now with frame, oil tank, primary chaincase normally in upper colour, lower colour for all dove grey. Upper colours for 88 Standard, cream, 88 De-Luxe, red, 88SS, green, 99 Standard, polychromatic grey, 99 De-Luxe, blue, 99SS polychromatic grey.

1962 Singles: as 1961. Twins: Jubilee, as before, with De-Luxe upper colour blue, Standard red, Navigator De-Luxe upper black, Standard blue. Others as 1961 with upper colour changes: 88 Standard and SS, green, 99 Standard and SS, polychromatic grey, 650 Standard polychromatic grey, De-Luxe upper blue, 650SS, cycle parts black, petrol tank silver.

1963 Singles: Model 30, ES2, as 1961 but for both black as upper colour, off-white as lower. Twins: Jubilee Standard as 1962 but with option of black cycle parts, flamboyant burgundy petrol tank, Jubilee De-Luxe blue upper, dove grey lower, or black upper, off-white lower. Navigator Standard, as 1962 but with option of black cycle parts, polychromatic blue tank, Navigator De-Luxe as 1962 but some models with all-black petrol tank. Electra, black cycle parts, silver petrol tank, oil tank, toolbox. Optional chrome plated mudguards. 88 upper green, lower now off-white, 88SS as 650SS, 650 black cycle parts,

polychromatic blue tank, 650SS as 1962. Optional chrome plated mudguards for all.

1964 Twins: as 1963; Jubilee, Navigator, Electra, as before but petrol tank single colour and chromed mudguards now standard on Electra, Atlas, black cycle parts, chrome plated mudguards, silver tank, with optional red or black for tank.

1965 Singles: Model 50 Mk II, ES2 Mk II, black cycle parts, silver tank with round plastic badges and lightning flash lining. Twins: Jubilee, black cycle parts, flamboyant burgundy petrol tank, mudguards, oil tank, tool box. Navigator as Jubilee but colours grey cycle parts, blue remainder. Electra as 1964. 88SS, 650SS as 1964. Atlas, black cycle parts, cherry red petrol tank.

1966 Singles: as 1965 but tank lining changed. Twins: Jubilee as 1965. 88SS, 650SS as 1965. Atlas black cycle parts, petrol tank Burgundy, chrome plated mudguards as standard.

1967 As 1966.

1968 Atlas, 650SS, as 1967, but seats with humped rear. Mercury, black frame, forks, headlamp shell; Atlantic Blue mudguards, primary chaincase, oil tank, toolbox; silver petrol tank. Chromed mudguards optional. Commando, black frame, cylinder barrels, seat. Dark green petrol tank, tail unit. Circular Norton badges on tank and on top of tail unit.

1969 Mercury, as 1968 but chromed mudguards standard. Commando Fastback, R and S, black frame, silver cylinder barrels, chrome front mudguards, silver side panels, chrome headlamp shell, Norton tank transfers, Fastback, black fork shrouds, green, or burgundy red and quicksilver tank, and tail unit. Side panel transfers on some models. R black fork shrouds, grenadier red tank, chromed rear mudguard. S as R, but forks now unshrouded, ungaitered and chromed, tank colours British racing green, quicksilver metal flake, grenadier red or burgundy and silver, with side panels in tank colour, and carrying machine type and capacity transfers.

1970 Commando as 1969 but colour schemes for S, Roadster (as S), tank and side panels, Fastback tank (panels remain silver) optional metal flake Fireglo red, Pacific Shimmer Blue, purple, bronze, silver or emerald green; or solid colour racing green, signal red, canary yellow.

1971 As 1970, but tangerine or orange now an option, all forks unshrouded and chromed, all rear chainguards chromed. Roadster available in black with single gold pinstripe panel outline on tank only. Fastback side covers in black, tail unit in tank colours. For all, side panels in black where tank colour is yellow or red. Interstate as

Roadster, but pinstriped outline of tank panels extended rearwards in shape of full tank.

1972 As 1971, with Interstate as Roadster, but pinstriped outline of tank panels extended rearwards in shape of full tank. Combat, cylinder barrels in black.

1973 750s as 1972, with Roadster, Interstate available in candy apple metallic red with silver lining. 850s as 750s, but for Roadster, Interstate 850 pinstriping in appropriate colour (gold on black, silver on red or blue, white on tangerine) is double. On Interstate simply double on tank, on Roadster back edge of panel shape not striped, and double striping continues back along tank top side to rear where the lines cross to join; on side panels, single striping on front edge becomes double for top edge.

1974 As 1973, but cylinder barrels now black, and Roadster now available in white with broad very dark blue stripe, angled on tank, horizontal on panels with a gold line close to its bottom edge, JPN, black frame, exhaust and silencers, side panels, chrome rear mudguard and chainguard, white front mudguard, fairing, tank and seat unit. Fairing either horizontally striped with broad red (top), white, blue bands, or red (top) and blue with a thin white divider starting narrow below headlamp, flaring out and turning downwards in broad bands to cut off before base of fairing.

Tail fairing rear with blue base, white middle section shared with Union Jack each side, red top.

1975 As 1974, but options now only candy apple red, black. For Interstate also new Manx silver and tank striping in broader outer black, thin inner red lining. Roadster 'blue stripe' finish modified, with gold line deleted and a red line, separated from the blue stripe by a band of white, following its contours just below.

Some approximate modern colour equivalents:
Silver (for International) — Volkswagen Beetle Silver
Polychromatic Grey (Wideline twins) — Talbot Steel Grey metallic 397 or Ford Granada Pearl Grey metallic.
Quicksilver (SS650, Electra, Atlas) — Ford Silver Fox GM 45411
Norton Red (88 De Luxe, Jubilee) — Ford Monaco Red
Dove Grey — BL Arabian Grey, or Volkswagen Pearl White.
Tunisian Blue/Atlantic Blue (99 De Luxe, Mercury) — Talbot Caribbean Blue 80 GL24435
Forest Green (ES2, Model 50) — Rover Cameron Green B266, or Vauxhall Laurel 4635.
(Commando colours are recent enough to be available from Norton stockists.)